THE ADVENTURES OF THE CRUMPSALL KID

THE ADVENTURES OF THE CRUMPSALL KID

A MEMOIR

MIKE HARDING

MICHAEL O'MARA BOOKS

First published in Great Britain in 2015 by
Michael O'Mara Books Limited
9 Lion Yard
Tremadoc Road
London SW4 7NQ

A CIP catalogue record for this book is available from the British Library.

Papers used by Michael O'Mara Books Limited are natural, recyclable products made from wood grown in sustainable forests. The manufacturing processes conform to the environmental regulations of the country of origin.

ISBN: 978-1-78243-452-8 in hardback print format
ISBN: 978-1-78243-453-5 in e-book format

1 2 3 4 5 6 7 8 9 10

www.mombooks.com

Designed and typeset by Design 23

Printed and bound by CPI Group (UK) Ltd, Croydon, CR0 4YY

CONTENTS

INTRODUCTION

It seems impossible to believe it now, but I was born into a world that was not just unlike the one that is lived in by today's children, but was, in truth, a different universe, another cosmos or plane of existence perhaps. When I tell my grandchildren about my life at their age I can see that they think it is another of my stories, like the one about Griselda Marrowfat the witch, who lives on Pendle Hill and who makes Wrigglety Boy Soup out of naughty boys, or the one about Ben and James, who go through a secret door to Candyland and get so fat they can't get out again. My childhood world was a street of terraced red-brick houses, and that street was surrounded by other streets that looked exactly the same; in those streets there was no central heating, no indoor sanitation, no TV, not many cars, hardly any private telephones and certainly no mobile phones; there were no iPods, no Xboxes, no trainers, no home cinemas, no computers and, for the working class at least, no foreign holidays.

To travel anywhere when I was a child you walked, cycled, got on a bus or boarded a train. You bought your food every day from a local shop instead of filling a trolley in a supermarket and carrots and apples went rotten after a few days because they weren't sprayed with chemical gunk. A suit lasted you several years and shoes were mended, not chucked away. Fashion was something you read about in magazines and most children grew up dressed as miniature versions of their parents. Churches were much fuller than they are now; pretty much everybody (even us republicans) stood to attention when they played 'God Save the Queen' at the end of the programme in the cinema; and most women were virgins when they married (though a great number of men did their best to correct this aberration – and mostly failed). Gay people lived in an underworld that was tacitly accepted, but were still regularly entrapped in public toilets by policemen. The two gay men who ran one of our local chippies were as camp as a bottle of coffee and were loved by the community, but they could have been given a long stretch in Strangeways for their relationship.

Revisiting the world of my childhood and beyond has been a strange journey back – not just in time but in every way: everything is different. The minds that delighted in dreaming up The Three Stooges, Flash Gordon, 'Bouncing Briggs the Demon Goalie' (he only lost one goal) and *Journey into Space* are no more; the new world is dominated by the slicker humour of US sitcoms, the gibber of people famous for being famous, and the *soi-disant* (as they say in Rotherham) 'free market' has turned the people from citizens to consumers. Were Descartes alive to see today's mega malls, cathedrals to the new religion of Money, he might proclaim the mantra, 'I shop, therefore I am.'

But I am a miserable old curmudgeon now and, when I was a nipper in the back streets of Manchester, the consumer society was all to come. Happiness then was a tanner 'spends' (pocket money) a week and a hot morning spent picking tar out from between the cobbles with a lollipop stick. Kids today! They wouldn't know a cobble if it hit them on the head.

I tried my best to write this as a work of 'miserabilia', part of that staple of today's literature that my local Waterstones has titled 'Unfortunate Lives'. But I failed. I wasn't kept in a cupboard with nothing but a sponge to pee in. I wasn't sent down the treacle mines at the age of six months, and I didn't spend my days on my hands and knees fighting the dogs for their Spratt's Ovals. I don't want to make light of the terrible lives that some people have led, but mine, while far from being that of Little Lord Fauntleroy, wasn't all that bad. We were poor – but not as poor as the starving children in Africa (as my mother reminded me when I said I didn't want to eat my stewed tripe and onions).

Indeed, the war was working its way to a close when I was born and for several years afterwards the country tried to rebuild itself physically and emotionally, both remaking the bombed infrastructure and coming to terms with a number of disagreeable facts: Britannia no longer ruled the waves; the days of Empire (quite rightly) were numbered; the colonised were in fact more than capable of taking over the reins of power and exploiting their own people; and things really were going to have to change.

The years of my early childhood, though difficult, were not disastrous. The middle class moaned about shortages and rationing and the Welfare State – but the middle class have always moaned about everything. The working class didn't moan, because they had nothing to lose and were in fact much better fed and better off at the end of World War II than they'd ever been. They had free education to secondary level and to university and a free National Health Service for when they were sick. So rightly they tended to get on with it. The ruling class didn't moan because they never want for anything anyway; like the poor, the über rich are always with us.

There was less fear and more optimism somehow; children played out unsupervised until all hours. True, some of them drowned in rivers or got run over by buses, but that was life, and mostly we kids led a charmed one. The terrible war that had brought both Hiroshima and Auschwitz was over, the men were back home (most of them at least) and people wanted no more of the world that had brought about this last mad conflagration. So they kicked out Churchill, nationalised the railways, coal and steel, gave the nation the NHS, created public footpaths and national parks, built council estates and new roads and looked forward to a brave new world.

They reckoned without the old guard of course, but they were lurking in the wings all the time: the same shadowy puppet-masters that produced Thatcher and Blair and the other know-nothing servants of the Establishment that still runs most of Britain and the world. But that's another story; my childhood days consisted of sunshine and lemonade and leapfrog, if not cakes and ale or wine and roses. Mostly my story is a happy one and, I am sure, is just one story among many such.

CHAPTER 1

THE CRUMPSALL KID

According to my mother I was born at 3 a.m. on 23 October 1944 in a place called Crumpsall, north Manchester (53.5167° N, 2.2417° W). My mum was there at the time because, as she explained later, she didn't want me coming into the world alone and naked, showing my willy to a roomful of strangers. According to some astrologers, my birth time makes me a Scorpio, and, to be perfectly honest, though I let my membership of the Holy Roman Catholic and Apostolic Church lapse many years ago and am no longer a member of St Clare's Manchester Scout troop, I have at least been loyal to my zodiacal sign. Finding out recently that some astrologers reckon I'm a Libran is a little like finding out you are Mongolian – which is fine if you are in fact from Ulan Bator but not if you're from Crumpsall. I shall ignore them and continue living as a Scorpio; Scorpios are much more fun than Librans – or Mongolians I suspect (unless you count Genghis Khan and he was only fun if you were on his side). In any case, I'm of the opinion that astrology, like economics and philosophy, is not an exact science. Perhaps, as Edmund crows in King Lear, 'I should have been that I am, had the maidenliest star in the firmament twinkled at my bastardising.' Not that I was a bastard, you understand, but the rest of the quote fits. That Shakespeare knew a thing or three.

The earliest thing I remember is my Uncle Bernard and Uncle Harry bouncing me on my nanna's bed. They were both in uniform, so I reckon it must have been late 1945 or early 1946 when they were waiting to be demobbed.

My nanna, Mary Alice Pyne, née O'Neil, was my great grandmother, and was just one of the people who lived in our house, 38 Hall Road, Crumpsall. The others were my mum and my

Aunty Julia, the cat and, from time to time, Harry or Bernard, who were only passing through on their way from the army back into civvy street. My dad, I knew, had also gone away to war but had never come back. The cat was a black and white tom called Mushy who featured large in my life. Mushy was given to us by the Jewish man my Aunty Julia worked for in town and was already quite old when I was born. He lived until I was ten or so and lost the last of his nine lives in a fight with a number 7 bus one snowy Christmas.

My nanna was from Ireland, born in the tenements near the College of Surgeons in Dublin. She must have been over eighty when I was born yet she helped bring me up; she was a strong woman both mentally and physically and was the one who filled me full of song and stories, all of which seem to have been of some help in my later life. She also filled me full of religion, which was not something I would go on to make a career out of. Much of my early pre-school years were spent with my nanna and the cat; my mother worked whenever and wherever she could because living on a war widow's pension was no great shakes.

My nanna was tall and slim and had long silver hair which she kept up in a bun with tortoiseshell combs and washed in paraffin as a precaution against nits. She would do this in front of the fire in winter, which struck me as more than a trifle risky: one spark and she would have gone from Dublin granny to Joan of Arc. When she wasn't washing her hair with inflammable materials she was saying her rosary, and when she wasn't saying her rosary she would look after me, cook me bubble and squeak for my dinner and sit me on her knee singing her songs. These ranged from nursery rhymes to music hall songs and Dublin street ballads about Patsy Fagan who was a 'harum, scarum, divil-may-carum, dacent Irish boy' and one called 'Mush Mush Aye Tooral Ayaddy' about treading on the tail of somebody's coat.

I loved the song about the poor fishmonger girl, 'Molly Malone', whose ghost – a grey, beautiful wraith, as I imagined her – pushed her barrow through the dark Dublin streets. Nanna also sang me the song of the 'Wild Colonial Boy', Jack Duggan, who was an Irish rebel who had gone to Australia and become a bushranger, robbing the rich to help the poor. When she came to the lines '"I'll fight but not surrender!"/ Cried the wild colonial boy', she would bang her hand down hard on the arm of her chair. I always shuddered at the lines, when 'a bullet pierced his proud young heart'.

She also sang a song about Lily of Laguna (which I thought was something to do with a lagoon like you find on coral islands) and of Kevin Barry, the brave rebel boy who died for Ireland:

Go on and shoot me like a soldier
Don't hang me like a dog in scorn
For I fought to free old Ireland
On that chill September morn.

She told me stories of tinker's curses and the banshee and the saints and blessed martyrs, of the Irish rebels, James Connolly and Patrick Pearse, and how they shot James Connolly tied to a chair because he had been so badly wounded in the Easter Rising he couldn't stand up. She told me stories about wonders and marvels and miraculous cures, which were sometimes to do with the saints and sometimes to do with mouldy bread. (Stick with it – all will be made clear later.)

Most of my growing years were coloured by Ireland and Dublin in particular, since my great-aunts Julia and Kitty were both born there at the Rotunda, though I'm not sure where my granddad – my nanna's son and their brother – was born. His accent was pure Dublin tinged with Scouse because he had lived in Liverpool. So between them all I grew up in a confused world that was like some kind of Irish enclave in Crumpsall. It wasn't until I went to school that I began to understand that I was in England and there was a king and a queen lording it over us. Even at school there was still a large Irish influence; some of our teachers were from Ireland and there were many children in the school who came of Irish stock. On St Patrick's Day the whole school sported the shamrock; my nanna was such a great fan of St Patrick that she got hold of huge bunches of the stuff, and I walked to school on Paddy's Day covered with so much shamrock that I looked like a Japanese sniper.

So there I was: Michael Christopher Harding, in a house full of strong women of Irish descent with everything that entails, and with no father figure to influence me or tell me that I was not in fact the best thing since sliced bread. Uncle Harry and Uncle Bernard floated in and out, and my granddad always appeared at holiday times like Christmas and Easter and at odd occasions whenever he felt he needed a few days drinking with Uncle Bobby and his pals in Manchester – but otherwise I was a prince in my own little princedom. I was quite ruined by the women in the family and on the street because I had fair hair, blue eyes and was half an orphan; so for the first few years of my life I grew up with the idea that the world revolved around me. School and our street soon got rid of that notion.

Uncle Bernard and Uncle Harry had gone into the army not long after leaving school. Harry was in the Long Range Desert Group where he had spent much of the war behind the German lines in North Africa, spying on enemy troop movements, blowing up airplanes, and generally getting up Rommel's nose while being bitten by scorpions and almost shitting himself to death. In between that he seemed to have spent a lot of his time in khaki carrying Randolph Churchill and Jakie Astor back to their tents blind drunk (them, not him). I doubted Uncle Harry's stories until I read a few books on the Phantoms and found that both Randolph and Astor had been out there at the same time as Harry. Harry was also a keen boxer who boxed for the army and never lost the ability to look after himself.

Uncle Bernard was sent to India to fight the Japanese. He got bored waiting for the Japanese to come and let him shoot them, and got himself into trouble by getting pissed and riding a horse into the officers' mess. Had he been an officer it would all have been regarded as something of a high-spirited jape; since he was simply an oik he got himself into a right load of manure.

In the mythology of the family, Uncle Bernard saw more than his fair share of trouble throughout his life, and all (according to Nanna) because he had been cursed by an Indian beggar woman. She had begged him for alms as he was marching through her village with his troop and he had thrown her some useless English coppers for a joke; if I remember the story right they were farthings. The Indian woman had cursed him, and carrying her hex and his Lee–Enfield rifle, Bernard had gone on to get into lots of scrapes. Almost immediately after being cursed he fell into a pit while marching through the jungle and was knocked unconscious. His companions marched on, not noticing he was missing, and Bernard, when he came round, found himself surrounded by dozens of cobras. Speechless and terrified, he sat propped against the clay wall of the pit, frozen with fear as the snakes reared up, spread their hoods and hissed at him.

My nanna, back home in Hall Road, Crumpsall, Manchester, had seen this happening in a dream at the exact time Bernard was in the snake pit in India. She prayed to the Virgin Mary, mother to mother, to see if she wouldn't mind asking Her Son, Jesus, to sort the situation out; after all, Uncle Bernard was a good Catholic boy who had regularly attended mass at St Patrick's, Collyhurst. She must have had a pretty direct line to the Virgin Mary because, as a result of her prayers, a bright light suddenly flashed out and the cobras all died (in some versions); or (alternative version no. 47) an angel appeared and chopped the cobras' heads off. I believed every rendition, of course, just as I believed in the devil, the tooth fairy, God, the Blessed Virgin Mary, all the saints and angels, Icky the Bare-Bum Fire Bobby and Jinny Greenteeth who lived down grids and would 'get you' if you went near. It seems that Bernard did get into some trouble with snakes but the angels that saved him might have been some Gurkhas.

My father, Louis Arthur Harding, a Devon boy from Ottery St Mary, was a navigator for Lancaster Bombers and had been killed while returning from a bombing raid on the night-fighter base at Munster on the night of 23/24 September 1944, just a month before I was born. According to my sister, Colette, the family archivist, the Lancaster V – for Victor – was probably shot down by Heinz-Wolfgang Schnaufer, a German night-fighter ace who was operational that evening and who claimed two 'kills' in the area. He survived the war but died in a road accident in Bordeaux in 1950 when his Mercedes convertible hit a lorry full of empty gas cylinders. Schnaufer's Messerschmitt was brought to England after the war and put on display in Hyde Park. A piece of the tail tallying all his 121 victories is preserved at the Imperial War Museum.

Whoever it was that brought the bomber down, my mother, Eileen, was a bride, a widow and a mother within a year, and though she remarried again – and my stepfather, Lou, was a good and kind man – I don't believe that she ever got over her loss.

A few nights before he flew on his last raid my dad had gone for a couple of pints with my Uncle Harry in the Woodlands pub, just down the road from our house. He told my Uncle Harry that he didn't believe that he was going to make it through to the end of the war. Harry told me the story many years later: 'Your dad's crew had flown all their missions and were due to stand down and become instructors, but another crew went sick and they volunteered for the mission. And that was that.'

Louis, that boy from the apple orchards of Devon, is buried in a small village graveyard in Holten, near Maastricht in Holland. The village schoolchildren put flowers on the graves each year on the anniversary of the crew's deaths. There is a strange twist to the tale, though. As my father's plane burst into flames, the fire spread so quickly that there was no time for any of the crew to get out – except the bomb aimer. He was in his pod in the belly of the fuselage and somehow managed to fall clear. His parachute brought him down safely and he was lucky enough to be picked up by the Dutch Resistance. He spent the rest of the war hiding in a barn playing the Dutch version of Monopoly with an escaped American airman (I'll give you four thousand guilders for Edam Straat and I'll put a houseboat on Van Gogh Canal). The burning plane, with the rest of the crew still in it, landed smack on top of another English airman who had parachuted out of his plane, so that when the Germans came looking for the dead crew they found the correct number of seven corpses and thus left the bomb aimer to his games of Monopoly.

Both Uncle Harry and Uncle Bernard liked the odd pint or two and used to come back from the pub very jolly and sit at the table playing mouth organs and singing songs. One of their party pieces was an old army song which I later discovered to be very rude, but which, at the time, floated over my mother's head and my grandmother's rosary beads like a cloud because they thought it was all Hindi – which some of it was (*pani* is Hindi for water or in this case the ocean, doo-lalli means mad or crazy and goolies was originally a Hindi word for testicles).

Fifteen years you loved my daughter
Now to the Blighty you must go.
May the ship that carries you over
Sink to the bottom of the Pani sahib.
Oh doo-lalli sahib, oh doo-lalli sahib.
Queen Victoria very fine man
Find her goolies if you can.

That and 'Molly Malone' were some of the earliest folk songs I learned.

Bernard went into the building trade as a plasterer's labourer and stayed there for most of his working life; Harry, as an apprenticeship for what was to become a lifetime of ducking and diving, went into the world of catering: he ran a butty wagon, selling sausage and bacon sandwiches and mugs of tea on a bomb site in Cannon Street in the centre of the city. German bombs had done a lot to destroy the heart of medieval and Georgian Manchester, but nothing like as much as the planners and developers would do later with their concrete and glass neo-Brutalist boxes. But that, dear reader, was all in the future, and before that there were still a few years of old Manchester left, and still plenty of bomb sites on which enterprising demobbed squaddies like Harry could run their businesses.

All the kids in the street thought Harry's butty wagon was simply wonderful. It was a large van with a drop-down counter in the side; when the counter was up, the side of the van showed a huge coloured painting of a jolly-looking fat man in chef's uniform carrying an enormous sausage over his shoulder. When Harry parked it in the street outside our house, kids from all around would come to stare open-mouthed at the fat man with the giant sausage. Harry also had a car: in fact, he was one of the first people I ever knew with a car. It was American and huge and smelled of leather and had an enormous imitation ivory steering wheel. He sat me on his knee and let me drive it once. We went off happily down the cobbled street, me steering, my mother running alongside shouting through the open window that Harry was a lunatic and would kill her child. I don't know why she was worried – I was three years old and could already drive a pedal car for goodness' sake!

My friend Pete Simmons lived next door and his Aunty Winnie was courting a Yank who was stationed at Burtonwood Aerodrome. The Yank used to ride over from the air base on a huge Harley Davidson motorbike, and one sunny afternoon, a few weeks after my ride with Uncle Harry, he sat me on the pillion, and with me holding on to his leather flying jacket we zoomed off down the cobbled street and round the corner with my mother running alongside shouting that he was a lunatic and would kill her child. She did the very same thing when the milkman let me up on the back of his milkfloat for a ride – strange creatures, mothers. Winnie eventually married her airman and went to live in America.

Manchester had quite a floating population of Yanks in those days. They made their way into the city on the weekends in special buses from Burtonwood, their pockets filled with nylon stockings and cigarettes, their trousers filled with quiet confidence. Their favourite drinking, dancing and fighting holes were the Ritz and the Long Bar, both in the heart of the city, and the Band on the Wall on the edge of what was then the market quarter and is now the very trendy Northern Quarter. The Band on the Wall, instead of a stage, really did have a balcony high on the wall where the band would sit and play. This was lucky for the band because the floor was often awash with beer, bottles, bodies and blood, after one of the many battles between our American liberators and the ungrateful native British servicemen who seemed to resent the fact that the Yanks – with nothing more than a flourish of a pair of fifteen-denier nylons and a pack of Lucky Strike – could melt knicker elastic at five hundred yards. Added to that, the Yanks could afford to whizz the girls off to one of the city's many hotels for a late-night omelette, a sweet stout and a night of rumpy-pumpy in a warm bedroom. A dripping butty and a mug of stewed tea from my Uncle Harry's butty wagon as a prelude to a knee trembler at the back of the fish market in the February fog and sleet didn't have quite the same allure.

All this, of course, I didn't know at the time because I was only little. My Uncle Harry told me all about it much later.

My nanna, like many another Irish migrant, had come over from Dublin looking for work. Like all my family on the Pyne's side she had worked in the clothing trade. Her husband was a tailor, Aunty Julia was a seamstress, Aunty Kitty was a shirtmaker while her husband, Uncle Bobby, was a tailor also; added to that my granddad was a tailor. Now this is where it gets complicated because my nanna wasn't my grandmother, she was my mum's grandmother. My mum's own mother, Mary Quinlan, had done a runner back to Ireland when her husband (my grandfather and Nanna's son) got the daughter of the landlord of the local pub in the family way. Stay with it – like most families, it's complicated.

In his defence, it seems that my granddad was just one among many whose trouser tadpoles could have been responsible, but he was the one left holding the parcel when the banjo stopped twanging. So my grandfather, Henry Pyne, did a swift one to Liverpool and my grandmother, who found herself with three children and no husband, did a similar swift one back to Tipperary, where her family told her they had neither the room nor the wherewithal to look after her and her three small children. So she did what any woman would do and stuck them in an orphanage in Dublin. Harry was seven, my mum was five and Bernard was a baby of two.

The minute Nanna heard what had happened, she got on the next boat to Dublin, went to the orphanage and told the nuns she was taking the children back home. Family legend has it that the nuns were none too happy about this; after all, they were used to having people do what they said, not the other way round. The Mother Superior tried to stop her and got the length of my nanna's tongue and, family legend has it, a clout from her fists.

As a result, Nanna brought the children back home to Collyhurst,

Manchester, where she and my great-grandfather were living at the time. So after bringing up seven children of her own she now found herself with three more, and being who she was, she rolled up her sleeves and set to. My mum, Uncle Harry and Uncle Bernard never saw their mother again. They never talked about how they felt to me but I suspect that my mother and her brothers were deeply affected by what had happened.

Many years later, at my Uncle Bernard's funeral, a woman approached us at the graveside to tell us she was related to us. It turned out that she was the daughter of my grandmother by her second marriage. (As far as I know my grandparents were never divorced so the marriage may have been bigamous.) The woman was a Mormon, which is a first for our family, and she was researching the family's history (as Mormons do). She had come across Uncle Bernard's name in the births and deaths column of the *Manchester Evening News* and, knowing that Pyne was an unusual name, had come to the funeral to tell us that my grandmother was alive and well, though in her nineties now. It seems she had married a wealthy man in Cheshire but not before she'd had another baby to an unnamed father and had given it up for adoption in the workhouse where she had given birth; all we know now is his name. So somewhere I have or did have an Uncle John.

After Bernard's funeral, my mum got in touch with the woman and asked whether my grandmother would like to meet her and Harry but was told no, too much water had flowed under the bridge and it would all have been too painful.

My granddad, Henry O'Neil, was a master tailor who worked sitting cross-legged on a table in the best gentleman's tailors in Liverpool. According to family mythology, he made hand-stitched and perfectly lined suits for such luminaries as Selwyn Lloyd. He also made suits for himself every bit as fine as Selwyn Lloyd's, and wore handmade shirts and lovely, handmade tan brogues, so that he looked more like an Irish racehorse owner than somebody who sat cross-legged all day with a tape measure round his neck and a lump of French chalk in his waistcoat pocket.

I thought my granddad was wonderful, though others in the

family were a little less enamoured. Uncle Bernard, with some reason, never forgave him for buggering off and with even more reason never forgave him for living on the pig's back in Liverpool while he and Harry and my mum lived on whatever Nanna and her husband could scrape together in Collyhurst. According to Bernard, he sent them very little – in fact he sent them the square root of bugger all. That's families for you. He lived with a lady in Wallasey called Elsie. He only came to visit at holiday time and on one occasion when he broke his ankle in Liverpool falling off a tram (drunk, my nanna said) and came home to be nursed. He drove my mum and Nanna potty sitting by the fire all day with his foot up on a cushion (although he did manage to stagger as far as a waiting taxi every night which would take him to the Mitre pub in town).

He never brought Elsie with him to Manchester because my nanna wouldn't have had her in the house. She was a 'loose woman' and my granddad and Elsie were 'living over the brush'. I overheard these phrases while sitting in front of the fire eavesdropping on the grown-up conversation going on around me. I didn't understand what they were talking about. Living over the brush goes back to the days of the navvies, when men and women who wanted to set up together when there wasn't a churchman for miles would jump over a broomstick together and would then be regarded as married by the community. My granddad wasn't a navvy and I misheard 'brush' as 'bush' so I pictured my granddad and Elsie living in a tree house on top of a big bush while Elsie, being a loose woman, would occasionally have to lie down when her arms or legs came out of their sockets.

On the three or four times a year that my granddad came to visit to get drunk with my Uncle Bobby, I didn't ask him about the tree house or Elsie's socket problem because I knew that it was grown-up stuff and I would get in trouble for listening in.

By all accounts, Elsie was a lovely woman who cared for my granddad until the day he died.

At the time, of course, I knew none of this and loved it when my granddad came to stay. He told me lots of stories and jokes and is probably more responsible than anybody else for me becoming a comedian. He also spoiled me quite royally, giving me two half crowns or a ten-bob note every time he came to visit – and ten bob was no small potatoes in those day. It would have bought you a slap-up meal, a seat at the cinema and a mucky woman – or a house in Salford (actually, the rent on the first house we lived in when I got married was ten bob a week). He also had one of the luckiest war records of anybody I know. Early in the First World War he joined the Manchester Regiment and was sent off to fight the Hun. The story goes that he was captured on the first day of the Battle of the Somme and put in a POW camp. When the German officers discovered he was a tailor they gave him a job making suits for them. And then when they saw how good his tailoring was, they began paying him in sausages, brandy and fine cigars. I think he was quite sorry when the war was over and he had to come back to Collyhurst. He was the only man in his regiment who came back fatter than when he went in.

There are no skeletons in our family cupboard; they're all out there in the street dancing the double jig.

My nanna had a very bizarre relationship with her errant son. He was a rabid socialist from the James Connolly/James Larkin school and was also a strident atheist; my nanna, while in no way, shape or form a conservative, was a very devout Catholic with a rock-solid belief in all of the Church's teachings. When I was seven or so my nanna began to suggest that I might like to consider the priesthood as a career opportunity. She used to read a magazine put out by the Holy Ghost Fathers called something like *The Word*, which was full of pictures showing smiling African children being baptised.

One Sunday afternoon I was sitting at the table reading the Beano and my granddad and Nanna were sitting either side of the fire. Everything was quiet and peaceful until my nanna slid a copy of the magazine across the table.

'Would you never think of being a priest now, Michael? It's a wonderful thing to have a priest in the family and the missionary fathers go out to Africa baptising the little black babies and saving their souls. It's a wonderful thing doing God's work.'

My granddad snorted down his long nose.

'Huh! What are ye doin' puttin' ideas like that in the child's mind? What are they anyway, these Holy Ghost Fathers of yours but the shock troops of imperial capitalism, giving the poor bloody darkies the Bible and while they're reading it they steal the land from off them! And what do they do anyway, only make them ashamed of their own culture, even the way they dress' – and I will never forget until the day I die this next phrase – 'putting brassieres on the black chests of Africa.'

I thought my grandmother was going to go for the holy water bottle and drown him with it but instead she shook her fist at him and said, 'What are ye doing, using language like that in front of a child? Yer not too old to have your mouth washed out with soap!'

I think she objected to the word 'brassieres' but I don't know why. I knew what they were because there were pictures of ladies wearing them in my Aunty Julia's fashion magazines. I used to look at them sometimes and my willy would go hard, though I didn't know why. But I did know I would be in trouble if my nanna caught me looking at them.

The Street

My world then was the street, our back yard and our back entry. The back yard held the outside toilet, a coal shed which had its roof under my bedroom window and a scrubby garden with a single rose bush that crawled up the wall which separated us from the next-door corner shop. That rose bush was my nanna's pride and it was my job to run out with the hearth brush and shovel after the rag and bone man's horse had done its shit, to collect the steaming turds before anybody else got to them. Very often this meant a race with the lady who lived across the back entry, Aunty Guy, who had a lovely garden and who always grew a beautiful crop of roses. The horse-shit race depended not just upon pace and timing but upon hearing. The rag and bone man had a bugle and he used to blast out a twisted half-scale on it before shouting out 'Hebone nolerags!', which thinking about it now probably translates as 'Any old bones and rags'. Like the milkman and the ice cream man he preferred the horse to the more costly and expensive to feed lorry. The rags went to be turned into shoddy and the bones went to make glue. As well as rags and bones he also collected any spare bits of brass and copper we might have hanging around. These he would weigh in at the local scrap yard.

In return for the rags and old scrap metal, we got – guess what? Donkey stones. These were soft chalky blocks of artificial stone, which the women of the house (blokes didn't do cleaning) used to scour the steps and the pavement outside the house as a way of both marking territory and as a statement of cleanliness. A proper donkey-stoned step was a sure sign of a woman's standing on the street. Later in my childhood, women stopped using donkey stones and began using Mansion Polish, a sort of red gloss paint that only needed slapping on once a month or so. The problem with that was that when it rained the Mansion Polish became very slippery. Milkmen used to find themselves flat on their backs surrounded by broken bottles and a lagoon of milk and before they could get up they would find a postman landing on their chest. Dangerous stuff.

However, back to the horse shit. My nanna was going quite deaf, which meant that I had to keep my ears open for the rag man's bugle. Aunty Guy must have had ears as good as mine because a lot of the time she won the horse-shit race outright.

I had better luck with the Italian ice-cream man's horse shit than the rag and bone man's because when Carlo Visci came round he always stopped in our street first and rang his bell to tell us he was there. I was able to get there first while Aunty Guy, across the way, had much further to come. This might all seem academic to you but horse-shit races were a huge part of my intellectual development.

Aunty Guy was a lovely lady, warm and generous, and she was married to Arnold 'Daddy' Edgar, a rounded, smiling man who played the tenor horn in the CWS Manchester Silver Band. Next door to Aunty Guy lived Aunty Cissie, a spinster and Aunty Guy's friend. She still had gas lights in her house. Aunty Guy and Cissie weren't my real aunties but that was the way of things then. I don't know how Aunty Guy and Daddy Edgar met but she was a New Zealander and told me she was part Maori. She did have a slight

Kiwi accent and used to joke with me all the time. If ever I asked her where she was going she would say, 'Up the Boo-Aye shooting pookakies.' This seems to be a Kiwi expression and gave me the inspiration when I was much older for a children's poem and the title of my first collection.

Next door to our house was the corner shop run by Mr and Mrs Hughes. They sold everything from clothes pegs to vinegar, from dolly blue for whitening whites in the wash to bacon, butter, cheese, eggs, biscuits, boiled ham, flypaper, sweets, bleach, candles and paraffin. My mum used to help out in the shop to earn a few bob, and I would go and watch her cutting butter off a big slab and wrapping it in greaseproof paper. She would slice bacon on the hand-driven slicer and when people wanted vinegar they brought empty bottles to the shop and she filled them from a huge barrel that stood on the counter. When I was about four I pulled the spigot out of the vinegar barrel while trying to turn it and flooded the shop. I thought I was going to be sent to prison and started wailing in fear but they told me I was too small to go to jail and gave me a barleysugar stick to shut me up. The shop stank of vinegar for quite a while after that.

Recycling came naturally, then. People brought bottles back to be filled, and saved brown paper and string to be used again and again. (My nanna had drawers full of smoothed-out brown paper and salvaged hairy string.) The milkman brought fresh bottles of milk every morning and took the empties back; the pop man brought the great stoneware bottles of dandelion and burdock, lemonade and sarsaparilla and took back the empties. Jam jars were recycled too, as were egg-boxes, packing cases and all kinds of wooden crates. If you saw us now, through the reverse telescope of time, you might think we were a thin, undernourished and badly clothed tribe. We weren't; we had enough to eat, and what we had was seasonal and wasn't flown in from some recently cleared tropical rain forest; and though our clothes might have been old-fashioned and not very exciting, they weren't made by small children in sweat shops in Vietnam.

Wartime rationing was still in place. Though it meant we had enough to eat and not much more, it also meant that sweets were rationed so fat children were an extreme rarity. Uncle Joe's Mint Balls were three for a penny and used up pretty much all my sweet ration for a week, so I used to try to make mine last and last by sucking each one very slowly and carefully. Then I'd forget and crunch it and it would be gone. Wooden liquorice root was cheaper and lasted longer. It looked like a short twig, six inches or so long and about as thick as a child's little finger. It tasted nothing like liquorice but was nonetheless quite nice and you could chew it for ages until in the end there was nothing left but a soggy, tasteless brush. Other magical treats that our gang lusted after in those post-war days were Flying Saucers (rice-paper domes filled with fizzy sherbet), toffee cigarettes, sherbet dips, humbugs, penny chews and gob stoppers.

I remember a recurring dream as a small child in which I went to a sweetshop and found that it had a hole in the window big enough for me to get my hand through; any notions of stealing or sin vanished in my somnolent greed and I would put my hand in through the hole, help myself to sweets from the display and stuff them into my mouth.

I had lots of strange dreams when I was small.

One night, when I was staying at my Aunty Kitty's, I had to share a bed with their son, who I called Uncle George. He'd come home on leave from army camp because he was courting a local lass, Thora Devlin, and had found his bed occupied by a small second cousin from four stations down the railway line. That night I had a dream in which not only did I get all the sweets out of the window, but I also found myself in possession of a brand-new bike which I proceeded to furiously dream-pedal all the way to the park and back.

Uncle George got up and went to sleep downstairs on the settee because (as he told everyone next morning) I'd spent all night kicking him, laughing out loud, making guzzling noises and shouting, 'Gerrout the way! Gerrout the way!'

Another dream I had which used to really upset me had me arriving at school wearing nothing but a very short vest that wouldn't cover my willy no matter how hard I pulled at it. In my dream I didn't discover this until I was in the school playground. I grew out of that dream eventually – thank God. My worst nightmare recurred throughout my childhood and on into my adult years. In my dream I was walking along a path between a river and a canal. It was a kind of towpath and, as I walked, the path grew narrower and narrower and the river and canal grew wider until finally I was walking on a strip not much wider than my two feet. When I looked back the path had gone and when I looked forward I saw that my way ahead had also vanished and I was now standing on a small platform of earth just big enough to hold me. All around me was an endless sea. I hated that dream. Somebody I spoke to said that it represented a fear of dying. I think it represents a fear of being left on a tuft of grass in the middle of a lot of water.

I know that poverty is comparative and in some ways we sons of sons of toil had 'never had it so good', as Harold Macmillan was later to boast. We did have health and education and much of our heavy industries and transport had been nationalised, but living on a war widow's pension and what few pounds my nanna's state pension brought in didn't mean that we were well off. On the other hand I don't think we saw ourselves as poor; we were pretty much getting by like everybody else in the street. It was only later when I went to grammar school that I realised that there was a whole tribe of people who went on holidays to places like St Ives, who had AGAs in their kitchen, who put Lea & Perrins Worcestershire sauce in their soup and who didn't wipe their arses on squares of yesterday's newspapers strung up in the outside loo.

Our house, like all the others in Hall Road except the corner shops, was a red-brick, slate-roofed terraced house with a small patch of earth in front and a bigger patch of earth, a coal shed and an air-raid shelter out back. There were two bedrooms and a small boxroom where I was to spend most of my life. Downstairs was the front room, only used when somebody was ill or dead or there was a party. There was an old upright piano in there that Aunty Julia played at parties and that was otherwise kept locked. When I was small I used to sit underneath it and push the keys up from underneath, pretending that the deep low notes were giants stamping their feet and the tinkly high notes were icicles falling.

The living room had a fireplace, a table and four chairs and two armchairs, one of which was occupied by my nanna, who would sit there most of the day saying her rosary and reading the newspaper. A smaller room off the living room was called 'the scullery' and it contained a sink, a gas cooker and a small press. It was crowded in the living room, particularly when Big Lou came to live at number 38, but we were used to it. Most of us were out at work or school during the week and of an evening I would sit at the table doing my homework or reading or playing with my toys while the grown-ups smoked and listened to the radio and the cat yawned on the hearthrug. Saturdays I would be out all day, off to the cinema or the swimming baths or just 'mucking about' with my pals; Sundays would be a wash at the sink followed by church followed by boredom followed by more church then tea then homework then bed. I loathed and detested Sundays and I'm not sure I'm all that delirious about them now.

Me, Cissy Worswick and the Cannibal Queen

One day my mother tricked me into going to school.

Until that day, my life had not been ruled by any clocks and nobody had made me sit in rows doing stuff; I had been at liberty to mooch around, dig dirt, sing songs, tell jokes, pick up worms, climb trees, ride my scooter, talk with old men sitting on their doorsteps, go to the market with Nanna and drink sarsaparilla from the man with one arm who sold drinks and herbs, and most importantly I could read and draw what I wanted and when I wanted.

That morning my mum woke me up early.

'You're going to school today.'

'I want to play out.'

'You'll like it.'

'But it's sunny. I want to play out.'

'You'll like it.'

'I won't.'

'You will.'

'I won't.'

'You really, really will.'

'I really, really won't.'

'You can have some Jelly Babies afterwards.'

Half an hour later, face washed, hair combed and shoes polished, I was on my way to school, hand in hand with my mum.

The baby class was in what had been the stable block of an old house and orphanage that was now St Anne's Roman Catholic School, Crumpsall. The Catholics of the area had bought them both and had turned them into a school for children aged five to fifteen. They built a wooden church in the grounds; I'd been there with my nanna to mass and benediction.

It was warm and sunny as my mum walked me to school and it seemed to me that it would be much better if, instead of going to school, I played in the street. It would probably be hot enough to melt the pitch between the cobbles and I could play with it, popping the bubbles and digging it out with a lollipop stick. Sometimes I got pitch on my legs and my nanna used to get it off with butter. When I mentioned my preference, though, my mother insisted that I would have an even better time in school. Like a fool I believed her. I've never trusted women since.

When we got to school there were lots of other children in the playground, running round squealing and playing tig. Several boys were joined in a long chain, huffing and chuffing and moving their arms playing trains, and some girls were playing whip and top. My mother held my hand while I looked at this whirling mass of humanity. Outside of the crowded beaches of Blackpool I'd never seen so many people in one place at the same time.

A lady (who I would later come to know as Mrs Barnett the dinner lady) came out with a bell in her hands and rang it and all the children ran and stood in lines outside their classrooms. We went over to the infants and my mum introduced me to a lady who I would later find was called Miss Worswick. She had steel-rimmed glasses and hair up in a bun like my nanna; I thought her terribly old but I expect that she was probably only in her forties, if that.

Suddenly I noticed that my mum had somehow dematerialised and left me alone on Planet School where Miss Worswick, the Empress Ming to my Flash Gordon, grabbed me by the hand and led me into a room that smelled of milk, plasticine and pee. To add insult to abandonment, Miss Worswick sat me at a table with a boy with a runny nose. Twin candles of snot slid down from his nostrils, slowly crawling earthwards until they reached the edge of his lip, at which point he would give a powerful sniff, jerking his head back at the same time so that the twin trails would vanish like panicking slugs back into the caverns of his nostrils. I found this disgusting and fascinating at the same time. He also had the strangest haircut I had ever seen: his thick black hair looked as though it had been cut at random and ranged in length from half an inch to three inches – in no particular pattern or scheme that I could make out. Years later when I saw reconstructions of Cro-Magnon man I always thought of that snotty table-mate of my first day at school. I would like to say that he went on to become a world-famous neurological surgeon, but that would not be true.

The room was painted green up to about three foot from the floor and was a dull cream above that. There were pictures of Jesus and Mary, a map of the world, big cut-out pictures of Humpty Dumpty and Little Bo Peep, and friezes telling the story of the Gingerbread Man, the Three Little Pigs and Jack tumbling down a hill while Jill ran after him.

Miss Worswick gave me some wooden letters to make words from. I could do that easily because I could already read, so I made the words and then rolled a plasticine snake. This together with counting cowrie shells and a strange thing called sleepy-time-blanket, when we were all made to lie down and pretend to be asleep, took up most of the day. At home time my mother collected me and took me back along the warm afternoon streets. I played out afterwards until tea time and bed.

The next morning she woke me up again and told me to get washed and dressed.

'Why?'

'Because you're going to school.'

'I went there yesterday.'

My child's mind saw school as an optional, one-day event, like going to the park or the zoo. You didn't necessarily have to do it again – only if you really wanted to. And I didn't. I didn't want to sit next to Cro-Magnon Snot Boy rolling plasticine snakes in a room that smelled of sour milk and pee ever again.

Moaning and wailing, I was dragged through the Crumpsall streets, howling my grief at my mother's treachery to the chimney pots and the heavens beyond. Old ladies clucked as my poor mother struggled with this snivelling ball of misery, shaking their heads and saying, 'He'll soon get used to it,' or 'Mine cried for a month before she settled down.'

Eventually we got to the entrance of that gloomy old building, arriving long after the other children had gone in.

Miss Worswick heard my wailing and came to the door.

'He won't go in,' my mother said.

'Oh yes he will go in,' said Miss Worswick.

She took a firm grip of my jumper and pulled.

I got one foot on each side of the door jamb and leaned back, flailing and screaming. I might have been small, but I was rough and tough and also half-mad with grief at being wrenched away from my clock-free world of play and fun. Throwing my head back, I screamed as loudly as I could, aware of the small faces staring at me over their crayons and cowrie shells.

'If you go, he'll come in,' said Miss Worswick.

My mum retreated and before she'd turned the corner I was most definitely in, with well-smacked legs, sniffling and gulping air, and staring at the head of the boy with the snot yo-yos and was reading some rubbish about John and Jane and a cat called Fluff. I never tangled with Miss Worswick again. She was one … mean … hombre.

The next day I walked to school with a pal from the next street, Colin Duff, who filled me in on this school stuff. Miss McWalter and Mrs Clark ran the infants' class, which he was in, and they were a doddle compared to Miss Worswick; so if I was good and showed that I could read and do my numbers, I might get sent up to the top infants. I resolved to work my way out of the Worswick gulag as soon as I could.

The boy with the snot moustache had been moved to another table so that morning I was seated with a couple of other children who seemed pleasant enough. In fact one of them, a dark-haired girl with huge brown eyes, I thought very pretty. When I got home that afternoon, quite an old hand at this school thing, my mother asked me who I was sat next to.

'Bernard Atlakeland, she's a girl, and there's a boy called Cannibal Queen.'

'Who?'

'Cannibal Queen.'

No matter how many times she asked she got the same answer. Her curiosity got the best of her and the next morning she asked Miss Worswick who these children might be.

'Bernadette Lakeland and Clement Mulqueen.'

Years later, when I did a routine about Miss Worswick and the school nativity play on BBC television, a woman wrote to me to say that she'd known Miss Worswick at teacher training college. Cissy Worswick and she had trained together and, after a long number of years working in primary schools, they had met up again. The writer of the letter had married and had children but Cissy had stayed single, living with her elderly parents and looking after them through their frail and fading years.

'Cissy told me that every Sunday after dinner, her parents would go upstairs for a nap and she used to pull all the curtains, take all her clothes off, pour herself a dry sherry and walk round the house naked for a couple of hours. She said it made her feel deliciously wicked.'

This lonely and loyal woman who walked naked round the shadows of a quiet suburban house of a Sunday afternoon with a glass of dry sherry in her hand, had, to my five-year-old eyes, been one of the fearsome giants of the grown-up world, and for most of my life I'd remembered her as a kind of ogre. We know so little of each other and nothing at all of what is in each other's hearts.

Within a few weeks I was moved up out of Miss Worswick's class into the infants. I liked it there and soon found that I'd graduated from making plasticine snakes to reading and writing and doing sums.

The Runaway

I don't know what made me do it – some imagined slight, I suppose (I took offence easily in those days because I was still a little prince-emperor at the epicentre of my own small world). Perhaps I'd seen something in the paper-shop window that was beyond the reach of my spends and my mother had refused to top up the difference, or perhaps I'd been shouted at for leaving my stuff all over the place. Whatever it was, I told them all I was leaving home, that I never wanted anything to do with any of them again, and I started to pack.

Thinking back now, it was most probably something to do with spends since it was definitely a Saturday when I ran away because my Aunty Julia was at home. If it had been Sunday she would have been at church or out with her friend Jessie. Saturday was also spends day. I do know for certain it was afternoon when I left because my mum had just finished washing and clearing the plates from dinner, as we called lunch back then. They didn't seem surprised when I drew myself up to my full six-year-old height and told them I was leaving for good.

'I'm not staying here any longer,' I wailed through my tears. 'I hate you all. You're all rotten to me so I'm running away.'

'Off you go then,' my mother said, laughing.

There she was laughing and there I was, six years old and breaking my heart!

I would show them. I would leave now, get on a ship at Salford docks and sail away to make my fortune.

I rooted in the glory hole under the stairs for the old gas-mask bag I used occasionally to carry a picnic to the park. I got my imitation leather flying helmet and wind-cheater, made myself a jam butty, poured some milk into an empty medicine bottle, stuffed everything but the jacket in the bag and left.

All the time I was doing this my Aunty Julia sat smoking a Pall Mall and reading her Boots penny library book. My mother got on with some ironing and Nanna sat by the empty grate saying her rosary. It was a hot summer's day so there was no need for a fire.

Nobody came to wave me off as I stormed down the lobby, flung open the door and flounced into the street, slamming it behind me.

Mushy was sat on the wall, snoozing in the afternoon sun and watching the antics of the girls in the street who were turning a big rope and skipping in and out of it, calling 'Betty Grable on the table, showing her legs to Clark Gable' in time to their skips. The cat looked at me in a vague sort of way, wondering if I were going to stroke him: then, sensing the mood I was in, he shut his eyes and nodded off again.

It was already very hot: my jacket felt heavy and itchy, and the bag, which was designed for a grown-up to carry, was banging against my short legs. I tried to adjust the webbing shoulder strap but only managed to tear my fingernail so that now I also had a split nail that caught on everything. There were scissors on the kitchen window sill that I could have cut my nail with and my Aunty Julia would have shortened the strap for me, but my departure had been grand and final, the end of my relationship with that unfeeling lot, and I was not going back.

I left our street behind, crossed the main road and made for Peg's Arches, which I knew led to Woodland's Road, Barney's Croft and on into town. All I had to do then was cross the Irwell into Salford, find the docks and get a job as a cabin boy on one of the big ships. My Uncle Bobby had been in the Merchant Navy and he'd been to somewhere called Nover Scosher in Canada and said it was a grand country. A man could make his fortune there. So that was what I was going to do: make my fortune.

I followed the old lane between the allotments. Old Man Corkett was weeding his potatoes. He waved me over to the fence as I walked past.

'Where you off to, then?'

'I'm running away to Nover Scosher.'

'Got any money?'

'A shilling.'

'You'll need more than that to get to Nova Scotia.'

He gave me a tanner and told me that if I got into trouble I should go to the police station. I knew this already because I'd ended up there once when Nanna and Aunty Kitty lost me in Manchester.

One and sixpence. I could get anywhere with that!

Bees hummed in the rosebay willowherb that lined the old footpath and, as I walked under the railway bridge, a shunting engine dragged some clanking trucks overhead, making for the ICI dyeworks down the track. I could smell the coal smoke and steam on the hot afternoon air.

I dawdled along until I came to Woodlands Road and decided I was thirsty and ought to buy a bottle of pop. The milk would keep until later. The shop was cool and dark after the heat of the day, and I waited while an old lady with wishbone legs was served. It was common to see people who had been crippled with rickets in those days: decades of poor food and overwork had produced a stunted population in those northern towns. The situation had got so bad that the government was eventually forced to act. By the time I was growing up, every child got a small bottle of milk at school and babies were given free cod-liver oil and orange juice. It was too late for many, though, like the old lady in front of me who, as my granddad would have said, couldn't have stopped a pig in a back entry.

I bought a bottle of Tizer and headed off down the road towards Barney's Croft.

I was out of my tribal boundaries now and fair game for any gang that might happen upon me, so I had to keep my wits about me. On my way to Queen's Road I would have to pass the notorious Queen Mary flats at Smedley. They were called that because, although they were only council tenements, they'd been built in the thirties in a modernist style and looked a little like the upper decks of an ocean liner. Ten years after Manchester Corporation had knocked them down I saw identical flats in Golders Green going for a quarter of a million pounds each. But the people in the Smedley flats couldn't have afforded a quarter of a million farthings.

They were a tough bunch; many of them were good-hearted and honest working people just trying to get by from day to day, but scattered amongst them were some real villains. Their kids were all rough hard-cases and we were terrified of them. Their gang was the fabled Black Hand Gang and they would come swarming over the

Hills regularly to raid us, particularly on the nights before Bonfire Night when they came to rob all the wood and old tyres we had collected for our bonfire. Years later, when I read *Lord of the Flies*, I thought that Golding, when he wrote of the boys' savagery towards each other on that coral island, must have seen some of the pitched battles between our gang and the notorious Black Hand Gang.

As I drew near the tenements, a lone figure came out from an alley and walked towards me. I crossed the road. He followed. I walked faster; so did he. I slowed down; he followed suit. I sat on a wall and drank some more of the Tizer. He came up and stared at me. It was one of the kids from my school.

'Wot yer doin 'ere?'

'Runnin' away.'

'Where to?'

'Nover Scosher.'

'Never 'eard of it.'

'It's in Canada.'

''Ow long will it tek yer?'

'Cuppler days.'

'They have Mounties there. Gizza drink.'

The kid seemed all right but he had a mouth that was crusted with sores so I drank as much as I could without bursting from the fizz, and gave him the bottle with a couple of inches of pop left in it.

'Here y'are. Yer can 'ave the rest.'

'Shall I get us some toffees with the money back?'

I nodded. I didn't know where the 'us' had come from or how we had become bosom buddies all of a sudden but I wasn't going to argue.

He drained the bottle, walked solemnly to a shop across the road and came back with two Black Sambo chews.

'I'll come wiv yer ter Barney's.'

He led me up a path between some garages and across some wasteland. We paused to throw stones at a pair of copulating dogs and to watch a couple of old tramps who were sitting on some empty crates drinking a mixture of methylated spirits and milk from a bottle.

When we got to Barney's Croft he left me, simply saying 'tarar' as I struck out across the wasteland. There was a lot of it. Part of it was a brickworks with clay pits and large ovens and piles of bricks stacked ready for collection. Tramps used to congregate there in the winter to sleep in the warm ovens as they were cooling down after a firing.

According to local legend, one night some tramps were in the ovens fast asleep. When men came early next morning to fire up the ovens they didn't see that the tramps were in there and roasted them alive. A few years later my Uncle Harry's brother-in-law, Jurek, on his way to work early one morning, found a dead man on Barney's Croft, lying where he had been bludgeoned to death. So it was not at all the place for a junior runaway.

I decided that it was time for my tea, sat down on a pile of rubble and opened my bag. The sun was settling in the west, hanging just above the far-off rooftops, and the evening air was cooling. I laid out my jam butty and bottle of milk and pulled on my imitation leather helmet. I had taken a mouthful of bread and jam and was just opening the bottle when I felt something tickling my head. I tried to ignore it but it got worse. There was something alive in my hat. I jumped up, threw it off and began screaming and dancing on the spot; the helmet was alive with cockroaches. They had crept in it while it was rolled up under the stairs and now they were in my hair and down the back of my shirt.

As a grown man I have few phobias but one thing that still chills my blood is a cockroach. Like a lot of houses in the street, ours was plagued with them. No matter what we did – putting Derris powder and DDT down the skirting boards, stuffing up the cracks in the floorboards – they were there in the morning when you switched the light on, scuttling for cover, their black-brown cases shining as they scampered across the lino. Worst of all, they scrunched when you trod on them, their pale yellow blood squelching out from the flattened casework of their bodies. Nanna hated them as much as I did and called them 'witch clocks', which made them seem all the more sinister. Years later I read that they are the only living things that can survive the radiation from a nuclear blast. Well, they didn't survive my boot that day as I shook them out of my hair and shirt and squashed them underfoot. In the absence of a convenient Boys' Own Pocket Hydrogen Bomb, it was the best I could do.

I sat down, shaking. All of a sudden this running away lark didn't seem all that great. I threw the butty away and poured the milk into the cinders. I would go back home and give them all one more chance.

Arriving at the door as the last of the sun vanished behind the slate roofs, I whistled my way into the room and flung the gas-mask bag back into the dark of the glory hole.

'How far did you get?'

'Nearly to Nover Scosher,' I lied.

'How far?'

'Barney's Croft.'

That got me a really good smacking because I wasn't supposed to go anywhere near there.

Lying in bed sniffling that night, I decided that I would run away again as soon as possible; but the next day Uncle Harry came and took me to town in his van with the fat man carrying the sausage painted on the side and I forgot all about Nover Scosher.

The Amateur Barber

There was a barber's on Cheetham Hill near the swimming baths, just down the road from the builder's yard where they made black mortar from slaked lime and coal cinders. Mackie Davies was the barber, a comical and popular Jewish ex-boxer who always had a joke for everybody, kids and grown-ups alike.

Mothers left their sons waiting while they went off to do their shopping along the main road. We would sit for ages as grown men were shaved and barbered, shuffling along the leather upholstered bench watching the scissors flashing while Abie, another ex-boxer (who I would meet again years later when I worked in a carpet shop on Cheetham Hill), swept the hair from the floor.

Men would slip furtively in from the bustle of the street, hand something to Mackie or Abie then slope off out again. There was a lot of whispering and talking out of the sides of mouths and, as in a

Damon Runyon story, the language was pure argot:

'Am I saying he's a schnorrer? Of course he's a schnorrer. He'd take your eye and come back for the socket already! I'm telling you, the schmuck blags the gelt and shpiels it all on something that should be lucky to pull a rag and bone cart! A pony, on the nose! A shlemiel, a nebbish.'

Yiddish and Manchester rhyming slang flew about the shop like an incantation and still we little kids waited. Mackie's was the front for a betting shop – in those days off-course betting was illegal unless you were rich and could place bets by phone with your bookmaker with whom, naturally, you had an account. So places like Mackie's were where bets were taken then dodged round to Demmy's, the bookmakers, by Abie, the bookies' runner. Pitch and toss was played on the streets and men would scatter when the police came running. I saw pitch and toss played many years later in the 1980s at Appleby Gypsy Horse Fair but there the stakes weren't pennies or a few bob but hundreds of pounds in twenty and fifty pound notes.

From time to time, mothers would stick their heads round the door, shout at Mackie to get on with it, then go for a hot Vimto and a fag at Lorenzini's, the Italian snack bar near the public baths.

When it finally came to your turn, little kids like me were sat on a plank that was set across the arms of the chair. We were then swaddled in a sheet and given the regulation short back and sides or a pudding-basin cut as we stared at our reflections in the mirror and watched Mackie with a fag hanging from one side of his mouth talking nineteen to the dozen out of the other. In those days, all kids looked like scaled-down versions of their fathers, and all the fathers looked the same. Post-war fashion amounted to a short back and sides, a suit for Sundays and weddings, and a boiler suit, a flat 'at and a gas-mask bag for the carry-out for working days. There wasn't much variation unless you were a bus conductor, a railwayman or worked for the water board, in which case you had a uniform. Otherwise it was work clothes and the same haircut you'd had in the army.

There were a few hardy souls that had their Brylcreemed hair cut and combed like Clark Gable or Jimmy Stewart or one of the other film stars, but men with hair like that were thought a bit fast and were equated with mucky weekends in Blackpool and the ruination of some innocent girl or other. Romance was for the silver screen and stopped once you'd come through the door after the honeymoon.

I remember when the first real Teddy Boy appeared in our street; Mr Dalton told him to go and get his bloody hair cut. Of course, Cliff Richard, Billy Fury and Tommy Steele would soon come along and change everybody's idea of what a haircut could look like – but that was in the dim future.

When I was fourteen I went alone to Mackie's and asked for a crew cut, which was all the rage then. My mate Andy Rigg had one – but he also had a good bone structure and would have still been good-looking if he was bald with one eye in the middle of his forehead. I had ears like a taxi with its doors open, a chin like a shovel and wore glasses. Coming out of Mackie's ('Are you sure your mum ain't gonner kill me for this, son?' 'No, she says it's OK'), I put my glasses on and looked at myself in a shop window. I looked like a hedgehog with wings and two jam-jars strapped to the front of its head.

When she saw me, my mother hit the roof, then went on to hit the wall, the floor and the lamppost. For weeks after she would only go out with me when it was dark and foggy. If I went anywhere with her during the day I had to walk on the other side of the road.

'I'm not being seen out with you until it grows out.'

'We had haircuts like that in the desert if we got lousy,' Uncle Harry said.

Her answer was short and to the point. 'He's not lousy and he's not in the bloody desert, he's in bloody Crumpsall, and anyway, the war's been over thirteen years.'

He just looked at me, winked and whispered, 'It'll grow out.'

Strangely, when it did grow back, it grew back curly. I let it get fairly long and one day a local girl said, 'You look like Billy Fury.' She was either mad, bad or worse-sighted than me. I no more looked like Billy Fury than King Tut but what she said went to my head and I spent ages with a water-damped comb slicking my hair in a quiff and practising the kind of sneery smile that passed for cool then (and now, I suppose). My mother caught me sneering into the mirror and said the last time she'd seen a look like that on somebody's face it had been Bell's Palsy.

When I was five, my mate Wharfie decided to set up as a barber. It was a hot summer's day, and he simply went down their back yard with his mother's scissors, turned a bucket upside down for the clients to sit on, then invited all the girls from the streets around to have their hair cut. His mother, who was a clairvoyant and fortune-teller, was inside with her crystal ball and tea leaves and a cabal of women from the neighbourhood, doing what my nanna said was 'the devil's work'. She can't have been much of a clairvoyant if she failed to see that her son had turned into an amateur Mr Teasy-Weasy. Word of Wharfie's impromptu barbershop soon spread and before too long customers were queuing up to get into Wharfie's back yard. There were a lot of girls in the entry that day, playing ball and doing handstands against the wall with their skirts tucked in their knickers, and they all decided to patronise Salon Wharfie at the same time. In those post-war years most little girls had long hair, some of them very long hair; it was often described as a woman's 'crowning glory'. But Wharfie only had one style: 'convict chic'. Pamela Dolmen's hair wasn't very long but it was thick and a mass of corkscrew curls like Shirley Temple's. She was the first girl under the scissors, and I watched, transfixed, as all those lovely curls fell onto the warm flagstones, and I watched on, still transfixed, as girl after girl, with long ginger plaits and straight blonde pigtails alike, were transformed into creatures that looked as though they were about to be transported to Australia after being found on the salt marshes with Magwitch, chapter one, *Great Expectations*.

As soon as the first mothers saw what had happened to their daughters, their wails began to echo round the summer streets. Wharfie's yard was ankle-deep in curls and plaits, and the mob was at the gates baying for blood. Sensing trouble, I made for home and was 'whistling dixie' in our kitchen. Once safely there, I said to my mother: 'It wasn't nothing to do with me, Mam.'

'What wasn't?'

'Wharfie's gone and cut all the girls' hair all off, and all their mums are all crying.'

Mrs Wharfe came out from her crystal ball and tea cups to find her yard covered in curls and plaits and a mob of screaming mothers at her gate telling her that her son was an imbecile. She told them all to bugger off, then when they'd gone gave Barry a good hiding. It was a bit pointless but they couldn't send him to prison – he was only six.

The girls were all taken to the hairdressers to have remedial work carried out and came back with feminine versions of the sort of crew cut that was to make my mother do a reverse Mrs Oedipus years later. Soon, like my crew cut, the girls' hair grew out and Wharfie gave up barbering in favour of jumping off high things like trees and garage roofs – which he was very good at.

CHAPTER 2

SHEER POETRY

Whatever storytelling ability I might have I must put down to my granddad and my nanna, but whatever poetic ability I possess is mostly due to my mum. When I was quite small, four or five perhaps, she read all the poems in Robert Louis Stevenson's *A Child's Garden of Verses* to me, over and over again, until I had some bits off by heart; when I was a little older I read them to myself. My favourites were 'From a Railway Carriage', 'The Swing', 'The Land of Counterpane' and 'The Lamplighter'. We were still on the edge of that world of Edwardian twilight and had gas lamps in our street.

My tea is nearly ready and the sun has left the sky.
It's time to take the window to see Leerie going by;
For every night at teatime and before you take your seat,
With lantern and with ladder he comes posting up the street.

And I found something unutterably beautiful in the lines in the poem 'Requiem':

Home is the sailor, home from the sea,
And the hunter home from the hill.

By the time I went to school I already knew dozens of poems; the nursery rhymes and songs my nanna sang to me were the base rock on which all the other poems settled. One song she sang to me from when I was a baby was:

There was an old woman went up in a basket
Ninety times as high as the moon

And where she was going I couldn't but ask it
For under her apron she carried a broom.
'Old woman, old woman, old woman,' said I,
'Where are you going up so high?'
'I'm going to sweep cobwebs off the sky,
And I will be with you tomorrow by and by.'

And I believed that an old lady just like Nanna really was going to sweep fine clinging spiders' webs from around the stars and the moon, and when the moon shone down on the cobbles in the street I imagined the old lady up there, working away with her broom.

I liked the poems we learned at school, too, though I wasn't all that keen on the hymns. Christmas carols were OK but I wasn't sure about 'Full in the Panting Heart of Rome', because I couldn't see how a city could have a heart, and 'Faith of Our Fathers', while it had a good tune, was all about dungeons and fires. But we were expected to learn them off by heart together with our Catechism.

Like most children I loved singing and there was one lesson we all looked forward to without exception: *Singing Together*. The programme was broadcast on weekday mornings and we all sat down on the floor near the radio and were exposed to some of the finest music the world has ever made. Most of the tunes were folk songs from these islands, but there was a fair smattering of songs from other countries, America and the West Indies in particular. According to folkie mythology, one of the BBC producers responsible for the content of *Singing Together* was the communist 'Bert' Lloyd.

The BBC (together with MI6 and MI5) spent much of the post-war years trying to root out any communists or anarchists in the corporation. Unfortunately many of the left-wingers were also highly intelligent and superbly talented people like Louis MacNeice, the poet, and Philip Donnellan, a wonderful left-wing documentary maker and thorn in the heavy foot of the Establishment. Perhaps the best known of them all was Salford street theatre Marxist Ewan MacColl, who together with his life partner, Peggy Seeger, and producer Charles Parker made the wonderful *Radio Ballads*, ground-breaking documentaries that used the voices and words of ordinary people to celebrate their lives; one of the programmes they made, *Singing the Fishing*, won the Prix d'Italia award.

Bert Lloyd, who I was to get to know well in later life, was a folk singer, folk song collector, musicologist, writer and broadcaster. He worked alongside that great photographer Bert Hardy, writing pieces for the *Picture Post*, and together they sailed Arctic waters with deep-sea fishermen and interviewed prostitutes in the slums of London. The BBC, fearful that Bert – as a well-known 'leftie' – would taint the minds of the general populace, put him to work in the schools' broadcasting department where he went on to taint the minds of a generation of schoolchildren by introducing them to the joys of traditional folk song. The BBC produced a series of handbooks for these programmes, which were very much in the style of the 1950s, well produced with beautiful pen and ink illustrations. My own favourites were 'Down in Demerara', 'Donkey Riding', 'Early One Morning', 'The Mermaid', 'Boney was a Warrior', 'Charley is my Darling', 'Paddy on the Railroad' and 'Li'l Liza Jane'. Other songs such as 'Cockles and Mussels' and 'Waltzing Matilda' I already knew because Nanna sung them to me and 'The Runaway Train' and 'The Big Rock Candy Mountain' I already knew from Uncle Mac's BBC radio programme on a Saturday morning.

By the way, Bert Lloyd later went on to produce the *Penguin Book of English Folk Songs* with Ralph Vaughan Williams. Not bad for an autodidact who spent part of his early life as a stockman in the Australian Outback and on board a whaling ship in the South Atlantic.

Miss Fisher

From the infants we went up to Miss Fisher's class. She was a shrike of a lady, thin as a rake with wild hair and bad nerves, and always seemed on the edge of complete hysteria. We were all frightened of her sudden outbursts, her high-pitched shrieking and her random and sudden slaps. I believe that she did have a full-blown breakdown not long after I'd left St Anne's, which is very sad. It was while I was in her class that I took my first communion and shat myself. Not, I might add, at the same time.

The first communion was easy; all we had to do was know our catechism and understand that now, at the fine old age of seven, we had reached the Age of Reason and were in command of our immortal souls. From now on it was up to us whether we went to Heaven, Hell or Purgatory. We were taught how to eat the Host and told not bite it because it was the real body of Jesus. It had come into the church as unleavened bread and during the mass the priest had turned it into Jesus's body. Since we were used to things like Santa Claus and the tooth fairy, transubstantiation didn't seem too much of a leap of faith.

We went to confession the day before and unburdened our seven-year-old souls of their black and disgusting accumulation of sins and then, on the day of our first Holy Communion we turned up early for mass; the girls in long white dresses, white gloves and shoes; the boys in black velvet shorts, white silk blouses and patent leather shoes with silver buckles. My mum made my shorts and blouse; there was no way we could afford to buy them. The consecration over, the first communicants made our way to the altar, grandparents and mums wiping tears away as we innocents progressed to the rail. I knelt and the altar boy held a silver plate under my chin as the priest put Jesus onto my tongue.

I don't know what Jesus thought He was doing because the daft ha'porth went and got Himself stuck on the roof of my mouth. God's Son was stuck there as though he had been glued to my soft palate and was not for coming off. I knew that if I touched Him with my finger I would go to Hell because that was a very bad sin; the priest had told us how somebody had once dropped the Host on the floor and when they picked Jesus up again there was a bloodstain there. I went back to my place in the pew and tried to peel Him off with my tongue but He just stuck there all the more. We had fasted since the night before and now I hadn't enough saliva to get the Son of God off the roof of my mouth. I looked around: all the other children had their heads down in devotion. I was choking. I looked desperately at the holy water stoops on either side of the altar. Which would be worse: to run and gulp down some holy water or pick Jesus off with my fingers? I began to weep silent tears and as I did I discovered that I'd also started to salivate. As soon as I'd enough spit I gave Jesus a good wetting and started to roll Him off. It took a while but eventually He was all done and dusted and the fires of Hell had been dampened for a bit.

We had strawberries and cream for our communion breakfast, which somewhat took my mind off the trauma. Talking to other Catholics over the years I have discovered that mine is not an isolated case and am convinced that the Vatican should have founded a Post First Holy Communion Trauma Department to deal with the millions of children whose lives have been blighted by fear of damaging Jesus and going to Hell for it.

Shitting myself had nothing to do with religion and everything to do with my granddad. I loved it when my granddad came to stay, because not only did he usually slip a few bob into my pocket but also his coming always meant bacon and cabbage. It was his favourite meal (and mine). My mum would go to the butchers for a sheet of spare ribs, which she would then place on the back step and whack with the kindling axe to make them short enough to fit in the pot. She would boil them for ages until the meat was falling off and then would dump a whole head of cabbage into the pan and cook it until it was soft. She served it up with mashed potatoes and butter and cups of very strong tea. My nanna didn't eat very much and neither did my mum, while Aunty Julia, on this occasion, was on one of her diets. There was quite a bit of cabbage left and I wolfed the lot.

The first lesson next morning was times tables. It was a winter's morning, the fire was blazing and the classroom was quite stuffy. Half way through the nine times table I felt a bit queasy; my stomach seemed very swollen and was hurting quite a lot. I needed to fart. I did fart but had what I later learned is called a 'follow through'. In this case it was quite a substantial one. Peter Gittins, my best pal, was sitting next to me. He gave an involuntary groan followed by a retching noise, and I can't say I blamed him. Other children around me were swaying and holding their noses. Miss Fisher immediately realised what was happening and sent me home. I waddled out of school like a bandy penguin, conscious of the load I was carrying. It was many a day before I would trust a fart again.

Our Gang

At the corner of our street there was an old gaslamp
And us kids used to meet there every night
We'd swing from its old bars and we'd play hide and seek,
In the shadows just beyond its yellow light.

'The Old Green Iron Lamp', the author

All the kids from our street and the ones that ran parallel formed a large gang that ranged in age from seven to eleven. Below seven you were 'a baby' and too young to join in many of the games, and past eleven you were on the road to becoming a teenager and therefore, to our eyes, 'dead boring'. So we played together and sang daft songs and formed an alliance against kids from other streets, boys and girls alike. In fact, the toughest of the bunch was a group of girls, the Carter sisters, all of whom could send you reeling with a slap and who we really relied on if there was ever a skirmish with another gang. But at the heart of it all was a smaller cadre of boys all about the same age who ran together and got into trouble together.

Albert Dalton lived a couple of doors away from me, Jimmy Hands lived across the back entry in the next street, Kenny Fullen lived in the same street as Jimmy, Wharfie the Barber lived down the bottom of our street near the greengrocer's shop and finally there was me. We didn't have a name for our gang, though for a brief period we called ourselves the Green Hand Gang, and we weren't an exclusive group so that other kids from our streets like Billy Perry and Kevin Leech came with us on lots of adventures, but we 'band of brothers' were the hard core that 'got up to things'. Albert was quiet and thoughtful with a bad scar on his shoulder where a pan of boiling water had fallen on him; Jimmy was solid and determined and the scourge of bullies. Kenny was one of the most cheerful people I have ever met; like his mum he was always laughing and always generous. He always called me Michelin after the Michelin man, for a bit of fun, shared his roller skates and his bike with me and was the first with any new jokes or mucky songs. We would all sit on the wall howling with laughter as Kenny went off into his performance, and all his life he carried on bringing fun into people's lives. He was a talented footballer and when I was writing a column for the *Manchester Evening News* I described how 'he was a fine young footballer of great promise who lost his way at the age of four when he discovered drink and women'. He would always help smaller children and protect them from bullying and it was Kenny who taught me how to ride a bike by pushing me down Duchess Road on his old rattler and letting go so that I either had to pedal or fall off.

Wharfie has assumed mythical status in my life and rightly so; not only was he able to climb higher and faster than any of us but he also seemed to have no fear. Wharfie's dad, Ben, was a tall slim man who didn't say much but always seemed to have a smile at the corner of his mouth. His fortune-telling mum was called Priscilla; my nanna suspected she was in league with the devil. In fact Nanna suspected that most people who weren't Irish and Catholic were in league with Old Nick; she would have preferred it if all the kids in our gang had been Catholics but Catholics were thin on the ground in our street.

We didn't care a toss about religion. Together, we would roam the streets, climb trees, kick balls, see who could pee the furthest (Wharfie) and get up to mischief. Playing cricket in the street was a favourite activity; it would be impossible now, but then there were few cars and we just stacked up some old cardboard boxes as a wicket and with a tennis ball and a crude wooden bat we played for hours, only moving the wicket when the very occasional delivery lorry came to the corner shop.

Our mothers didn't mind us being in a gang but kept an eye on us all the same.

'Where are you going?'

'Playing out.'

'Well, don't go climbing any trees. If you fall and break your legs then don't come running to me.'

How could I go running to her with my legs broken? I wondered. Mothers were always coming out with stuff like that.

When you were sniffling and moaning about something your mum would ask, 'Do you want something to cry about?'

What answer did she expect? 'Oh, yes please!'

When I wouldn't eat my tripe and onions my mum would tell me, 'Children all over the world are starving that would be only too glad of that.'

When I asked her to name one I got a clout for being cheeky.

If I got in trouble for doing something that Wharfie or Kenny had done she would say, 'If he put his hand in the fire, would you do it, too?' To which the answer was obviously 'no', since scrumping apples or cheeking a park keeper was nothing like sticking your hand in the fire, that would have been really stupid.

My nanna would just sit by the fire shaking her head when I got into trouble and mutter something about how it was all because I was playing with Protestants.

She herself was full of sayings that were supposed to help me on my way through life. 'If you'd any more mouth you'd have no face to wash,' she would say if I was being cheeky. 'Street angel, house devil,' was her reply to anybody who told her what a nice boy I was and if any woman walked down the street in new clothes she would mutter, 'Huh, fur coat and no knickers!' Best of all, if somebody got above themselves and started to 'lord it a bit', she would say, 'Well, the higher a monkey climbs, the more he shows his arse.'

All sayings which have helped me greatly on my way through this vale of tears.

In the mythology of those days there were more goblins and demons than saints and angels and everywhere you went there were things that wanted to kill you or at least hurt you.

If you swallowed chewing gum it would make a knot in your stomach that would kill you – and this was true because Kenny knew somebody who knew a kid that had died from chewing gum.

If an ambulance went past you had to touch your collar for good luck or you would end up in an ambulance too.

If you played near grids you would get fever and Jinny Greenteeth the water witch would get you. Telling me now (as urban folkorists do) that Jinny Greenteeth was an urban version of a dryad or water sprite and that Jennet was a name often associated with witches, doesn't do anything to lessen the terrors we felt then. Also I have recently discovered that she appears in other cultures as a child-snatching water demon – so we were probably right to be scared crapless by her.

Another monster we had to avoid was Icky the Bare-Bum Fire Bobby. 'Fire bobbies' was what us kids called firemen but why Icky wore no trousers or underpants and was to be feared is beyond me.

Other things to be avoided were orange pips, which grew into trees in your stomach; cow parsley, which we called 'Mother Die' because if you touched it your mother would die; dandelions, which would make you pee the bed if you ate them; and hawthorn, as a prick from a bush would kill you.

Rats were poisonous: one bite and you were dead and they always went for your throat. Earwigs could tunnel into your brain via your ear and then would eat it away. Big worms were called 'blood-suckers' because that's exactly what they would do, given the chance.

The edges of some of the millponds attached to the cotton mills and dyeworks often had leeches in them and one kid had got that many leeches on him all his blood had gone and he'd died and that was true because Wharfie knew somebody who knew a kid that knew that kid's brother.

Dogs would bite you without provocation and were a constant hazard in our street. Dogs seemed to have a dual function: chasing motorbikes and biting children. Chasing motorbikes always puzzled me because I couldn't work out what the dogs would do if they ever caught one? Savage it? Tear off its exhaust and gnaw its innards? Drag it back to feed its kids?

When it came to bites on the bottom or the leg, we were always told that it was our fault for running. Apparently that got the dogs excited – they must have thought we were small, pink motorbikes. Bees and wasps were another constant danger. Before biotechnology came along there were many more bees than there are now. We used to get stung quite a lot and would have to be fixed with 'dolly blue', the little bags of whitening my mum used to put in the wash.

Kevin Leech's dad Bobby kept bees and I would watch him sometimes taking out the honeycombs using a bellows with burning newspaper in it to make the bees drowsy. One day I found a dying hornet and, thinking it was a king bee (I knew there were queens so there had to be kings), I put it in a match box, gave it some sugar and took it to Mrs Leech who took it off me very solemnly and thanked me for saving its life.

Bees and wasps and dogs were a constant worry, but there were other terrors particular to Crumpsall – one of which was 'the mad people'. Springfield Hospital was part of the Crumpsall Hospital complex; it had once been a workhouse and later, when the old-age pension was introduced and people were no longer committed to institutions, it became an asylum for the insane. It still functioned as such when I was growing up and the inmates would regularly escape and be found roaming around in their pyjamas, dazed and hopeless, while us kids screamed blue murder and ran like billy-oh when we saw them.

One patient famously got out and nicked the school lollipop man's coat and cap from the hut where he stored it. Thus garbed, he walked to the junction at Crumpsall Green, stood in the middle of the crossroads and started to direct the traffic. He flagged two cars on with great gusto, one from the main road another from a side road. They crashed into each other and, undeterred, the amateur traffic bobby flagged more cars on with even greater enthusiasm until there was total gridlock. This didn't make the national press but it was the talk of Crumpsall for quite some time afterwards.

Uncle Bobby said there were lots of people in Springfield who shouldn't have been there: girls who had had babies without being married, feckless lads that kept getting into trouble and people who had just been put there because their families found them a burden; one doctor's signature later and they were incarcerated for the rest of their lives.

The Hills Are Alive

Between the hospital and 'the village' of Crumpsall (people still called it that, though the village had long been swamped by the sprawl of Manchester) was Crumpsall Park. You could play in the tennis courts if you had racquets (we didn't) and you could play a round on the putting green if you had sixpence (we rarely did and in any case preferred to spend any money we had on sweets). The park was a place of amusement, certainly, but it was structured and overseen by a park keeper who stopped you doing most of the things you wanted to do. For real fun and adventure we had the Hills.

If you ran to the bottom of our street, crossed the main road and climbed a short path worn into the grassy bank behind the number 7 bus stop you would find yourself going through the back of a wardrobe into a sudden bit of wild countryside. It was a small piece of countryside but countryside nonetheless; it was all that was left in fact of the old Crumpsall. It was probably no more than a dozen or so humpy acres of sandy hills stretching between Crescent Road and the Bury-to-Manchester railway line but it was green, had insects, wildflowers and frogs and it was ours to play in. There were sandy mounds and ponds and, most important of all, close to the railway line, the Hidden Valley. This was our secret place, a hole a hundred feet or more across and about forty foot deep with a pond at the bottom and the only way in was through a narrow defile. There were rumours as to how it had been formed. One was that a landslip had created it when an underground river running through the sands of what had once been a prehistoric sea washed the valley out. Another was that the Hidden Valley was the result of one of Hitler's stray bombs. However it came to be, it was a very special place for us kids. The Hills had somehow escaped the blight of industry and housebuilding and was all that remained of the estate belonging to a large mansion house, the Woodlands. In Edwardian days, the house had been the home of somebody called Madam Mont who seems to have been a bit of a one; she had a daughter called Maud, an actress which was not very PLU in them there days when actresses showed their legs. The only history of the house I could find tells us that in 1893, Maud was Principal Boy in *Robin Hood* at the Theatre Royal in Manchester. I remember the old people talking about Madame Maud when I was small and the feeling I got was that there was something risqué about the place.

I believe the family sold the house to the ICI in the 1920s. It was a very swish place which, at the time I'm writing about, the 1950s, the ICI used as a club/guest house for its executives and visitors. Many of them were from overseas and were brought up from Blackley in shining, chauffeur-driven cars to dine in the old manor house. When I was bigger and had a paper round I used to deliver papers there on my bike, pedalling all the way up the long drive. When I was even bigger and worked on the buses, one of the guards who had been a council worker in the sanitation department told me that they regularly had to go and clear the drains at the Woodlands because they were choked with used condoms, the after-effects one presumes of nights of passion with convenient ladies brought in by the guests of the ICI – it was Crumpsall's version of the Hellfire Club. Such goings-on! If my nanna had known she would have burned the place down. The house was demolished not long ago but back then the Hills, a.k.a. the old Woodlands Estate, was our Never Never Land.

We played in the Hidden Valley for hours every day of the holidays, weekends and long evenings after school in the summer. We made dens, played hide and seek, dragged old tin baths all the way from home and sailed them on the pond. We caught frogs and newts and even some massive toads and saw damselflies and dragonflies, waterboatmen and wildflowers. I suppose if I saw it now it would seem ever so small but back then it seemed huge. We played war games there, too, pretending to be Germans and English, and of course the English always won. And later we played other games that were a sort of extension of 'you show me and I'll show you' and were much more fun than war.

The ICI, which had bought the land with the manor, was gradually but determinedly covering the grass and hills with toxic dumping from its factory at the bottom of the hill. The company built a road into our Shangri La, down at the far end, away from our valley, but day after day lorries would grumble along it to dump chemicals onto the land. Lagoons of dye stuffs spread out across the grassy sand-hills and men with face masks, rubber gloves and aprons opened huge drums of toxic waste and let the contents spill into the poisoned lakes. When they had gone we would creep up and stand on the edge of these pools, watching bubbles rise and break through the scummy crust on the surface to burst with a foul stink that we called the Devil's Breath.

The worst of these toxic ponds lay further into the Hills and were looked over by a uniformed watchman in a cabin who checked the wagons in and out during working hours. His name was Rushton; we called him Specky and we were the bane of his life. He would regularly come haring across the Hills to chase us off because we were getting too close to his patch and would threaten us with the 'approved school' when he got hold of us. He rarely did because we knew the Hills like Native Americans know their prairies and could be off the rough land and back in our own back yards before Speck had made it to the road.

Like all kids we loved to light fires. We lit fires to bake potatoes or cook sausages on sticks but mostly we just lit them for fun. Sometimes we would light a 'spreader', running with burning grass torches and setting fire to dry grass to watch the flames spreading like a wild animal across the hillocks. We would start the fires with matches stolen from the kitchen or, in the hot days of summer, with shilling plastic magnifying glasses, which we shone on dried leaves and grass until they burst into flame.

When the fires spread beyond control we ran away and the fire brigade would have to come and put the fires out. Not the Manchester Fire Brigade but the ICI's own company fire bobbies with their own little fire engine. Hoses were useless because they couldn't get the engine up onto the hills so they had to beat the fires out with big paddles. We, meanwhile, were back on our own turf 'whistling dixie' and were well ready to deny all charges of pyromania. Eventually, at the end of one long hot summer, we got a real 'spreader' going and this time they called out the Manchester Fire Brigade too. They put the fire out with water pumped from their big engines and then went round the streets knocking on doors looking for the culprits. Our parents were not amused; firstly because, although we all denied it, our smoke-blackened faces and hands grassed us up, and secondly because the firemen told our mums and dads that if the flames had reached the chemical dumps Crumpsall would have had to be evacuated. I don't think they were saying this for effect.

Nowadays the Hills are covered with a school and community centre and I assume that the toxic lagoons have been dealt with, but who knows? How deep down did the chemicals percolate? Did they hit the water table? No one in those days seemed particularly worried about where the toxins went.

Marrying Bricks and Mouldy Bread

If you tread on a nick
You'll marry a brick,
And a beetle will come to your wedding.

And we believed it, or at least half believed it, and, since the pavements round our street were made of great slabs of York stone with lots of nicks in between, you would totter across them in delicious fear, jumping from flagstone to flagstone, imagining yourself in church standing in front of Monsignor Aspinall having to marry a big lump of fired Accrington clay while a large cockroach sat in the front row singing hymns along with the best of them.

We lived in a world where such things were possible. When you are small, witches really do live in every derelict house; swallowing chewing gum really will tie all your insides in knots; and Jinny Greenteeth really does live down grids. Such stuff was no more unbelievable to us than Santa Claus, the tooth fairy, the Red Sea parting, dead men rising from their beds, and a man filling a big boat up with animals of every kind before sailing off across the floodwaters to land on what I thought was Mount Arrowroot. This really confused me because arrowroot was what my nanna had when her stomach got upset.

We children moved constantly in a world where myth and fable walked hand in hand with reality, and the borderline between them was at all times nebulous and shifting. The violent world of fairytale with its Bluebeards and shirts made from thistles wasn't that far from ours. A boy called Victor showed us the scars on his back once; they ran from his neck to his waist, marbled and knotted like the fat on a piece of meat. He had been thrown on a Guy Fawkes bonfire by some bigger boys who later claimed they thought the fire was out. Then there was the boy from our school, David Poulton, who went playing in the cellar of an empty, half-derelict bombed-out house. David made the mistake of playing with the broken fusebox and touched the mains cable. He never touched anything again. When we got to school that morning, not yet knowing that he was dead, there was a bleak air about the playground. People spoke in whispers and the story flew from child to child. His dad was the local chimney sweep and the family was well-liked.

Everybody knew some kid who had died, or knew somebody who knew somebody. There was the kid who was supposed to have drowned at the deep end in Harpurhey Baths when he got his finger stuck in the drain at the bottom; there was the kid who died swimming in the millponds at Rhodes when his legs got tangled in the weeds; and there was the kid who fell under a steamroller and who had to be 'scraped up off the road'. Unlike Tom in the Tom and Jerry films, he couldn't suddenly reinflate back to life.

Diseases were all about, too. Play on the grids in the street and you got scarlet fever, go to the swimming baths and you got polio, eat raw bacon and you would get tapeworms. One kid I knew, knew another kid who knew another kid whose brother got a tapeworm and the only way they could get it out was by holding a bacon sandwich as a bait near his bare bum and when it came out they got hold of its head and pulled it out and it was fifty feet long – and that's really true!

Then there were days of general terror when we all went into a raw existential panic because the world was going to end at a quarter past ten, or ten to eleven, or three minutes past; the times varied but the pattern was always the same. You would arrive in school to find everybody already in a state of lunacy. Nobody knew who started it or why, but everybody knew – because it had been on the radio/in the paper/the Virgin Mary had appeared and told some kids – that the world was most definitely going to end for ever at the stated time. The teachers would arrive in the playground to find a mob of gibbering kids on the edge of meltdown, and no amount of persuading could bring them down. Once the dreaded time had passed a feeling of relief would run through the school and the kids would get back to reading about Janet and John and Fluff the cat.

As if all this wasn't bad enough, my torments were increased by my nanna. She had stories galore about people dying after eating cockles, banshees appearing just before somebody died, crocks of gold at the rainbow's end and then there was Old Nick, Satan, the devil himself. Old Nick had cloven hooves and a tail and horns but could disguise himself in many ways so that at times he could look like an ordinary man. Only when one of his shoes fell off and you saw his cloven hoof, or his tail fell out of his trousers, or the wind blew his bowler hat off and you saw his horns, would you know that it was Old Nick. Then you had to throw holy water on him and he would vanish, leaving behind two perfect hoof prints burned into the place where he had stood. Terrified that Old Nick might turn up at our house, I made a special study of all our visitors, giving the rent man, the tally man and the man from the Pru a very thorough going-over before I let them in the house in order to see if they had a tail poking out through the back of their raincoats.

The devil came in many strange and terrible ways, I was told: he appeared to people on country roads in the black of night; he came when they were playing cards (cards were the devil's Bible); or he met them at the crossroads coming home from a dance (dancing also was the work of the devil).

She was pretty much against a lot of things, was my nanna. Although she liked the odd bottle of stout herself (and would 'mull' it with a red-hot poker), she didn't approve of heavy drinking: her husband had been an alcoholic until he got the DTs and saw rats climbing the house walls. She wasn't wild about Protestants (which was a bit rich seeing as we were the only Catholic family in a street of forty houses) and of course she was against sex in any shape, kind or form. Mostly she railed against ladies showing their bits and if there was a picture of a lady in a swimsuit in the papers, such as Jane Russell, she would rip it out. Some weeks the Sunday paper was all holes.

When we eventually got a television, and *Sunday Night at the London Palladium* came on with the Tiller Girls opening the show with their high-kicking dance routines, Nanna (who for some reason seemed to be caught out by it every week) would reach for her bottle of holy water and would drench the television, shouting, 'Holy God! Would ye look at them now, showing their timbers!' You were well advised not to touch the TV for a while after one of Nanna's attacks in case you earthed yourself and were killed. She also spat at the television whenever Churchill came on the screen (which wasn't all that often because by then he was on his way out). She blamed him personally for the Irish Civil War and (with more truth) for bringing in troopers to fire on striking Welsh miners at Tonypandy. She had quite a good aim and what with the spit and the holy water our Bakelite TV set was a bit of a mess.

The only thing my nanna was frightened of was tinkers. She was a tough woman who would face anybody: milkman, bus conductor, teacher – anybody but a tinker.

She would watch the coalman from behind the lace curtain and would count the empty sacks as he laid them down in our back yard after dumping the coal into the coal shed. Then if he told her he had delivered ten sacks when she had counted nine she would rear up on him and give him a tongue-lashing. I did see him once drop an empty sack hidden under the full one and she saw it too, she only paid him for the sacks he had delivered and told him he could go and whistle for the rest of his money.

Men trying to cheat her on the market would get short shrift from my nanna. She wasn't even afraid of the Sikh hawkers in their turbans who came with their suitcases full of dishcloths, dusters and tea-towels – but tinkers were another thing altogether.

They would come from time to time, arriving at the door selling clothes pegs or wooden flowers they had made by cleverly paring a piece of wood and leaving the shavings on in delicate curls, so the end effect was that of a chrysanthemum which they then dyed in the juice of berries collected from the hedgerows. They would offer these for sale and then tell your fortune. However, my nanna was terrified of getting 'the tinker's curse' and would peep through the curtains to see who was knocking, and if it were a tinker woman in a shawl she would give me sixpence and send me to the door to get the curse instead. Thanks, Nanna.

This is one of my nanna's tinker stories.

'Back home in Ireland there was a pregnant countrywoman and she was standing at her cottage door one day when a tinker woman came by with a small baby wrapped in a shawl. The tinker woman was hungry and her baby was starving.

'"For the love of God would you give me a sup of milk for my baby? He's sick from hunger and I have nothing to give him."

'"Get away from here and take that pig with you!" said the woman of the house and that was the worst thing she could ever have said because the tinker woman turned, with fire in her eyes, and just said, "Pig yourself!" And she went away and was never seen again.

'And do you know what happened?'

I shook my head, mouth and eyes wide open.

'Well, when that cruel woman had her own baby, it had the head of a pig – a perfect little pig. The body of a baby boy and the head of a small pig.'

'And what happened to it?'

'They kept it locked up for the rest of its life.'

'Can we go and see it?'

'It's away in Ireland and dead and buried now, because it was a long time ago.'

'Did they baptise it?'

'How could they baptise it, and it with the head of a pig?'

'But it had the body of a boy and it might have been human.'

'Not at all! Would ye come out of that! Go and fetch me my medicine off the shelf in the scullery and less of yer malarkey.'

And that was that.

Another of my nanna's stories.

'There was a woman lived near us in the tenements in Dublin and her little boy fell and cut his leg. It started to fester and she took him to the hospital. "It will have to come off," they told her.

'Well, I found her crying her heart out one day and I asked her what was the matter and she told me. "Well," I said, "Come in the house." And I found the mouldiest piece of a loaf and tied it on the wound and I told her to keep doing that every day. Put mouldy bread on that sore every day. And she did, and do you know what?'

'No.'

'That boy never lost his leg at all and within three weeks he was cured of it. All he had was a bit of a scar.'

Aunty Kitty told me that the story was true, my nanna really did cure that boy.

Now penicillin is supposed to have been discovered by Alexander Fleming in 1928. It wasn't. It was discovered by my nanna before the First World War.

Actually, like a lot of my nanna's remedies, the mouldy bread cure was known to country people all over Europe. Nanna was full of such cures. I remember spraining my ankle badly once while playing on the Crumpsall Hospital fields. My nanna went out and found some comfrey leaves, made a hot compress with them and sorted my ankle out in no time. I did the same thing myself forty years later when I ended up with inflamed Achilles tendons after going jogging one icy morning without warming up. After three months of expensive heat and ultrasound treatment, all of which had proved worse than useless, I got a handful of comfrey leaves, made a hot compress and slapped it on. In three days the tendons were back to normal.

Most of her knowledge of folk medicine came from her own mother and the aunts and other women she had known back home. In her day there had been no National Health Service (there still isn't in Ireland) and the doctor, who would charge for everything, was seen as a last resort. So, even though I was born into a country that was soon to have the best free health service in the world, we always tried the old ways first before calling in Dr Dolan or Dr Bernstein.

I hated having earache – not just because of the pain but because of the folk medicine cure that my nanna treated me with. She would drip olive oil into my ear and then cover it with a slice of hot toast, which she would bind firmly onto my head with a scarf. She would then put me to bed and expect me to sleep with half a loaf on my ear and a load of crumbs on my pillow.

Sore throats were cured with Friars' Balsam taken on a spoonful of sugar. It was bitter and foul but seemed to work. Coughs were cured with a knob of butter melted in a glass of hot milk. Minor cuts were covered with a spider's web; 'heat lumps' (hives) were treated with calamine lotion which left you covered in pink chalk; and if you had a bad chest you wore red flannel and breathed the fumes that came off a tar-boiler when the workmen were laying setts in the street. Styes were cured by rubbing them with a gold wedding ring or wiping them with pee, and warts were cured by rubbing them on a tree or with a raw potato which you then had to bury so that as the potato rotted away so went the wart. You've no idea how thankful I was that small children, on the whole, didn't get piles.

Spiders' webs, toast on your ears – that's what made a man of me.

My nanna herself took Fennings' Lung Healers, little pills in a twist of paper sold by the corner shop. I've no idea what was in them but she swore by them; they were supposed to make breathing easy. Since most Mancunians in those days spent their lives trying to breathe in a chemical soup they needed all the help they could get.

Constipation was a great worry. As a hang-over from things Victorian it was thought that regular bowel movements were the only thing that could keep you from an early grave. There were various cures, most famous being syrup of figs, Andrews Liver Salts and Fam-Lax. The liver salts fizzed up in water and tasted quite refreshing; Famlax was a sweet chocolate laxative 'for all the family'; and syrup of figs was a kind of liquid Pickfords – it could move anything.

I didn't particularly like Famlax since it was pretty boring for chocolate but one summer's day I ate a whole slab of it and drank a large pint mug of Andrews Liver Salts because I was hot and thirsty. The results were disastrous. I was playing out on the Hills with the gang and thankfully it was the time of the year when there were lots of dock leaves. I went home a good stone lighter.

Dust and Uncle Bernard's Bunny

I didn't understand death then. You don't when you're only seven or eight. Cowboys fell off roofs when they were shot, soldiers got blown up by Japanese shells while fighting on the beach. They were dead – only that was in the cinema and wasn't real dead. I'd been told that my dad had died in the war but a small part of me wouldn't accept it and for a time I believed that one day my dad would get off the number seven bus and all that stuff about him being killed in a bomber would be wrong and it would be him that got out of the burning plane and not the bomb aimer. I would wait at the bus stop in the hope that my imagined reworking of the tale was true, but I grew out of that belief as I got slightly older. I saw that he would never get off the bus – not now. So death was something that had happened to my dad and that happened in the films to cowboys and to soldiers.

And then one evening Uncle Bernard came to our house looking as though he had come straight from work, plaster dust all over him, the white floury powder softening his overalls, his jacket, his skin, the black curls that poked from under his workman's cap. He sat at the table in the living room and in a half-choked voice said, 'I've lost my baby.' And then he cried and I'd never seen a man cry before. My nanna and my mother stared at him. I didn't know what to do.

Between his bouts of sobbing, he told how Bunny (Bernadette), his little girl toddler, had been outside their house at the travelling greengrocer's van with her mother while she bought some fruit and vegetables. A plum had fallen from the open side of the van into the gutter and the baby, unseen, had gone to pick it up. The driver had reversed over her and killed her.

I still remember that afternoon, the sun coming in through the window, the man crying at the table, his body bent, his rough, lime-scarred hands held together, and I remember that neither my mother nor my nanna went to put their arms around him. Both women were crying and my mother went and mashed a pot of tea because that was what you did whenever there was an emergency, but those weren't the days of hugging and kissing. You just took what came to you and got on with stuff. I think hugging and kissing is a good deal better for the soul than getting on with stuff. Sorrows came and somehow people got on with their lives with courage and a simple dignity, but you knew that they never forgot. I know for certain that my mum never forgot her Devon boy with his curly hair and his lopsided smile.

CHAPTER 3

THE FAMILY BUSH
(WE COULDN'T AFFORD A TREE ...)

When I was seven my mother got married again to a Polish ex-serviceman who was living in the Displaced Persons Camp in Lower Crumpsall near the CWS Biscuit Works. His name was Lucian Bilek and his story, though not unique, is a remarkable one. This is how I remember it. 'Lou' was one of ten children born and brought up on a small farm somewhere near Warsaw. It was not a wealthy farm and from the photographs he showed me they seemed to be farming fairly marginal land. There were photographs of his father poling a raft with a cow on it out to an island in a lake to make use of whatever grazing might be there. Lou's father was very strict and beat him a lot. He hated farm work but was forced to do it. One night after a very bad beating he climbed out of the window and ran away to join the army; he was sixteen years old.

He joined the cavalry and spent the next couple of years learning to charge on horseback and fight with a lance and spear. It seems that the story of the Polish cavalry charging German tanks on horseback is a myth, which sprung up after the Battle of Tuchola Forest on 1 September 1939 when a cavalry unit attacked soldiers of the German 76th Infantry Regiment, taking them by surprise. The Germans retaliated by bringing in armoured cars and employing heavy machine guns. One third of the Polish force was killed. I would like to believe the story that the brave Poles had gone out on horseback with lances and swords against a German Panzer division but it seems this just wasn't true; the cavalry regiments may well have been on horseback but they were equipped with anti-tank weapons.

According to Lou, his horse was shot from under him. Together with another young soldier who had also lost his horse, he made his way overland, sleeping by day and walking by night. The pair made their way across the Romanian, Czech and Yugoslavian borders and got on a ship to North Africa. From there they were shipped on again to Scotland where what was left of the Polish fighting forces regrouped under General Sikorski. The army, including Lou, was under the command of General Anders and when Lou was placed in the Polish 1st Armoured Division, sometimes known as the 'Black Devils', he went from riding horses to fighting in tanks. After training in Scotland he was sent with his regiment to fight on the European mainland. The bravery of the Polish soldiers, sailors and airmen has been well documented; they were fighting to free their country and they fought with immense courage and intelligence. The 1st Armoured Division helped to liberate France, Holland and Belgium and became part of the army of occupation in Germany. Ironically they never made it home. Under the terms of the Yalta Conference, Poland was ceded to the Russians; arguments go on to this day about Roosevelt and Churchill's part in what many Poles in exile saw as arrant betrayal. It isn't my job here to throw petrol on the fire but I can say that Lou sincerely believed that if he went home the Russians would kill him. In 1940, Soviet forces had executed 22,000 Poles in the Katyn Forest; many of them were officers and the rest described as 'the intelligensia'. Stalin denied this but the Poles in exile knew the truth and rather than risk being killed or sent to the gulags they chose to stay in exile in the UK. Manchester had a large Polish community, with many of the exiles based around Crumpsall and Cheetham Hill.

So my career as a little prince came to an abrupt end and I found myself having to share a bedroom with my Aunty Julia when Lou came to live in the house. And then, not long after the marriage, my sister Christina was born. I hadn't noticed that my mother was getting bigger and was wearing a maternity smock – so engrossed was I in my own small universe that I only realised something was different when I got home from school one day to find that my mum wasn't there. When I asked, my nanna told me that I had a baby sister and that her and my mum would be in the hospital for another ten days. Ten days! Who was going to give me my spends? Who was going to feed me?

The answer was my nanna and for ten days we lived on bubble and squeak, finnan haddock, coddle and boiled egg chopped up in a cup with butter and salt. I loved bubble and squeak and wolfed it down, thanking the Lord that Nanna hadn't taken it on herself to get on the bus into town for a yard of tripe and some pigs' feet.

After ten days of being spoiled rotten, my mum came home with my baby sister and the house began to get even more crowded. No wonder that my Aunty Julia eventually left to marry a complete barmpot. As for me, I can't say that I took kindly to being ousted by a Polish ex-serviceman in the cock-of-the-house stakes, or by a new sister for that matter. In fact I became a bit of a pain in the bum and took to sulks and moods, which are partly understandable but nonetheless must have been hard for people to put up with. But Lou bore it all with good humour, went on working and supporting the family and, though we were never rich (his jobs were mostly unskilled even though he was a trained mechanic), we were slightly better off than before.

One thing Lou did bring with him to the house was a better cuisine. Now our traditional fare of pigs' bits and potatoes with fish on a Friday was supplemented with great soups, Polish salamis and dark rye bread. Lou was a good cook and his Sunday roast – a rack of lamb braised with parsnips, carrots and onions – would, as they say in Lancashire, 'put fur on your back like velvet'.

The kids in our gang really liked Big Lou, because he was kind to them and smiled a lot. His English was really quite poor and hardly improved over the years; we could understand him and the people at work could understand him and that was just about all he needed. He would cod his accent up even more for us kids and would read storybooks out loud in the most fractured English, enjoying watching us roll around the floor on the edge of hysteria. 'Hickory Dickory Dock' would end up:

High cory die cory doke
De mow ooser ran op de cloak
De cloak stroke wan
Un downey run
High cory die cory doke.

'Can we come round and hear your dad read to us?' was a regular plea from the gang.

Lou handed all but ten bob of his wages over to Mum; the ten bob he kept back for the horses. He was convinced that one day he would hit the big one and it was no use me pointing out to him that it was Selwyn Demmy who was riding round in the Rolls-Royce and not him. He used to work out incredibly long accumulators where the winnings from one horse went on to bet on another and if that won then the winnings were placed on another horse and so on. When we eventually got a TV I would watch him white-knuckled, eyes bulging as his horse galloped its way towards the finishing line. Several times he came close to scooping the pool but the last horse always fell within sight of the finish; had it won, the pot would have been several thousand pounds. It was always a good idea to be out of the house just as the last horse fell since there would be lots of 'buggery, buggery, buggery!' going out over the air.

Aunty Kitty and Uncle Bobby

It was about this time that I began going to my Aunty Kitty and Uncle Bobby's house for 'adventures'. They may have sensed that I wasn't all that happy at home, or perhaps they felt a bit of country air would do me good – whatever the reason I began to spend school holidays and the odd weekend in the far-off countryside of Besses o' th' Barn. Besses is four stops and about four miles north/northwest of Crumpsall on the Manchester–Bury line and now has the M60 orbital motorway running through its borders. Tell people it was countryside now and they laugh, but back then it was a small piece of what for me at least passed for Paradise; I went there regularly until I was twelve or so.

It really was a trip into another world. The house where Kitty and Bobby lived backed onto a large golf course, and a short walk down an old footpath led into the Philips Park estate and on eventually through the clough (Lancashire for a valley) to Prestwich Hospital. So all I had to do was go down the garden and through the back gate and I was in a land where you could find hedgehogs, lost golf balls and blackberries in the hedges; where the lane led in one direction to a cluster of old buildings that included a smithy where I once watched a smith fitting shoes to a great shire horse, and in the other direction to a great red-brick viaduct that Robert Philips, the Earl of Derby and the East Lancashire Railway had built to take carriages over the clough to the nearest railway station. There was an old Edwardian tea-room at the western end of the bridge that served scones and jam and, if you continued in that direction you eventually dropped into the valley of the Irwell and came up against industrial filth and pollution again.

I caught gudgeon and roach in the millpond near Prestwich Hospital, paddled in the beck under the viaduct and saw damselflies and dragonflies like flying precious gems flit from flower to flower. I watched hawks circle over the clough and saw rabbits scuttering away on the path ahead of me. I know it rained occasionally because I remember staying in, sitting in the front room reading bound copies of *The Strand* magazine from Uncle Bobby's book collection. There were other kids in the streets near Aunty Kitty's but often I preferred to be alone, just wandering through the hot summer days, happy to just be there.

When I think about those times I remember more than anything else the great and unstinted kindness shown to a small boy who was not very happy at home. Uncle Bobby was a tailor who made suits for the male patients at the mental hospital in Crumpsall and Aunty Kitty, Aunty Julia's sister, had worked as a buttonholer all her life though she now stayed at home and did all the housework. She was smaller than Julia, had wavy hair and wore glasses and to me always seemed to be busy baking, washing, gardening, dusting and polishing. Her home was a neat orderly gem, a small 1920s semi-detached house and I always felt welcome there. Kitty was strict about things like mud on your boots and making sure you had a good wash but she was never unfair and what I remember most about that house is the warmth and the love.

Kitty, like my nanna, was very religious and used to take me to church on a Sunday morning in nearby Prestwich. Uncle Bobby, like his drinking pal my granddad, was an atheist socialist who would have nothing at all to do with churches or religion. He was a tall, slim man, always smartly dressed, who wore glasses and smoked a pipe, and who talked to me as though I were a very much younger equal. I used to meet him after work and we would walk together to the station to get the train to Besses. All the way he would tell me the stories of the places we were passing through, or tell me about how as a boy he had joined the merchant navy and had crossed the sea to Canada and up the St Lawrence Seaway: it was Bobby's stories that inspired me to head for Nover Skosher when I ran away. Later, when I got to nine years old, I would take the tram myself and that line north from Crumpsall always seemed an escape into a freer and more welcoming place.

Bobby was born in the Hightown area of Cheetham Hill, just up from Strangeways Prison and in the same street as Louis Golding, the author of more than forty books including the book that made him famous in the 1940s, *Magnolia Street*. Few know his name now but like Walter Greenwood's *Love on the Dole* and Howard Spring's *Fame is the Spur*, Golding's novel is a classic of Manchester life, following on a tradition of writing about that great city that was begun by authors like Elizabeth Gaskell (*Mary Barton*) and Linnaeus Banks (*A Manchester Man*).

Bobby used to like a pint of a night, and often went for the last hour to the Junction, a pub just up the road in Whitefield that was run by the hangman Harry Allen. Allen was the assistant to Albert Pierrepoint for many years, and when Pierrepoint retired he became chief executioner in his turn. Like Allen, Pierrepoint also ran a pub: his was in the Oldham Street area of Manchester and was called Help the Poor Struggler, which has always seemed more than a little ironic to me.

Uncle Bobby and Aunty Kitty had a dog called Vic, a black Labrador that I used to take walking with me and always had trouble with whenever there were hedgehogs about. I developed a summer cold once at Aunty Kitty's, probably because I'd got myself soaking in the brook in the clough, and I ended up with a bad chest and a barking cough. My mother used to walk to the phone box at the bottom of Oak Road every couple of days to ring up and see how I was getting on. I had heard Bobby and Kitty discussing my cough and deciding that the answer was to rub Vicks on my chest. When my mother asked me how I was, I cried and said I wanted to go home because they were going to rub the dog on my chest. They soon sorted it out. (Vicks VapoRub, by the way, is still sold and, according to Wikipedia, is an effective cough medicine for guinea pigs.)

It was Uncle Bobby who bought me my first real fishing rod and set me off on a life of maggots and worms and hand-tied flies. I'd been fishing for ages with our gang on the mill lodges in Bowker Vale but our rods had been bamboo canes pinched off the allotments. At first we tied nylon fishing lines on the ends of the canes but later we got more sophisticated and tied cheap shilling reels on the thick ends and fashioned rod rings out of thick copper wire. They were clumsy and we couldn't cast more than a few yards but we caught tiddlers with them using maggots bought from a pet shop and bread paste for bait.

Uncle Bobby took me walking whenever he could and on one of our walks I took a cane and some line with me and when we got to the lodge near the hospital I fished for a while and caught a few gudgeon. A week or so later, Bobby gave me a second-hand split cane rod and wooden reel he had bought from somebody at work. I have fished ever since. At first it was on the Bury Bolton canal with Uncle Bobby sitting smoking his pipe outside a towpath pub keeping an eye on me. I didn't catch much but that didn't stop me. I loved the thrill of the possible: that there might just be that monster perch or roach out there that would take my float under. Now I fish for trout using flies I tie myself and still have that same sense of the possible, or what some people might call 'incurable optimism'. I believe there is a nursing home somewhere for the incurably optimistic, I must try and find it.

Along with their son, George, Bobby and Kitty had two daughters, Pat and Maire, both smart women who worked in town. Maire was secretary to one of the bosses at Kemsley House and Pat was a secretary in one of the big insurance companies in Manchester. Both were good-looking women, strong and intelligent, yet they never married. Pat was tall and dark-haired, saw through people and while friendly and caring didn't suffer fools gladly. Maire was shorter with a beauty spot and a husky voice and was very lively and funny. She was engaged for a while to somebody called Tony but he jilted her a few months before they got married and I think that must have put her off men for good. I never asked them, and by the time I was old enough to ask them about such things they'd emigrated to Canada and I saw very little of them after that.

Both of them were immensely kind to me. Maire kept me supplied with notebooks and pencils from work; I used these for my stories and my drawings. They both loved books and Pat in particular seemed to have the knack of finding books that really captured me: *Huckleberry Finn* and *Tom Sawyer* weren't standard fare for kids then but I'd read both of them several times over by the time I was ten; *Ti-Coyo and his Shark* by Clement Richer is an amazing, almost amoral story set in the French West Indies about the 'friendship' between a boy and a shark and I loved it. Another book that entered my world completely was *The Valley of Song* by Elizabeth Goudge, a strange mystical tale about a girl called Tabitha who finds her way into a valley where all the creatures of the Zodiac live; I didn't let the fact that it was a girl having the adventure put me off and I read the book over and again. Both *Ti-Coyo* and *The Valley of Song* are, I believe, neglected classics of children's literature.

When I look at quizzes in the Sunday supplements that ask questions like, 'Where or when were you happiest?' it is always that house in Lime Avenue I think about, and the fields and the clough and that strange little old-fashioned tea shop.

Mad Uncle Len

All the time I was swanning it up in the far-off land of Besses o' th' Barn, my Aunty Julia was getting herself lined up for the marriage stakes with a really dubious bloke in the shape of a hairy-eared, Methodist, right winger with a farting dog.

People are like onions; there are many layers to them and as you peel the layers off and discover what lies beneath you will invariably cry – and the tears will mostly be of pity. Some day, no doubt, I will look at people like Thatcher, Pol Pot and Uncle Len like that – but not yet.

Uncle Len was barking mad. Of that there can be not the slightest doubt. He had the hairiest nostrils and ears and the bushiest eyebrows I have ever seen; he also had a nervous tic that had him rubbing his hairy right eyebrow with his knuckles every fifth second (on average). Facial tics and hairy noses of course don't make you a bad person, but Uncle Len was also a very strict and severe Methodist who had once driven a tram during the General Strike, two things that didn't exactly endear him to any of us in the family; we were Irish Catholic socialists to a child, never mind a man. How he ever made his right-wing racist way into our family is something of a mystery.

Aunty Julia, in spite of her mother and father's high hopes, worked as a machinist at Demmy's gaberdine factory. The Demmys were a well-known Manchester Jewish family who were involved in the clothing trade, the boxing game and running off-course racehorse betting shops before – and after – they were legal. They were wealthy manufacturers, and Christie's auction of Selwyn Demmy's collection of L. S. Lowry's paintings and drawings in 2010 realised £5 million.

Julia took the bus to work every morning and that is how Len must have met her because the only other social occasions he went in for – the Methodist Church and the Crumpsall Conservative Club – were not in my Aunty Julia's orbit.

The problem with my Aunty Julia was that her mum and dad had brought her up to be a lady. She was well read, played the piano and the violin, had red hair down to her waist, was tall and pretty and was not, if they could help it, going to end up married to a dustbin man or a turret lathe turner at Mather & Platt's engineering works. Since most of the eligible blokes round Crumpsall, Collyhurst and Harpurhey were destined to work in exactly those professions, this narrowed the gene pool down somewhat. Her friend, who I called Aunty Jessie, though she was no blood relation, was in the same boat. From a Manchester–Italian family, the Cashanellas, Aunty Jessie also had red hair and high hopes.

Long before I was born, the pair of them would go off on 'the Monkey Run', the Sunday afternoon promenade along Oldham Road that gave the youngsters of Manchester the chance to 'click', and both of them would disdainfully brush off the advances of the hopeful hoi polloi that trotted along beside them offering them Woodbines and Park Drive, and asking them where they worked. Unfortunately, Cheshire millionaires were a bit thin on the ground on the Oldham Road Monkey Run so both Julia and Jessie grew slowly and inevitably into spinsters. Loving and kind women and great friends all their lives, they nevertheless must have seen motherhood and marriage fading further away as the months and years went by, which is probably why Aunty Julia ended up with Uncle Len. The life of a spinster maiden aunt in a crowded house in the 1950s can't have had much appeal, and when a short, bushy-eyebrowed, hairy-nosed, Methodist Tory with a semi-detached house in the leafy suburbs of Higher Crumpsall turned up, it must have seemed as though all her spinster prayers had been answered – but by a God with a very strange sense of humour.

I don't know how and where they did their courting (they were both in their forties, and then being in your forties meant you were middle-aged) but they finished each night snogging in the lobby of our house, directly under my bed, and no matter how tightly I pulled the pillow over my ears I could still hear his breathless, 'Oh Julia! Oh Julia!' and the noises of smooching and fumbling. They can't have been up to much because if they had, my nanna would have been out like a shot with her stick at the ready, a bottle of holy water in her hands and her hearing aid whistling like a boiling kettle.

They got married eventually, after Uncle Len took 'instruction' in the ways of the Holy Roman and Apostolic Catholic Church and promised that any children would be brought up in the faith (thankfully there were none) and my Aunty Julia went to live in the manner she had been brought up to expect with a man who was a combination of Adolf Hitler and Mr Bean with none of the humility or humour thrown in.

Leonard Arthur Watkinson, to give him his full title, came from quite a well-off family who were owners of one of Manchester's main car dealerships and also had something to do with Wessex Fireworks. Somewhere along the line they realised that he was a complete fruitcake, gave him some shares and a bit of brass and told him to bugger off. So from a senior management position and a big detached Edwardian house with a tennis court in the back garden, he went to a job as a wages clerk in Manchester Town Hall and a 1930s semi in Crumpsall.

He seemed to blame the Jews, or 'the sheenies' as he called them, for this – I don't know why since they patently had nothing to do with it. I had row after row with him, once I realised what he was talking about, but there was no way you could have a civilised discussion with him. Frothing at the mouth, he would go on and on spouting complete rubbish about the Protocols of the Elders of Zion and how the Jews were running (and ruining) the country, his face getting redder and his eyes sticking out like a dog's balls after it has jumped a barbed-wire fence. He was also an Empire loyalist and when I got a bit older and knew my history I was able to shoot him down in flames. But the facts were as nothing to Uncle Len. He simply knew he was right and any argument he couldn't counter he would dismiss with, 'That's all stuff from books – how do you know it's true?'

He dressed like a petit bourgeois government inspector, hated anything remotely to do with socialism – even the public library was a step too far, it smacked of collectivism – and kept a pan of herbs on the stove which stank like a festering pond. The herbs were for his stomach, which troubled him a lot (probably because it was always churning over with ire and hate), but ironically he died of a heart attack in bed. He got thrown out of the local Methodist Church after some row or other and so spent Sunday mornings churchless, singing along to the BBC Home Service's *Act of Worship*, *Hymns Ancient and Modern* spread out on the table, a one-man barmpot congregation. In fact, thinking about it, he didn't just fall out with the Methodists, he fell out with pretty much everybody over the years. He had worked implementing the Means Test during the Depression, and I bet he was pretty damn good at it too. I can see him now telling somebody they didn't need six chairs when there were only four of them in the house, and they didn't need that armchair either; orange boxes were perfectly good to sit on.

He was also one of the pillars of the local Conservative club and mingled with the various shopkeepers and clerks who made up the membership – Little Englanders to a man and woman (come to think of it, Nigel Farage is very like a non-teetotal, joke-telling version of my Uncle Len). In the sixties, the BBC finished its TV broadcasts by playing the national anthem and Len would stand to attention every night, in the living room, stiff and patriotic. Aunty Julia would disappear into the kitchen and I would go and help her, anything to get way from Len and HMQ and the God who was supposed to be saving her.

By now it was the 1950s, the atom bomb had vapourised hundreds of thousands of Japanese, Coca Cola and bubble gum were available in the toffee shops, Frank Sinatra was warbling his way into the collective psyche and novelists, film-makers and painters were dragging the sink out of the kitchen and shoving it up on the wall for all to see – but Uncle Len still behaved as though it was the 1930s. Somewhere in his head a clock had stopped one summer's afternoon in the gardens of a large, detached, Edwardian house in Crumpsall where the tennis nets were still up and young men and women in flannels and shingle cuts were taking tea in the shade.

He was also a camera freak with a fine collection of half-plate and folding film cameras and had turned one of the bedrooms of his suburban villa into a darkroom. It was largely through this caterpillar-eyebrowed rajpot that I first took an interest in photography.

When my 'aunts' Pat and Maire bought me a Brownie 127 for my birthday, Len gave me *The Ilford Boys Book of Photography* – all I can remember is a piece of advice about not photographing people in front of lampposts because it made it look as though the pole was coming out of the top of their heads. I went out and took some photographs of Highland cattle in the mist. When they came back from the chemist all you could see were dark grey blobs in a sea of paler grey. I got better eventually.

Looking through his own photography books I found several on nude photography and a book of advice on the physical side of marriage written by some Methodist sex specialist (rhythm Methodist?) that was covered in brown paper and which I didn't understand. Though I did understand the nude photographs – from an aesthetic viewpoint, of course.

In case you think I'm being too harsh on him, I found out while I was writing this memoir that Len was quite capable of completely lunatic, not to say criminal, behaviour outside the house too. Some of you will have heard of 10cc, one of the wittiest and most literate of bands to come out of the Manchester rock scene. Lol Creme, of Godley and Creme, who wrote many of their hits, was a Crumpsall lad from a Jewish family and his aunty lived a few doors up the road from my Aunty Julia's old house.

'Your uncle was a very strange man,' she told my brother John (who was not born until after the events in this book). 'If we were ever sitting out in the garden in the summer, he used to come and march up and down outside, singing Nazi songs and shouting terrible things.'

Nowadays they would have locked him up for race hate crimes.

John also met a woman who lived opposite Uncle Len as a young girl. 'He used to come to the window if he saw me and expose himself.'

So there you go. What my lovely, gentle, intelligent Aunty Julia was doing marrying an Empire loyalist, anti-Semite, hairy-eared Methodist flasher is beyond me.

They say love is blind but in this case it must also have been deaf, dumb and have no sense of smell because, though Uncle Len didn't stink, his dog did. You can't blame dumb animals for the way they end up but Dinah, an old, festering Labrador, whose farts could make you want to throw up at a hundred yards, should really have been put down and buried somewhere deep and far away in a very strong lead coffin. He fed the dog on horse meat which he boiled to a mush in the kitchen alongside his stomach herbs (the dog had bad teeth and couldn't chew) and mixed it up with toasted brown bread to give her some fibre. Nothing can describe the farts that came out of that dog. They would make you dizzy, nauseous and hysterical all at the same time and since she reserved her best farts for mealtimes when she lay under the table, slipping them out soundlessly one after the other, you would find yourself rendered speechless and gagging, eyes streaming and hands shaking as Len, immune and insensate, munched away.

He drove a lovely old Lea-Francis 14HP saloon car, a true classic, in English racing green with tan leather upholstery and a walnut dashboard. It was a superb piece of engineering; Uncle Len managed to drive it like a lawnmower. Peering forward over the wheel, constantly brushing his eyebrows with his knuckles and jabbering on about 'sheenies' and 'nig nogs', he would put his foot down and aim the car at any available gap. Miraculously he never seemed to crash into anybody: they all seemed somehow to sense a madman coming and get swiftly out of his way. Roundabouts were a real challenge to him and he would often spend half the afternoon going round one, screaming at Julia to tell him which exit to use. He once travelled several miles down the wrong side of a dual carriageway with everybody in the car screaming at him and approaching cars hurling themselves out of his way onto the soft verge. He couldn't understand why they were all honking and shaking their fists at him. When he did find out he maintained it was the local council's fault for not making the road signs clear enough.

Uncle Len, being middle class, was a great believer in picnics. Only a picnic to Uncle Len wasn't a simple affair of a few sandwiches, a flask of tea and a walk round somewhere nice; with Len it was a major expedition.

The picnics usually took place in the summer on Sundays, and were supposed to start early. I would turn up at the house at half past eight to find Uncle Len tapping the barometer and arguing with it while Aunty Julia was in the kitchen preparing the picnic basket. This she would fill with tomatoes, lettuce, spring onions, hard-boiled eggs, cucumber, boiled ham, salad cream, a loaf of bread, a pack of butter, apple pie, tinned cream, sugar, tea, milk and biscuits. The dog meanwhile would be lying somewhere close by, farting silently.

Len would then get out the folding chairs, the folding table, various rugs, various bats and balls and stuff to play with; sun shades, umbrellas, the wind break, towels and finally the portable radio – a valve affair the size of a carry-on suitcase. None of this, I must add, was put together with any sense of order. Things would be carried out randomly and piled up near the boot of the car. Trips into the house and back were almost always for single objects and sometimes stuff that was brought out would have to go back only to be brought out again when he changed what was left of his mind. By now it would usually be approaching eleven o'clock and we should have been away two hours ago.

Uncle Len would then discover that he had put the car keys down and couldn't remember where. He had taken them to open the boot, remembered to do something else, had gone off to do it and had put them down somewhere.

Julia would take off her coat and we would then begin a thorough search of the house. Uncle Len, meanwhile, would march round (he never walked), muttering and moaning and trying to pin the blame on somebody else.

'If you'd gone and got that bally chair (bally was the closest he got to swearing) when I asked you I wouldn't have put them down and lost them.' Or 'I had them in my hand when you gave me all that bally stuff to carry. I must have given them you – and you must have put them down somewhere.' We would usually find the keys in the garage somewhere, set down while he looked for something, or up in the box-room where he had gone for the portable radio. On one memorable occasion after hours combing the house from roof tiles to kitchen floor he found them in the dashboard and said that Julia must have put them there because he 'bally well' hadn't.

Once he had the keys he would set about the mysterious ritual of packing the boot. I would watch from a distance, amazed, even as a small child, at how stupid a grown-up human being really could be. Several attempts would be made to pack in a mountain of stuff that was obviously not going to go in there. Uncle Len would get hotter and hotter and his face would be almost purple with frustration. His face was almost a litmus indicator as to how mad Len actually was at any given time: it would range from pink through vermillion to puce and finally a dark purple.

When we finally got away we would find that we were stuck in queues of traffic trying to get to Delamere Forest or Ingleton Falls and would get there just in time to have a quick sandwich and listen to the teatime news on the Home Service before loading all the stuff back into the car and heading home again. Not long before he died, Len sold the Lea-Francis and bought a Ford Escort Estate, which he drove straight into the gatepost when he brought it home from the garage. Len blamed the driveway for being too narrow.

Being a Methodist, Uncle Len was teetotal, to such an extent that at his own wedding, while the guests were toasting the happy couple in Pomagne, he drank the maid of honour's health in dandelion and burdock. The problem with his teetotalism was that Aunt Julia liked a tipple from time to time. She was no heavy boozer, she just liked a little of what she fancied in the belief that it did her good; her favourite drink was a small sweet sherry. The only way she could get a tipple at Christmas without provoking a major domestic scene – including fist-bangings and readings from Holy Scripture – was in the trifle. Each year she'd lace it very generously with sherry and get a little merry that way. Uncle Len never noticed her eyes glazing over after four helpings and he rarely ate puddings himself – they smacked of hedonism, brimstone and Popery.

He did make an exception for Julia's rice pudding and would boast to everybody who bothered to listen that Julia made the best rice pudding ever. 'None of this tinned rubbish; just rice and milk and a lovely skin on it, nice and crisp and brown.' What he didn't know was that my Aunty Julia would buy two tins of Ambrosia creamed rice pudding, put them in a shallow dish, heat it up in the oven then put a crisp skin on it under the grill; she would take the labels off the tins and batter them flat with a coal hammer before hiding them in the dustbin under a pile of potato peel.

One Christmas she made what my mate Wharfie would have called a 'whamdinger' of a trifle. There must have been a bottle and a half of sherry in it. The Christmas party was at our house and the front room had been cleaned and a fire lit for the occasion. Uncle Len broke the habit of years and had a bowl of trifle. He liked it so much he had four more.

'You know, Julia,' he slurred, 'I don't know why I never tried this before. It's delicious.'

The fire in the front parlour that we used only for funerals and Christmas was howling up the chimney. You could have roasted a turkey on the hearthrug. We all stood around the piano and sang along with Aunty Julia as she played a selection of Irish ballads.

Half way through 'Biddy Mulligan, the Pride of the Coombe', Uncle Len sank slowly to the linoleum like a deep-sea diver going down to a wreck, speechless and paralysed from the teeth down. He was as drunk as a bishop. To the day we buried him he thought he'd been overcome by coal fumes.

Christmases and Coronations

Christmas, of course, was always the best time of the year. Easter was for chocolate eggs, Bonfire Night and Mischief Night for adventures, Halloween for roast chestnuts and bob apple, but Christmas was when Granddad came to stay and when Uncle Bobby and Aunty Kitty came and it was also of course when Santa Claus came. I believed in him until I was nine or so though I had half-suspected that Santa wasn't real after my nanna and Aunty Kitty took me to Lewis's Christmas Grotto to sit on Santa's knee and tell him what I wanted for Christmas. Santa was there again at a Christmas Fair in Crumpsall a few days later and he asked me again what I wanted for Christmas. I thought then that he wasn't up to much if he'd forgotten what I told him a few days before.

I woke one Christmas morning, when I still believed in Santa, at something like four o'clock, wide-eyed and fully awake. In the dim light that came in from the landing I saw my pillow case at the bottom of my bed. I grabbed it, daft with excitement, and shoved my hands in to see what I'd got. The first thing I found was a flat torch with three glass bullseyes on a slider, red and green at the outside and clear in the middle. I switched it on and shone it into the pillow case. Santa Claus had brought me a *Rupert* book, a *Beano* annual, some crayons and a drawing pad, an orange and some nuts, a comic book copy of *Oliver Twist* done by Dudley D. Watkins, the man who drew Lord Snooty, Desperate Dan, The Broons and Oor Wullie. And there was something else, a little box with a picture of a boy blowing a trumpet across a lake and the words 'Hohner' and 'Echo'. I opened it. Inside was a shiny mouth organ. I was so excited, I'd never had anything like it before and it was no use telling me that it was four in the morning and everybody else was asleep because I was going to blow it. At first I breathed gently into it, listening to the tremolo reed's sweet sound, then I discovered quite quickly that I could play, by ear and by instinct, the first bars of 'The Happy Wanderer' and I began to blow loud and hard. I'd just got to the bit about 'my knapsack on my back' when the door was flung open and my stepfather Lou was there in his pyjamas, shouting, 'You buggery crazy? Buggery Christmas not buggery start till buggery nine o' clock!'

As well as the great feasts of Christmas and Easter, other one-off events loom large in the Pathé news of my memory.

On 6 February 1952, the King died. This didn't bring much in the way of mourning to our house because my nanna didn't reckon a great deal to kings and queens, while my mother was too busy keeping the wolves from the door to pay any attention to what was happening to a family of Greeks and Germans down there in London. We stood for a minute's silence in school which gave Keith Moylan a great excuse to stick a split pen nib into Pat Lee's bum so it was a minute's silence with a yelp in the middle followed by more yelps from Keith as Miss Fisher whacked his bare legs with a ruler.

As a result of the old King popping his clogs we had a coronation a year and a bit later when we all got a china cup and saucer from HMQ with a picture of her on it. My nanna used it to keep her false teeth in. The coronation was on 2 June and all the kids in our street crowded round Mrs Whittaker's black and white, nine-inch telly to watch it. Stan, her son, an ex-Desert Rat who had come back from the war a quiet and thoughtful man, had bought a weird contraption to enlarge the picture: a glass, water-filled magnifier that hung on straps over the front of the screen and increased the viewing area slightly. The only problem was that the top and bottom edges of the magnifier distorted the picture so that the wheels of the coronation coach were distinctly oval and the Queen's head was egg-shaped when the crown went on it. Still, courtesy of the magic conjured up by John Logie Baird, we were able to watch Betty Battenberg be anointed and crowned, surrounded by all the pomp and circumstance that the British Empire could muster.

A few days later the whole school was taken to the ABC Cinema on Cheetham Hill Road to watch it all again in full colour on the big screen. The event was shortened to make it watchable and the crowning itself was followed by a film of HMQ and her Danish–Greek hubby, going off to visit the far-flung outposts of the Empire. My memory tells me that part of the film showed the conquest of Everest. Apparently the summit had been reached on 29 May, three days before the coronation, but the news had been held back until Coronation Day. We sat there in the cinema, we children of the Empire, quite happy to have the afternoon off school and particularly amused when bare-breasted native ladies of one of our Pacific Island colonies did a dance which incorporated a lot of what Vinnie Evans called 'titty wobbling'. Every child in the cinema screamed with laughter and, as we looked at our teachers to see if we were in trouble, we saw that they were trying to hide their laughter too; so that was OK.

But, even as we watched the Queen being crowned, even as we watched Edmund Hillary and Sherpa Tenzing grinning into the camera on the summit of the world, there was a ghost in the attic shuffling its chains.

What we didn't know, because the Great British Ostrich had its head well and truly up its own jacksie, was that the Empire was falling apart. Twilight was already gathering around the great Victorian edifice that had turned huge parts of the globe red-pink on the map, signifying that they were 'ours'. All empires are unsustainable, all empires in time decay. It always seems strange to me that politicians never seem to understand this, or perhaps they do and carry on maintaining the pretence as long as the loot is still rolling in. However, I digress.

Television had entered our lives in that coronation year but Mrs Whittaker's was the only one in the street. Very kindly she would let us kids in each night to watch *Children's Hour* and a circle of half a dozen or more kids would sit on the floor watching *Muffin the Mule*, Mr Turnip and a puppet called Billy Bean who operated a crazy Heath Robinson-like machine. And then there was Mr Pastry, who was always putting his foot in buckets of whitewash and getting his head stuck in ladders. We thought he was hilarious and used to run around the street afterwards pretending to be him, falling down and making 'boink' noises.

Kid's programmes were confined to an hour between 5 and 6 p.m. but that was the time when there were trees to be climbed and cans to be kicked so we gave up the goggle-box once the warmer days came and went back to falling out of trees, collecting caterpillars in matchboxes and getting up to mischief in bombed-out houses. There were quite a few ruined houses, courtesy of Adolf, and we were always being told to keep away from them, which just made us want to play in them all the more. We were convinced that most of them were haunted and one day, one of the brightest sparks in our gang sloped off ahead, covered himself with a white sheet and hid in the cupboard of the house we were aiming for. No sooner had we got in the big, dark and damp-smelling room than the groans started and as we ran for it, screaming and gibbering with fear, the ghost emerged ahead of us. We all scrambled through a blasted-out window and shot off home, delirious with fear.

Every empty old house was haunted and every old lady living alone dressed in widow's black had to be a witch. There were two truly ancient ladies who lived on the main road in one of the bigger Edwardian houses who mystified us. They must have been sisters, perhaps twins, because they seemed to be carbon copies of each other. They were small, dumpy and always dressed in black from head to toe. We never saw them out, even on the hottest summer days, without their black hats, umbrellas and coats. Their legs were covered in thick brown lisle stockings, always wrinkled, and on their feet they wore black old-fashioned lace-up boots. They were from a bygone age and I often wondered what their story was. We were, of course, convinced that they were witches and ran for cover whenever they appeared.

There was another lady who looked like a man, who dressed always in pencil-line skirts, matching double-breasted jackets and a man's shirt and tie. She wore expensive tan brogue shoes, smoked cigarettes in a long ivory holder and had her hair in a shingle with a cowlick across her forehead. I used to see her at the bus stop every morning when I was walking to school and years later, when I was working on the Manchester buses, I would see her on my early morning runs into town. In all those years she never seemed to change and nobody in the street remarked on her. I think the war had taken my mum's generation and thrown them together in the services, the factories and support organisations like the Land Army, and people who might have been otherwise bigoted and judgmental learned to have understanding and tolerance of the sexuality and life choices of others.

CHAPTER 4

THE SINGING STREET

As well as the songs my nanna and my mum had taught me there was a whole canon of street songs that all us kids learned while out on the cobbles taking the fresh Manchester smog; many of them were clean, some were dirty but innocent childish ditties, while others were based on traditional ballads and airs or on more recent popular songs.

To the tune which Lonnie Donegan used for 'My Old Man's a Dustman', we sang:

Lulu had a baby, she called him Sonny Jim,
She put him down the lavatory
To see if he could swim.
He swam down to the bottom and swam up to the top
Lulu got excited and grabbed him by his ...
Haircut, shampoo, ring the barber's bell
And if he doesn't like it, tell him to go to Halifax!

We had daft songs like:

Made you look and I made you stare
Made the barber cut your hair,
He cut it long he cut it short
He cut it with a knife and fork.

While anybody who went to an adult and told tales was treated with:

Tell tale tit,
Your tongue will split

And all the little birds
Will have a little bit.

One we really delighted in was:

Abba dabba custard, green snot pie,
All mixed in with a dead dog's eye.
Slap it on a butty, nice 'n thick
And wash it all down with a cup of cold sick.

And there were songs that still have a rare beauty to me now, sometimes because of their melodies, other times through association. One song which is found all over these islands still seems beautiful to me because I remember hearing it coming over the early morning air as I walked to school on a breezy March day:

The wind, the wind, the wind blows high
The rain comes scattering down the sky,
She is handsome, she is pretty,
She is a girl from the windy city,
She goes a courting, one two three,
Pray won't you tell me, who is she?
Michael Harding says he loves her,
All the boys are fighting for her,
Let the boys say what they will
But Michael Harding loves her still.

As I walked into the playground one spring morning I could see the girls in a ring singing that song. The girl in the centre of the ring was Sheila Bevan and I was quite excited because I did like her very much. She gave me a Love Heart toffee a few days later, which meant that we were engaged to be married, but she broke off the engagement when somebody told her I liked Bernadette Lakeland too.

Many of our songs and rhymes were secret to us and you would never sing them when grown-ups were near. To the tune of 'Knees up Mother Brown' we sang:

Don't eat Whatmore's bread,
It makes you shit the bed.
No bloody wonder you fart like thunder
Don't eat Whatmore's bread.

To the old traditional tune 'In and Out the Windows', we sang one of my favourite songs of all, favourite because it had rude bits in it. The first verse, by the way, is almost identical with a verse in the American old-time song, 'Old Dan Tucker':

Dan, Dan, the dirty old man
Washed his face in a frying pan,
Combed his hair with a donkey's tail
And scratched his belly with his big toe nail.

Chorus:
Early in the morning
Early in the morning
Early in the morning
Before the break of day.

Micky Plum with a cast-iron bum
Went sailing down the river,
Caught his belly on a lump of jelly
Which made poor Mickey shi-hi-ver

To the same tune my nanna taught me another verse:

You know last night and the night before
Three big tomcats knocking on the door,
One had a fiddle, one had a drum
And the other had a pancake stuck to his bum.

Which of course was mightily risqué, and what an Irish Catholic granny was doing teaching me verses about cat's bums and pancakes is beyond me.

And then there is the verse my grandchildren still laugh at:

My brother Billy had a ten-foot willy
He showed it to the girl next door,
She thought it was a snake so she hit it with a rake
And now it's only five foot four.

I was always getting sent home from other kids' parties for chanting rhymes like those. For some reason parents would invite me to their child's party, feed us on fish paste sandwiches, orangeade and trifle and then would get all the kids in the front room, form us into a circle and go round the ring inviting us to sing or do a recitation. I usually started off with something innocent we'd learned in school like 'Early One Morning' or 'Boney Was a Warrior' but then a demon would grip me and out would come Billy with his ten-foot willy and I'd be on my way home with a slice of cake and a promise that my mother would be told.

It was during this time, and partly because of the erotic nature of many of the rude songs, that I began to take a more studied interest in sex. I had always been interested in girls, but without knowing particularly why. At the age of four my Uncle Harry had caught me and a girl called Brenda playing in the back garden on a sunny summer morning. She had watched me peeing standing up while I had watched her peeing squatting with her knickers round her ankles, and as he walked down the path we were in the act of examining each other's bits. Sensibly he didn't make a fuss about it and told us to play at collecting dandelions. But even then I sensed that there was something more exciting in what we were doing than collecting dandelions; no doubt a Freudian analyst would say that summer's morning explains the rest of my life, but I'm more of a Jungian myself.

As we grew older, sex grew to be even more of a mystery and a fascination to us. We knew that boys and girls were made differently and often showed each other the difference; in fact we used to check on a weekly basis just to make sure that the difference was still there. We also played doctors and nurses, which entailed the raising and lowering of clothes, lots of examinations with lollipop sticks and prescriptions of privet leaves and grass to be put under the liberty bodice or down the knickers or underpants. As anybody knows, when you are five years old, grass and privet leaves are the universal panacea. When one of the girls was getting ready for bed and several handfuls of vegetation fell out of her underwear, questions were asked, answers were given and the Hall Road Amateur NHS Drop-in Clinic was shut down, for a while at least.

But in spite of our best efforts we had no real knowledge of anatomy. Sex education was a thing of the far-off future; we had a vague idea where babies came from but, as yet, no idea how they were made. One of our explanatory rhymes went:

Milk, milk (pointing to our chests), lemonade
(pointing between our legs),
Round the corner (pointing to our bums) chocolate's made.

I now know, of course, that chocolate is made in Belgium but when I was five the rhyme seemed appropriate.

We were beginning to understand something about sex, though since it was filtered through the lens of childhood it looks innocent enough:

John and Mary went to the dairy
John pulled out his big canary
Mary said, 'Oh what a whopper,
Let's lie down and do it proper.'

Not quite understanding what it meant, we would also chant:

Long and thin
Just slips in
Doesn't please the ladies,
Short and thick
Does the trick
And produces babies.

It was a while before I would understand the import of that Shakespearian sestet.

Lucifer and the Polo Mints

Alongside sex, religion was a source of much trouble and worry to me from childhood right through to my teens. When I was small it was mostly the guilt and fear that was drummed into me by my nanna; when I got a little older, it was the guilt and fear hammered into us by the priests at St Onan's Roman Catholic College, a.k.a. St Bede's. I once joked on stage that at St Bede's we did O level Guilt and Damnation, and thinking about it after the show, it seemed that much of my life as a boy had been taken up with contemplating a job as a stoker in the furnace room of HMS *Hades* as a likely career choice for my afterlife.

The religion we got in school was orthodox stuff: the usual bit about how Jesus was his own son but in spite of that was a good boy who ended up doing miracles and teaching people how to be kind to each other – with the exception of money changers, to whom he gave a good kicking. St Joseph, we were taught, was a kind man, and the Virgin Mary was a lady who would help you if you prayed to her. Jesus was betrayed by Judas who then ended up being hated; this is strange really because without Judas betraying Him there would have been no crucifixion and Jesus wouldn't have died to save us all from Hell. I found this very puzzling but shrugged it off as yet another mystery like the Trinity, which told us that God the Father, God the Son and God the Holy Ghost were one and the same person. Mind you, that mystery wasn't too hard to swallow because Clark Kent was also Superman and if he'd been able to be Batman too that would have been a Trinity. There was Wakefield Trinity rugby league club as well, but Nanna told me that had nothing to do with the Holy Ghost.

There were quite a few saints we had to take notice of: Christopher, which was my middle name, meant 'Christ Bearer', and he'd been called that because he'd carried Jesus across the

Jordan when God was a small boy. I wasn't sure that made sense, since later on in the gospels Jesus showed that he was quite good at walking on water, so why he had to have a big beardy bloke to carry him across the river puzzled me. St Michael, who I was named after, was the archangel who thrust Satan down to Hell; secretly I didn't think Michael had done that much of a good job because my nanna and the teachers at school told us that Lucifer was still knocking around out there, tempting and tricking us.

My nanna, though she had a rock-solid faith in the redeeming power of Jesus, was still worried about Old Nick. His other names were the devil, the Prince of Darkness, Satan, Beelzebub and Lucifer – which was also, confusingly, the name for a match. But, whatever name he went under, Old Nick was incredibly real to me and I had no doubt that he was waiting to get hold of me and drag me down to Hell with him, particularly since I seemed to be the most sinful boy I knew. Other lads in our gang like Kenny and Wharfie did bad things too, but it didn't matter so much for them, my nanna said, because they were Protestants and didn't know any better. I, on the other hand, was a 'Child of God' and had a higher standard to keep up.

On the other side of the fence from Old Nick were God, Jesus, Mary, the Pope, the saints, the angels, the Holy Ghost, Bishop Marshall the Bishop of Salford, Monsignor Aspinall our parish priest, and my nanna.

Jesus I liked for obvious reasons: there were presents on his birthday at Christmas and chocolate eggs at Easter when he rose again like a chicken from an egg. I wasn't too happy about the mass on Good Friday, though; it went on for ages and invariably some soppy girl would faint and have to be carried out of church. I wasn't too happy with benediction either, come to that. Benediction was a strange kind of mass without communion; we sang songs and there was incense. The main part of benediction was when the priest took Jesus's body out of the tabernacle and put it in a monstrance, a strange round glass container on a stand with gold flames surrounding it. He then held it up on high for us all to see; only we had been taught that we weren't worthy enough to look at

Jesus as bread and had to show our unworthiness by bowing our heads. I did sneak a peek once or twice and all I could see was a white bit in the middle of the monstrance, which could have been anything. The altar boys would have a triple ration of incense at benediction and would swing the thurible with mischief in their minds until parts of the altar vanished in an aromatic fog. My nanna made me go to benediction most Sundays and often midweek too. I don't know why she liked it so much; the chances are that she might have been a frankincense and holy water addict.

Holy water was my nanna's WD-40. It was good for headaches, sore eyes, keeping demons out of the house and would protect you on journeys. I seldom left the house to go anywhere further than school without a liberal shower of holy water. Lourdes water was a kind of holy water that was especially efficacious and my nanna used to keep any she managed to get her hands on for her rheumatism.

I quite liked God the Father, because he was Jesus's dad and gave us lots of holidays of obligation when the school closed because the day was special to some saint or martyr (they were literally 'holy days' when we were 'obliged' to go to mass). One holy day was called the Feast of the Annunciation and was special because Jesus's mother had opened the door to an angel who wasn't selling wooden flowers but instead had come to tell her that she was going to have God's baby. This must have come as a bit of a shock to her because, as far as I could tell, they hadn't even been out on a date.

Another holiday was special because Jesus had told his Father that he didn't want his mother dying like other mothers had to do – he wanted her brought straight to Heaven without passing Go or collecting £200. This was a new Holy Day thought up and declared infallible by Pope Pius XII on 1 November 1950. I had seen lots of pictures of the Assumption, which I misheard as the Feast of the Consumption. You could buy the holy pictures in the church porch for sixpence; they were mostly copies of Italian baroque paintings and showed the Blessed Mother of God half way to Paradise, rising up through the clouds with lots of cherubs flitting round her like pink-bottomed, curly-headed bees.

These holy days of obligation meant that we got more holidays than the Protestants and could get more of a go on the swings and the roundabouts in the park because there weren't any other kids off school. On the whole I thought God was a good thing, and that Jesus had some great ideas, like whipping the money changers (some translations have 'lenders') out of the Temple, walking on water and feeding lots of people on a few loaves and fishes. One thing puzzled me, though: if he could raise Lazarus from the dead, why couldn't he do that for all of us? Was he Jesus's best pal? If so, why couldn't I be His best pal too and never have to die? Come to think of it, if God knew everything then He presumably knew how many sins you would have on your soul on the day you were born, so why didn't he skip the bit in the middle and send you straight to Heaven or Hell or Purgatory?

Limbo was another strange place – invented, it now seems, by the Church to explain where any good non-Catholics went who hadn't been baptised. It was chock full of pagans, my nanna said, which was why we had to collect money to give to St Joseph to baptise the black babies in Africa so they could go to Heaven or Hell instead of Limbo. By the 1990s the Church had stopped preaching about Limbo and was quietly hoping that nobody would notice the fact that it had gone. Kieran Halpin, the folk singer and songwriter, spotted that it had vanished and wrote a song called 'Where Did all the Limbo People Go?' which is well worth finding and listening to. On the basis of the non-existence of Limbo may I suggest that the Holy Roman Catholic Church must owe me quite a few quid by now because of all the money I raised to get black babies out of an imaginary place. In one month alone I raised fifty quid and was invited to tea by the Bishop of Salford for my hard work. There were a few hundred other kids my age there and the tea was dry sandwiches and weak orange squash so that was a bit of a con, too. With compound interest I reckon I'm owed well over a grand in today's money on brass I earned the Church from 1951 to 1955. So if the Bishop of Salford is reading this he can either send me a cheque or leave the cash at my mate Dimitri's Greek Café in Deansgate, Manchester. However, I digress.

I liked the look of God in the picture books with his big white beard and his long robes. He was like Santa without the reindeer. I also thought he was pretty smart because, as the catechism taught us, God always was, is, and always will be – which would look pretty good on anybody's CV. I didn't like it that God knows and sees all things, even our most secret thoughts, particularly since most of my secret thoughts were about naughty things like bare-naked ladies.

The member of the Trinity I had no time for at all was the Holy Ghost, either as a dove, tongues of fire or as a ghost. I knew what ghosts looked like because you saw them in the comics I read: they were white and had big heads and hands but no legs. They looked like flying bedsheets and nothing at all like a dove or tongues of fire. The Holy Ghost seemed pretty rubbish to me though the sin against Him, which was losing your faith, was the very worst sin of all and was a bit like not believing in Communism under Stalin.

I shall deal with my own particular battle with the Holy Ghost later – that battle was mostly to do with bosoms. What I want to talk about now is Old Nick and one simple sin. First, Old Nick. On the edge of the Hospital Fields there was a squat concrete building with steps going down to an underground door while the flat concrete roof ended in a pitched slope, down which we used to slide. The building was overhung with trees and was something to do with the water board. I think it was some kind of pumping house. It was also quite spooky and we called it the Devil's Knock because every so often, probably due to some change in water pressure, spasmodic groanings and bangings would come from within. We would go down the damp steps to the locked door and stand in the wet leaves at the bottom waiting breathlessly; on hearing the bangs and clanks we would run off shouting that the devil was coming, wailing and hysterical yet deliciously excited at the same time.

But the devil in the waterworks was as nothing to the Satan conjured up by my nanna and the priests and teachers at school. He didn't moan and bang; he tricked you into losing your immortal soul, which, once gone, was lost forever. Robert Johnson, the great blues singer, is said to have sold his soul at the crossroads for the gift of music. I sold mine for a packet of Polo mints and later sold it again for some innocent and completely natural fumblings of girls' bosoms. The jury is still out as to whether this was a good bargain or not.

I wasn't a particularly good or holy child but on the other hand I wasn't a particularly bad one. On a sliding scale of angel to devil I probably wobbled around somewhere in the middle with occasional forays along the lines either side of the spectrum. One thing I do know, however: because of a moment of selfishness I have not eaten a Polo mint for more than sixty years. No use in me blaming Old Nick, I made the choice of my own free will, and though I did confess it later, I have the feeling that if ever I get up there to that place above the clouds I will have to account for the thruppence and the Polo mints.

I had begun to realise, by the time I was nine or so, that, though the arse wasn't hanging out of our collective trousers, my family was not very rich. We had just about enough to live on and nothing more. My mother's war widow's pension had ceased when she married Lou and he was earning pitiful wages at Clayton Aniline chemical works. Aunty Julia didn't earn much as a machinist and my nanna's pension wasn't a bounty. My mum wasn't working because Christina was still small so there was six of us to feed, clothe and keep warm on not very much. Like everybody else in the street we ran up tick at the grocer's shop. Mrs Hughes kept a small red notebook for each customer and entered in it the stuff you had taken; then on the following Friday, when the wages had come in, you would be expected to pay it off. We just about managed to pay off our weekly debts each Friday, slept under old army greatcoats in winter and got new clothes once a year at Whitsun.

The trouble was that I had a serious Polo mint problem. I loved them, but my Saturday spends of a shilling (5p in today's money) was usually spent on a seat at the 'Thruppenny Rush', the kid's matinée in our local cinema, and anything over had gone by Sunday. I knew it was no use moaning and badgering for money during the week because every penny was earmarked for food, rent, the insurance man, the tally man and Lou's bus fare to work.

I could have collected empty pop bottles and got the money back on returning them but competition was fierce round our streets and the pickings varied from slim to bugger all. Nobody wanted any odd jobs doing, and since most of our gang were in the same straits there was no point trying to sell them a dinky car or a batch of comics. So, one day, driven mad by a craving for Polo mints, I did the unthinkable. I opened my mum's purse and stole a threepenny bit. Before remorse or guilt could grab me by the neck I raced down the road to the paper shop and bought a tube of Polos.

I stuffed three or four mints into my mouth standing outside the shop, but for some reason they didn't taste as good as they usually did. I had a couple more as I headed back towards our street, then I realised that if I was caught eating them in the house my mum would want to know where I'd got the money to buy them. I ate a few more but by now I had lost my love for them and I put the remainder of the roll down the nearest grid. I was filled with guilt and shame; my mum needed that money more than I did and what I had done was wrong, really wrong.

I confessed it to Father Thorpe the next Saturday when Nanna dragged me with her to confession in that long wooden hut that was then St Anne's Church, but even after the absolution I didn't feel too good about myself and I've never been able to eat a Polo mint since.

The stuff about the bosoms comes later, and by then I was already a hardened sinner of eleven.

Stewed Tripe and Rotten Eggs

Polo mints aside, our diet was limited but it was a healthy one. Meat in our house was a Sunday affair and was always the cheapest cut: neck end of lamb or some such. We might get the odd tea of curried eggs during the week, which would play havoc with my nanna's bowels, but it was always fish on Friday because of the Catholic thing and often fish on other days too, my least favourite being cold pilchards served up with boiled potatoes. Friday often saw us munching on finnan haddock and every time we had it, my nanna would point out to me the mark on the fish, which was where St Peter, the fisherman, had held it by his thumb and finger. I found this a bit mysterious since the fish came from Scotland and not the Sea of Galilee. I could accept that all donkeys had a cross on their backs because Jesus had once ridden one, but how St Peter had caught a Scottish fish was beyond me.

One day a week we would have coddle, a Dublin dish which is mostly made up of anything you had to hand, but in our case was usually scraps of fatty bacon and sausage with sliced potatoes and onions all cooked together with bruised tomatoes which we got cheap from the greengrocer's at the bottom of the street. It was actually very tasty and according to my mum it was a great favourite of Seán O'Casey and James Joyce who she told me were two of Ireland's greatest writers – although Joyce had written a dirty book that had been banned by the Church. The one dish I hated and which usually appeared midweek when my mum's purse was emptying was tripe. In the winter it was stewed with onions and milk and in the summer it was served raw with salad. When we were having tripe my nanna would have crubeens (boiled pigs' trotters), which she loved. She would sit by the fireside and attack the pigs' trotters with her gums in quite an alarming manner, looking not unlike Goya's painting of Saturn devouring his son.

The other meal I hated was macaroni boiled in milk, which we had when the cupboard was bare. I did like a dish called Egyptian Eye that my mum made. This was basically fried bread with a hole cut into the middle into which you broke an egg. You then flipped it over and sealed it, making sure you didn't break the yolk. My mum said it was supposed to look like the eye of Horus but I thought it just looked like a fried egg in the middle of a slice of bread.

If it wasn't my mum trying to kill me by feeding me bits of cow's innards, it was the weather having a go at shuffling me off the mortal coil: frost, ice, thunder and lightning and smog were all likely to send you off to where Old Nick could get you. Thunder and lightning and the frozen stuff you couldn't avoid because God made them, but smog was something man-made and deadly. You don't get them now but then they were common: thick yellow industrial smogs that would descend on cold wintry days to cloak the city with a freezing acrid soup that brought visibility down to the end of your nose, and meant that it was often quicker to walk home than sit on a bus stuck in a long snake of traffic, pumping more crap into the air while it waited. This crap came both from the bus engine and from the forty or so people upstairs that were smoking Capstan Full Strength and Wills Woodbines as though their lives depended upon it – which in a negative way they did. But that was as nothing compared with the industrial miasma outside the bus where cold and warm air mingled with all the SO_2, NO, HNO_3, CO_2 and all the other noxious O level chemistry gases that were pumped out of millions of chimneys and exhausts to make a thick chemical broth which everybody, high born or low, breathed in; part-payment for the benefits of living in an industrial society.

God knows how many thousands the smog attacks killed each year in the northern cities but nothing was done about it until the dreadful Great London Smog of the winter of 1952 when as many as 12,000 Londoners are thought to have died of chest complaints. After a small bit of research by the Department of the Fecking Obvious at Kew it dawned upon scientists and politicians that it might just possibly be the shite that heavy industry and domestic fires were pumping into the environment that was causing people to cough up bits of lung. After much consideration and political argy bargy they brought in the Clean Air Act in 1956. If only they had gone up to Manchester and talked to doctors there they would have been told about something called the 'Manchester Chest', a condition prevalent amongst people in that fair city, brought on by a high concentration of poison in the air they breathed. The filth came from the many mills, foundries, dye works and chemical plants in the Irwell, Medlock and Mersey valleys, and so well known was this complaint that the owners of these self-same mills and factories lived far away from the foul air in mansions on the Cheshire plains.

If it had just been northerners dying the government wouldn't have given a bugger and we would still have the same old pea soupers every November to March, but once all those Beefeaters and pearly kings and queens started popping their clogs, the government got on the case and, within a few years, the poisonous fogs had pretty much gone.

When the smogs enveloped Manchester we were sent off to school with handkerchiefs tied round our mouths and noses. Like a gang of small coughing bandits we would fumble our way to St Anne's and sit in a classroom that smelt of coke ovens, coughing our way through the nine times' table. Later when I was at grammar school I would splutter my way to the bus stop and wait for a Manchester Corporation galleon to come sailing down the river of gloop. If a bus did eventually turn up, we would pile on and sit there looking out at bugger-all as it crawled across the city at three miles an hour; we would arrive at school anything up to two hours late. If it persisted, as it often did, or if a bad smog came while we were in school, we were usually sent home early – though it still meant that sometimes we got home just in time for bed.

I found some interesting things in the airing cupboard one morning and thought they would be just the thing for dealing with the fog. They were thick gauze pads with loops at each end. To a ten-year-old boy they looked like smog masks and the loops fitted neatly over my ears. I got as far as the door before my mother noticed that I was wearing a sanitary towel and it was suddenly yanked from my head. It was years before I understood what all the fuss was about.

If the air was bad, the rivers were worse. As a keen little angler I used to buy the *Angling Times* occasionally and after peering longingly at all the great fishing rods and reels and baskets that I could never afford to buy, I would turn to the pages of news. Amongst the pictures of smiling men in flat caps with fags clamped between their lips holding prize-winning carp up to the camera, there would be pictures of rivers covered in foam caused when a factory poured loads of detergent into the water, and other pictures of rivers carpeted with dead fish, all floating belly up; the result of arsenic or concentrated bleach being dumped into the river. The paper did its best to campaign against this pollution, as did the various angling clubs who owned the fishing rights to the waters, but industry, like cotton, was king. The River Irk, my own local small river, was a tributary of the Irwell and before the Industrial Revolution was chock full of salmon, trout, sea trout and grayling. In fact salmon was so plentiful that on some apprentice indentures drawn up in the late eighteenth century it was stipulated that the apprentice was to be fed salmon on no more than three days a week. We often played along the banks of the Irk and used to watch it change colour throughout the course of the day, sometimes red, sometimes blue or purple. It was nicknamed the Rainbow River and common mythology had it that if you fell in and managed not to drown, you would have to be taken to Crumpsall Hospital to have your stomach pumped. The river was also home to massive scabrous rats and we used to go and sit on the bank trying to pop them off with our catapults and air guns. The Irk never caught fire like the Tees did but it was often man high with foam from the detergents dumped into it by a bleach and detergent manufacturer further upstream.

Watch the 1954 film *Hobson's Choice*, starring Charles Laughton and directed by David Lean, and look out for the part where Willie Mossop and Maggie are out 'courtin'' and are sat on the banks of the River Irwell. Great bergs of foam sail downstream in a constant flotilla and the air is speckled with bird-sized flakes torn off and flung helter skelter by the wind.

It's hard to believe that in 1681 James Chetham wrote his *Angler's Vade Mecum*, a book of angling and fishing flies based on his experience of fishing the river when the Irk valley was described as one of the most beautiful places in the whole of England. In the days of my growing up it was home to a Dark Satanic Mill, a Dark Satanic ICI Factory and a Dark Satanic Brake and Clutch-lining Works where they made asbestos pads (and where, as well as a brass clock, they gave many people who worked there a generous dose of asbestosis for their years of loyalty). There was also a Dark Satanic Biscuit Works where they made the world-famous C.W.S. Crumpsall Cream Cracker. These really were world famous, unlike Bernard Manning's World Famous Embassy Club just up the road at the top of Factory Brew, which was unknown outside Harpurhey.

Nobody seemed too concerned about pollution then, even though it was patently obvious that the reason so many people in Manchester had bad chests was because of the shit air we breathed. It was assumed, I suppose, that the working class actually liked breathing all that crap. Strange that the only time things changed for the working class was during World War I, when medical officers, alarmed at the terrible physical condition of the new recruits, notified the government. The government promised to do something about getting a better physical specimen of soldier to be shot, and in the meantime formed Bantam Battalions of small blokes who, like bantam cocks, were supposed to be small and yet good fighters. Being small probably meant they were just slightly harder for the Germans to shoot and also cheaper to keep since they didn't eat much; also, of course, their coffins would use less wood.

The ICI, not wanting to seem slacking in the pollution stakes, did their bit when it came to poisoning the Crumpsall air. One of the processes carried out in Quatermassville down the hill in Blackley required a great deal of hydrogen sulfide to be produced and contained in sealed retorts. H_2S is the stuff they put in stink bombs to give them their rotten-egg, fart smell. The ICI seemed to have problems keeping the lid on their autoclaves because the regular stomach-turning stink of rotten eggs would come up the hill from the factory, particularly on warm summer days. A gang of us kids would find ourselves standing at the bus stop alongside people who had come from visiting time at the nearby hospital as one of these industrial megafarts made its way up the hill.

'Pooo! Who's let Polly out of prison?' one of us would shout, and you could see the strangers wondering how such a small group of children, with presumably quite small bowels, could make such an incredibly disgusting and powerful stink.

The stench was truly nauseating, but whenever the government alkali inspectors who were supposed to spot such pollution came round to sample the air the atmosphere was strangely normal. As soon as they had gone – shazaam! The Rotten Egg Fairy would come and Crumpsall would magically turn into Fartsville UK. Hydrogen sulfide is pretty dangerous, but the ICI knew that we Crumpsalites were built of strong stuff; that's why they made beta-naphthylamine in the factory, a known cause of papillomas of the bladder which, while they didn't always kill you, didn't do you any great favours either; anybody who drew more than a few years of their pension after leaving work there was thought to be exceptionally lucky. In *Brave New World*, Huxley describes how the Epsilon Minus clones are subjected to chemical pollution while in the foetus stage to enable them to work in lethal conditions later. I think the ICI was trying to do that to us.

We were lucky in one way, though, because our part of Lancashire, at the foot of the Pennines, seemed to attract quite a lot of wind. This wind came in off the Atlantic, having first dumped a lot of rain on Ireland, then would run around Manchester for a bit, taking most of the really poisonous stuff over the hills to Yorkshire. This is probably one of the reasons why Yorkshire folk tend to distrust Lankies and why the Wars of the Roses is still going on – though now it's mainly on the cricket pitch.

Rain was quite common in our neck of the woods (they don't call Manchester the Rainy City for nothing), which was a bit of a bugger because if it rained heavily you stayed in and watched the steam condense on the windows but if you drew faces in it you got told off because it would 'leave marks'. The worst day to get stuck in was washing day, for then there was no escape from the steam and my mum would already be fractious with having to wash sheets and clothes for the whole household with no prospect of getting them out on the line. Mushy the cat and I always found it best to keep a low profile on such days. My nanna would be sat near the fire with her rosary beads earning time out of Purgatory with a rattle through of Hail Marys and Our Fathers and I would be sat by the window looking out at the rain, the coal shed, the sooty privet and the grey, weeping Manchester sky.

It was on days like that I began to suspect that there was no God. How could He let it rain when there was no school?

Things were already conspiring to turn me into an agnostic.

During school holidays, even if it was raining fit enough to worry

Noah, there was always the baths and the flicks and if things got really bad and the rain went on for more than a couple of days, mothers would relent and let other kids in to play or swap comics.

And what comics they were: *The Dandy*, *Beano*, *Beezer*, *Topper*, *Film Fun*, *Radio Fun*, *Knockout*, *The Victor*, *The Hotspur* – and, best of all when we were a little older, *The Eagle* with its classic strip Dan Dare, Pilot of the Future, featuring strong-jawed Dan, Digby, his Yorkshire sidekick, and the Mekon – the green-faced Treen ruler who is the dead spit of William Hague.

Flea Pits, Bug Huts and Bare-Naked Ladies

Before television came blundering into our lives like some kind of Genghis Khan of the intellect, there was only radio and 'the flicks' or 'the pictures' as the cinema was known to us Crumpsall kids. Listen, I know that the Great Khan did bring some good things such as silk and spices and creches for working mums to the lands he harried and looted, but his influence, on the whole, was less than good. Thus it is, I believe, with the Haunted Fish Tank, and that's from somebody who once worked in the media and may well be accused of biting the hand that feedeth. Before any sociologists write in to tell me that I am elitist, and that *Topless Gardening*, *Big Brother on Ice* and *Celebrity Come Dancing and Cooking* are part of the common culture, may I say, 'bollocks'. In the eighteenth century the common culture celebrated cock-fighting, bear-baiting, public hangings and bare-knuckle boxing. As mankind grew up and became slightly more civilised, we realised that having a good laugh while somebody swung and jerked on the end of a hemp rope might just have a general tendency to brutalise us. For most of my early life the popular media had some sense of what was fair and good and produced entertainment that might seem dated and simple now, but which worked with the spirit of the time. That world seemed somehow a gentler place. On the rare occasion I watch the box today I surf the channels looking for something that isn't the modern equivalent of a public disembowelling ... and mostly fail. Here endeth the moan.

The cinemas that dominated our streets were a motley lot. The ABC Premier on Cheetham Hill Road was the poshest of all; you mostly dressed smart to go there and they had a regular Saturday morning club for kids called the ABC Minors. None of the kids in our street were members because you had to pay to join. Across the road was the slightly scruffier Greenhill, our favoured celluloid dream cathedral, while close by were the Shakespeare and the Temple, the latter built on land which had originally belonged to the Knights Templars and where some of them were said to be buried. Little could they have known, as they were whacking off Saracen's heads on the road to the Holy Land, that six hundred years later, little boys in short pants would be jumping up and down on dusty plush seats several feet above their mouldering bones, shouting at Hopalong Cassidy to look behind him because the 'baddies' were coming.

Last of all there was the Globe, a.k.a. 'the Bug Hut' or 'the Flea Pit'. It was the cheapest of all the picture houses, and kids I knew reckoned that if you hadn't got any money you could get in for two empty two-pound jam jars, which made it a sort of cross between a rag and bone shop and a cinema. The Globe was situated up a side street at the back of Woolworth's and right by a graveyard. The cemetery was overgrown with weeds and clinging ivy and was dank, damp and dark even on the brightest of summer days. To us it was a place so ghoulish that after watching particularly scary films on winter nights we would run past screaming in self-induced terror. All it needed was for one kid to shout 'Ghost! Ghost!' and we were off.

The 'Bug Hut' got its name from the denizens of its seats and many's the time I emerged after a good night at the pictures itching and scratching, courtesy of the 'mechanical dandruff'.

Infestations were common in those times: nits and bed bugs, lice and fleas were not unknown and most houses in our street had a tribe of cockroaches and a mouse or three living somewhere behind the skirting boards. Head lice or 'nits' were regular visitors and the Manchester Education Committee health people sent a nurse round regularly to check us for nits and ringworm. The nurse, 'Nitty Nora the Bug Explorer', as we kids called her, would stand in front of the class and one by one you would go up to be examined. She'd assess your overall health then look at your fingernails and arms to see if you had scabies or ringworm; last of all she would have a good root through your scalp looking for 'visitors'. If she found them you were given a note to take home to your mum. In most cases a nit comb and a dose of Derbac would get them out. Some kids didn't bother with that fancy stuff; they just had their hair shaved off. If you had a 'full house' (nits and ringworm), your head was shaved and also painted with purple ointment. I remember two brothers in St Anne's who seemed to spend their entire school careers walking round looking like blackcurrant lollies. Since they were the hardest kids in the school and wore studded leather boots (provided free to kids who had no shoes by the Lord Mayor's Boot Fund), nobody made any comments.

The Greenhill Cinema was where we went on a Saturday morning for the 'Thruppenny Rush' but the Bug Hut was our cinema of choice for weeknights. It cost kids just sixpence to get in and had the added attraction of a great chippy close by where you could get a bag of chips for threepence and a poke of scrapings for nothing. I'm sure that chaps of our own age in Eton or Rugby would have envied us had they seen us stood under the gas lamp, our heads full of nits, a bag of chips and a poke of scrapings in our hands, reliving the sagas we had just seen: *Treasure Island* with Robert Newton, Norman Wisdom coming up trumps again in spite of all, *The Dam Busters*, *The Cruel Sea*, *The Lavender Hill Mob* and *Hobson's Choice*. It wasn't enough simply to see the films, we had to retell them over and again under the old, green iron lamp, acting out our favourite scenes with all the energy and fervour of baby seannachies.

'Where Norman Wisdom gets that candy floss stick stuck to his fingers and he gets in the orchestra and waves it about trying to get it off and everybody thinks he's the conductor and they play the music.'

'No, this is it – where he escapes from prison in his underpants and vest and ends up doing that road-walking with them athletes and the police don't see him.'

Scenes like this would usually be followed with full-blown enactments accompanied by our own sound effects. If the film we'd been watching had been a war film we would be Lancaster Bombers,

Messerschmitts, Ack-Ack crews and machine gunners and we would scoot round the lamppost, gaberdine macs flying, shooting each other down until somebody stuck their head out of an upstairs window and told us to 'bugger off!' back to our own streets.

Saturday mornings in winter saw the whole tribe of us leaving our street heading for the Greenhill. Up along the sand hills we would go, singing and shouting, past the spot where two kids got killed when the den they were digging caved in, and up past the chicken farm where they threw dead chickens out to rot and stink in a maggot-riddled heap, and finally onto Cheetham Hill. There we would make our final gallop to the picture house singing our gang anthem:

We are the mystery riders,
We fight the spiders
From off the walls.

Then we would join the queue with hundreds of other pushing and shoving kids under the eyes of a uniformed commissionaire who spent all his time marching up and down hauling kids out of the line for fighting or giving him cheek, only to find that they had slipped back in again elsewhere.

At 11 a.m. the doors would open and we would stream in, a tide of smelly, shouting, raggy-arsed kids who immediately set about making their own fun as they waited for the film to begin; singing snatches of songs such as:

I went a walkin' with my Uncle Jim
And somebody threw a tomato at him,
Tomatoes don't hurt when they come in the skin
But this one it did 'cos it came in a tin.

Fed up with the row coming from the stalls, the usherettes would flash their torches and shout for us to be quiet; it would have been as much use shouting at the wind. The only thing that caught our attention was the dimming of the lights which signalled the film starting, at which point we started to stamp and cheer like good 'uns. Most weeks there was a cowboy film featuring Roy Rogers or Hopalong Cassidy or some such, and that was usually preceded by our favourites: the cartoons and the shorts. The cartoons we most loved were *Tom and Jerry* and *Mr Magoo* and I can still hear the howls of hysteria from the stalls as Magoo went though his short-sighted antics, walking off tall buildings onto girders that just happened to be swinging past on the chain of a crane or talking to petrol pumps thinking they were men.

With luck we might have an episode of *The Three Stooges*, *Our Gang* or *Flash Gordon* between the cartoons and the cowboy film. All the kids loved Flash Gordon, even though (in true comic-book superhero tradition) Flash wore his underpants outside his trousers, and the rocket ship looked as though it were made from a couple of dustbins. We lived every moment of it and booed the Emperor Ming as though our very existence depended on it.

The Three Stooges were a different kettle of fish. The daft noises they made and the crazy scrapes they got into had us hooting and furthermore had us imitating them on the way home. 'Nyim nyim nyim nyim!' we would go, before pretending to bop each other on the head.

We liked the cowboy films, but only so long as there was lots of chasing and shooting and falling off cliffs. The minute Roy Rogers got his guitar out or Hopalong Cassidy looked as though he were about to kiss some busty woman we would all start booing and stamping our feet. We hadn't come there to watch Hopalong snog some lady or hear songs about silvery moons and little doggies 'gitting along'; what we wanted was shooting and fighting and heading them off at Dead Man's Gulch – and plenty of it. In our dandelion days the goodies wore white hats and baddies wore black hats and the worst baddie of them all was Jack Elam, the one with the wall eye and the grizzly chin who chewed tobacco. He was the baddie I dreamed about in my nightmares.

Some of the more adventurous kids worked out a scam that as far as I can remember was never detected. The emergency doors were located in the corridor that led to the boys' toilets and they were not alarmed. Some of the harder kids from Kennet House

'Queen Mary' flats would go to the toilet, open the door quietly and let dozens of their mates in, cleverly slipping back one or two at a time so the usherettes weren't made suspicious by the sight of one small boy going for a pee and twenty-five coming back again.

There was something about us all being kids together in 'the flicks' that the coming of television changed. We watched the movies together and were united in our loves and our hates, united in our belief that the world was black and white and we could all sing the same songs; we learned from each other, and we also learned how to give and take.

The cinema inspired us to play games together, too; on the Hills away from the toxic ponds was a mound of old granite cobbles that had been torn up and dumped there by the ICI. We rearranged them into space ships and racing cars, castles and kingdoms. The girls made little houses and collected wild flowers to put on the stone shelves of their imaginary cottages. We took the dials and wires and transformers of old laboratory consoles we found on the tip nearby and turned them into the controls of our flying saucers, while bits of covings and sheet steel were bent into the shape of our rocket nose cones. For hours we would roam the universe in our stone and scrap vessels fighting battles and rescuing each other until, with the coming of dusk, we heard our mothers calling us from the streets below and, one by one, we would peel off out of formation, dock our spacecraft, and step out of the cosmos of the ICI tip and back into Crumpsall.

In the summer, Saturday mornings would find a shouting, laughing, joking mob of boys and sometimes girls too on our way to the swimming baths, to Cheetham Hill or Harpurhey Baths. Harpurhey had a washhouse attached and women with their hair in turbans would push prams piled high with washing up the hill to do their weekly wash. We paid our tanners, went in through the turnstile and rushed to get changed in the small cubicles that lined the sides of the pool. When we got older, around ten, we would try and peep under the doors and see if we could catch a glimpse of any bare-naked ladies.

Bare-naked ladies were becoming a bit of an obsession with our gang, ever since Kenny had found a copy of *Health and Efficiency* somewhere and brought it to the den we had made in the Hills. *Health and Efficiency* was (and still is) the house organ of the British nudist movement. It had lots of pictures of ladies bare and naked but with their bottom bits either covered up with a strategically placed beach ball or towel, or airbrushed out so that there was nothing there. Jimmy reckoned that grown-up ladies actually had hairs there but we rubbished the idea. The magazine was pored over and the lads reckoned that by standing close to the pool's edge we would be able to look under the doors and see the girls getting changed. We stood there until Wharfie wolf-whistled at something pink he said he had just seen. A big girl came out and whacked him with her towel. I got whacked too which was unfair because I couldn't see a damn thing without my glasses.

You could get in the baths a bit cheaper by going in the 'Men Only' pool. That had a smaller, shallower pool and allowed nude bathing; it also had hot slipper baths at the top end where you could wash the muck off with a cake of soap before taking a cold shower and diving in the pool. I remember more than once colliers from Bradford Road pit asking me to scrub their backs for them, which I did. There was nothing remotely dodgy about this since it was all done in broad daylight; it was just that the blokes couldn't reach. I remember noticing the scars, healed over but blue from the coal dust that lay underneath the healed skin, like random tattoos traced across their backs.

Talking Blackpool Blues

We had no family holidays because we simply couldn't afford it. We weren't alone in that; most of the families in the street couldn't afford to go away for a fortnight. There were one or two families that went to Pontins or Butlins (apparently they were run just like an army camp – you had to get up at reveille and do keep fit every morning) or went to a boarding house somewhere for a week, but we didn't. We went to Blackpool, or Southport or Llandudno for the day on a charabanc ('We're just going away by the day – seeing how the weather pans out' – was the accepted excuse that saved families the embarrassment of admitting they were too poor to afford a boarding-house holiday). Poor we might have been but those day trips to the seaside were the most exciting days of my childhood; almost up there with Christmas and definitely better than first Holy Communion, in spite of what my nanna said.

Mrs Howarth at the corner shop arranged it all. She collected the money week by week, booked the coach and organised a stop halfway for the kids to have a pee and for the grown-ups to stretch their legs and have a pint. We almost always went in one of the coaches owned by my friend Kevin Leech's dad, Bobby, who ran the local funeral parlour; as well as carting the dead off to Moston Cemetery, Bob took the living out on day trips away from the factories that were more likely than not making sure that they would be customers of the other side of Bob's counter before too long.

I don't doubt that there were days when we went to Blackpool and the sun didn't shine, I don't doubt that there were days when an icy wind drove us off the Great Orme in Llandudno into a bus shelter, but I don't remember them. All I remember is the sun shining, the waves shimmering, and the fish and chips tasting like the best food I'd ever eaten; all I remember is getting sunburned, making sand castles with paper flags on the top, and dropping my ice cream in the sand.

On the morning of our 'charabang' trip we would dress quickly in our best clothes. My mum would make a picnic lunch and pack it in a shopping bag together with my swimming trunks, a towel and spare underwear for me in case I fell in the sea (it had happened before – lots). Then we would stand with everybody else outside the corner shop waiting for the charabanc to come. There was always a last-minute panic as somebody realised they'd forgotten something: a thermos of tea, their purse, a child.

I can still see their smiling faces coming down the aisle of the bus towards me: Mrs Lee, as plump as her husband was thin; Mrs Dalton, who always seemed to be smiling, and her husband Sam, a gentle giant of a man; Mrs Lane, a slight good-hearted woman; Wharfie's mum, the fortune teller, and his dad, Ben, with his curly hair and gentle manner. There were more whose faces and names now are lost in the winds of the years. On the best of days, Doris and Eddie from the chip shop in our street where my mum worked from time to time would come on the trip, bringing their music with them: Doris on the ukulele and Eddie on the piano accordion. They would play us to the coast and back leading the singing all the way.

And then there was Old Man Corkett. He seemed immeasurably old to me then, though he was probably only in his fifties. He had a whiskery chin and a long thin face and always wore a cap. I don't remember if there was a Mrs Corkett on those trips. There was a son, Brian, a few years older than me, a tall good-natured lad with black curly hair who later became a painter and decorator. At the time I'm writing about I would have been about seven and my mother would have only been twenty-four or five. I would think of her as a girl now. The seasons roll and the years melt like the snows and nothing lasts for ever.

All us kids would pile on the front seats and the grown-ups and some of the older sisters, who would later mind us while the mams and dads went in the pub, would fill the others. There would be laughing, joking, chatting, even shouting, as some kid went too far and would be given a crack with: 'There! And that's before we've even got going.'

Eventually somebody would count heads, the doors would be closed and those that weren't coming would wave us off. Mr Swindells would be sat outside his front door in his chair, looking like Smuts the Boer War general, and the sad boy who lived near the chip shop and had something wrong with his brain would wave from his wheelchair.

Out through the morning we'd roll, rumbling over the cobbles and on towards Swinton and the A6.

I loved those charabancs: all plush and leather inside, the outside all chrome and sparkling coachpaint, mostly cream with a maroon or blue trim. The back of each seat had an ashtray and a metal plate for striking matches. In those days when every film star smoked, most of our parents were smokers too and by Cheetham

Hill the bus would be a fug of smoke. I would sit happily, the plush of the seat tickling my bare legs, my nose pressed on the cold glass, watching the streets slip by.

The cobbles gave way to asphalt and the charabanc picked up speed. All along the way people were going to work: men made their way to the factories with brew bags over their shoulders; women in shawls could still be seen going to the mill and shopkeepers were raising the blinds. How was it, I wondered, that they weren't all on holiday too?

Through Chorley towards Preston we went, singing all the way. The morning was time for jolly songs: 'One Man Went to Mow', 'Ten Green Bottles', 'The Quartermaster's Store', 'We're Off in a Motorcar', 'Run Rabbit Run'. I really liked it when they sang 'Sons of the Sea', and everybody bobbed up and down when the line came round.

Mr Corkett would sit me on his knee and sing:

There was an old man called Michael Finnegan
He grew whiskers on his chinnegan.
The wind came out and blew them in again
Poor Old Michael Finnegan – begin again.

Around and around it would go, and he would rub his whiskery chin against my cheek and it would hurt and his breath smelled of beer and tobacco. But he was a kind man and seemed to have a soft spot for me, probably because I had no dad. He slipped me a sixpence even though I wasn't the first one to see Blackpool Tower. There was a prize for the first kid to spot it. I never won: though I didn't know it at the time, a bout of measles had begun to make me very short-sighted.

'Are we nearly there yet, Mam?' would echo up and down the bus as us kids got fed up and the grown-ups would shout back, 'Not far now. Stop your mitherin'. Driver's goin' as fast as 'ee can.'

Eventually somebody would see the tower and after another eternity or four we would roll into Blackpool and park up somewhere near the station. It was a race then to the sands because if you didn't get there soon enough there would be nowhere to sit. The men would go and get the deckchairs and make sure the women and kids were all well sorted before heading off to the Golden Mile and a swift pint or three in one of the pubs. The more adventurous might make it to Yates Wine Lodge, which amongst other things sold draught champagne.

Us kids would be straight in with our tin buckets and spades making sandcastles and digging a channel for the sea to come up and make a moat, though it never did, it always somehow sank into the sand instead. Swimming in the sea was only for the brave or daft: the sea was freezing and always looked mucky to me. But everybody paddled, even the mums. Bessie Lee, who was quite a big lady, would tuck her dress in her drawers and get out into the sea with the best of them.

On almost every trip some kid would get lost and there would be a frantic search until they were found again, either at the Lost Children hut or wandering around weeping. If it rained we would either sit it out or head off for the Fun House. I hated the Fun House. I didn't mind the Hall of Mirrors but I found the rest of it with its slides and spinning roundabouts that threw you off really dangerous. And I hated the laughing clown outside. It was a macabre rocking model of a clown that laughed with a false maniacal cackle that seemed more evil than funny. If you've ever watched the 1960s film *A Taste of Honey* you can see the Laughing Man in the scene where Rita Tushingham goes to Blackpool with her mum and the fancy man. That nightmarish laughing man outside the Fun House was still there years later when I went to Blackpool with my own kids.

As the day wore on, the grown-ups would start to gather everything together, the dads would take the deckchairs back and get their deposits and we'd all go back to the charabanc. As the sun slid down into the Irish Sea we'd head for home, sunburned and tired, candyfloss rings round our mouths, chewing on sticks of rock as the sun flashed between the trees that lined the road.

We'd stop for another drink somewhere along the way and this time the grown-ups would spend a lot longer in the pub. If it was warm we would sit outside with bottles of pop and crisps, if it was cold we stayed on the bus and waited, and waited. And then out they would all come, a lot noisier than when they went in, and the singing would start before the coach was even out of the pub car park. But now they would be sad romantic songs: 'Red Sails in the Sunset', 'Who's Sorry Now', 'Carolina Moon', 'The Tennessee Waltz', 'Heart of my Heart', 'Lily of Laguna' and my favourite, 'Barefoot Days'; my favourite because I liked to imagine all the grown-ups as barefoot kids and because it had a swear word in it, 'bloody'.

This was nearly always followed by 'On Mother Kelly's Doorstep', but when they got to the lines 'She's got a hole in her frock, hole in her shoe, hole in her stocking where her toes peep through', sometimes, if they'd had too much to drink, the men would sing, 'hole in her knickers where her bum peeps through' and the women would shout at them for being rude in front of the kids.

There was one song that everybody knew that seemed to have a special relevance, perhaps because of all the partings that had taken place during the war. It was my mum's favourite song and she used to sing it to me when I was very small. It is an old Maori song of leaving and farewells, 'Now is the Hour':

Now is the hour, for us to say goodbye.
Soon you'll be sailing far across the sea.
While I'm away, oh please remember me.
When you return, you'll find me waiting here.

I love you dear, but duty calls you now
How I will miss you, when far, far away.
God guard you dear, and guide you safely home,
When you return, you'll find me waiting here.

I'm sure my mother thought of my dad when she was singing this.

I would usually fall asleep somewhere the other side of Chorley and would wake up as we turned the last corner into our street just before midnight. We would all fall out onto the pavement, checking that we'd got all our bags and calling goodnight as we headed to our doors. Then for me it was a quick 'cat lick' of a wash before pyjamas and bed, and as soon as my head sunk into the pillow I would be deep in the 'arms of Murphy' (as my nanna pronounced Morpheus).

Mushycat

In the winter of my tenth year, our cat Mushy died. He was a black and white moggy who did more fighting than mouse catching and spent most of his time killing sparrows, duffing up other tomcats and, I heard later, fathering kittens up and down the street. He was always there through my childhood, stalking in when I got in from school, miaowing for a saucer of milk and rubbing himself up against your legs as you poured it out for him. There was no cat food then; we fed him on scraps and the odd bits of fish we got from Rennies' the greengrocer's and fish shop at the bottom of the street. Like my nanna and my mum, Mushy was a permanent fixture.

Then he vanished. It was not long before Christmas, there was snow deep on the ground and the nearby Hills were now a white frozen sea. I looked out into the yard before I went to bed and called, 'Che, che, che, che, che.' I waited but he didn't come. I tried again but there was still no Mushy.

I put my coat and wellingtons on and told Mum I would only be half an hour. There was nobody about, no children, no grown-ups, not a sinner out. I walked our street and the streets about then crossed over the main road to the Hills. There was no point looking there; it was getting dark and the Hills were so big he might be anywhere. I looked back at our street, the gaslamp throwing its yellow light onto the snow near our house and set off home, looking left and right, before I crossed the road near the bus stop. Then I saw him, stretched in the gutter under the street lamp's amber light. I picked him up; he was stiff as a piece of wood and as ice-cold as the snow he was lying in. A small trickle of frozen blood was the only sign that something had happened. He must have been hit by a bus.

I carried him back in my arms, tears running down my cheeks, and we buried him next morning near the rose bush in the garden.

We got another cat after Christmas, in fact there was never a time during my childhood when we didn't have a cat, but none of them was as important to me as Mushy.

CHAPTER 5

POLYGONAL PEARS AND PROJECTIONISTS

The Amateur Projectionist

One day, when I was ten, Uncle Len gave me a projector.

Comics like the *Hotspur* and *The Wizard* used to carry advertisements on the back page for things like 'Seebackroscopes', a kind of periscope that enabled you to spy on courting couples, itching powder that you could put down your gran's vest, and courses on hypnotism that would turn you into the Svengali of your street. One advertisement I remember in particular showed a group of happy, laughing boys surrounding another boy who was the centre of their undivided attention and hero worship. The boy had a slide projector and was showing pictures to all his friends; I remember the look on the boys' faces and remember too that for one golden afternoon at least, I was that boy.

Now in keeping with much of what went on in Uncle Len's strange life, the projector he gave me was no ordinary electric projector with a tray for the slides: this was an acetylene carbide-powered, hand-cranked job that could show both hand-painted glass slides and 35mm film. It was an Edwardian relic – like Len himself. The rocks of carbide went into a brass container, which you then put into a bucket of water. Once the water seeped into the brass container, via a cunningly placed spigot, the carbide gave off acetylene gas, which travelled up a rubber tube into the projector where it burned with a bright light and a distinct smell. Nowadays I think carbide is only used in caving lamps and is classed as an explosive; in those days it was still used in some bicycle lamps and any kid could buy it from the high-street chemist. Anybody with half a brain would have put the projector with its japanned black body and its long brass lens on a shelf and kept it there as a showpiece. They would not have given it into the hands of a ten-year-old.

I spent many happy hours boring the crust off my family showing them magic lantern slides while the carbide bubbled away and the gas jet hissed and spluttered. The slides were mostly Victorian and Edwardian hand-painted scenes of missionaries being chased by lions and small boys getting chased by schoolmasters with canes. They would probably be worth a fortune nowadays but ended up in the bin after one of my mother's many clear-outs. A dozen film loops came with the projector, early comedy shorts a half-minute or so in length showing scenes from the very first Popeye and Felix the Cat films. I would lace these in and crank them round. Believing that anything that kept me out of mischief was a good idea, the adults in my life humoured me.

One day, in a fit of lunacy, I mentioned to Miss Biesty at school that I had a projector and some slides. 'Bring it in,' she said, 'and you can give the class a slide show.' Next day with the cold winter winds of Manchester whipping about my frozen knees I carted my projector and its boxes of hand-painted slides and film loops through the gates of the school.

After playtime that morning the school screen went up in our classroom and I, the showman in me bursting forth, commenced the performance. Slides of missionaries being chased in the African jungles were accompanied by a running commentary that had kept my mother enthralled but which bored the school in minutes. Sensing that I was losing the audience as the first paper pellets fired from rubber-band catapults started to smack me on the head, I quickly spooled the Popeye film through the gate. I cranked the film too fast in my nervousness but instead of boos and hisses this drew a good laugh. Encouraged by this, I cranked it even faster. More laughs. I knew (because I'd done it before) that if I cranked the film backwards so that the spinach came out of Popeye's pipe and back into the tin like grassy smoke I would get an even bigger laugh. This was my downfall. I cranked it backwards and the class erupted: they laughed, they wept, they choked. So I cranked it backwards some more, then forwards, then backwards again.

The essence of good comic timing is knowing when to leave the stage. I didn't have it. In a manic burst of showmanship I sent Popeye's spinach in and out of his pipe in double-quick time. Then the film jammed, the sprockets ripped and the school laughed even louder as Popeye and Bluto melted and slid down the screen. Two seconds later the film caught fire. It was made of cellulose acetate, a material so highly explosive in its own right that film libraries are now working round the clock transferring old stock onto safer materials. As the film melted, the flame in the projector backfired into the rubber tube that brought the acetylene gas to the projector. The tube melted and a tongue of flame some four feet long took part of Miss Biesty's carefully combed bun away. The school had to be evacuated and we spent the rest of the afternoon in the playground, while the fire brigade made the school safe by dismantling the projector. I got a telling-off, of course, but for that gold-dusted afternoon at least, show business had waved its magic wand and turned me into the most popular boy at St Anne's. I had won them an hour in the playground.

I won myself a lot more trouble a few days later when I discovered that sticking a needle into a cigarette lots of times made it impossible to smoke. The secret was to use a very fine needle and to just prick the paper with the end so that the holes weren't easy to see. What happened then was that the adults in the house would light their fags but then would find that no matter how hard they sucked all they got was faintly tobacco-flavoured air. I thought this hilarious but the three grown-ups sucking air round the fire didn't, particularly when they found I'd done the whole pack. Result – lots of whacks.

Mischief I suppose was in our genes, and we took every opportunity to get up to a bit of malarkey. Tickawinda was one of our favourite winter japes and required a fair bit of engineering. For Tickawinda you needed a spool of strong, black cotton, a large button, a drawing pin and a corner house. In the dark of night you crept up to the window of a corner house with the stealth of an Apache warrior. You tied the button onto the thread and then pinned one end to the top of a window frame, positioning the pin exactly where the button would tap against the glass when you pulled it. You then spooled the cotton round the corner and all grouped quietly together while one of the gang tugged on the thread. Using just the right amount of tension you could make the button swing and tap on the window. Hankies stuffed in mouths, you would huddle in the dark listening for the door opening. This would be followed by, 'There's no bugger there!' from the victim and the door would close again. You would tug the thread again and the victim would come out again shouting, 'I know you little buggers are up to something! I'll give you what for when I catch you.'

We also had quite a bit of fun with dog shit. Our favourite trick involved putting a large dollop of fresh dog shit into a couple of paper bags, which we then put on a doorstep and set alight before knocking on the door and running like mad to a safe position from which we would watch. The door would fly open, the victim would come out to find a fire on the doorstep which he would then stamp out. The moans of disgust as the various victims examined their shoes were often long and followed by threats and curses. We never did this trick anywhere near our own street.

On the whole most of our crimes were victimless (pretty much) and involved nothing worse than scrumping a few apples or nicking a bamboo cane off the allotments for a fishing rod. One expedition in search of illicit pears, however, did not go as smoothly as expected and the Green Hand Gang found themselves up against a platoon of baby rabbis.

I don't think I'm alone in thinking that one of the most beautiful sounds in the world is the song of a blackbird on a summer's evening, and nowhere is it more sweet and mournful than when it's echoing round the quiet old suburban streets of some city at the dimming of the day. The suburbs of Higher Crumpsall, around Middleton Road and the Half Way House pub, where the big houses were, had once been fields with mansions dotted about them: mill-owners, lawyers and doctors had lived in the big houses, together with their servants and carriages. Over the years the city had crept up on them and the gentry of Higher Crumpsall and Higher Broughton had moved out to Cheshire, or into the Lancashire hills, and the great houses with their walled gardens, carriage houses and tennis courts had been divided up into flats or sold off to become private academies. Later when I went to St Bede's, I would pal out with a lad called Peter McGawley, son of my old St Anne's headmaster. Peter's grandfather was a self-taught man who set up such an academy in an old house on Rochdale Road where he taught Latin, German, Science and Bookkeeping to the clerks of North Manchester who, like H. G. Wells's Kipps, wanted to get on in the world.

In a private enclave off the leafy Seymour Road was a cluster of large houses called the Polygon. In their prime they must have been wonderful: five stone-built merchants' houses forming a polygon, cut off from the world by high walls, and at its heart a small round copse. The houses were early Victorian or late Georgian with portico columns, great sandstone steps, tiled hallways and massive doors; each had a separate carriage drive leading to its door.

When I knew them they had slipped down the social ladder into the shabby genteel, and had been broken up into apartments housing a mixed bag of residents: the Bensons, an elderly married couple, lived in one of the houses and rented rooms out to two old ladies; my friend Pete Gittins used to get twopence a bucket for fetching coal out of the cellar for them. In one of the other houses there was an artist who used to paint his wife and daughter in the nude. I was constantly risking my neck with my friend Pete and his brother Anthony, climbing a big sycamore tree to hang over the wall and see if could we get a peep. But although Pete reckoned he and his brother (who went on to become a Holy Ghost Father) had seen both ladies bare I don't remember ever being so lucky. I was so short-sighted I could only just about see the wall of the house anyway.

One of the houses of the Polygon had been bought by the Jewish community around Cheetham Hill and had been turned into a rabbinical college. We watched a lot of young men dressed in black suits and overcoats with strange beaver hats and long curling locks going in to be turned into rabbis. I was fairly used to the exotic (after all, half my family was Irish, my stepfather was a Pole and my friend at school was a Ukrainian girl called Bernadette Nevaskaty) but these young men that we always called 'the baby rabbis' were different from different.

I would later come to understand from Jewish friends that they were 'frummers' (very orthodox Jews) and in fact I went on to work for the orthodox community occasionally myself: lighting fires for them on the Sabbath when they were not supposed to do such things and earning myself the title 'fire goy'.

But that was in the future. Here and now, as a ten-year-old ragamuffin, I was about to go into the Polygon (forbidden ground anyway), climb a tree in the garden of the baby rabbis' college and scrump a load of pears. In my own defence I have to say that it was Wharfie's idea that we should do this; I wasn't slow coming up with mischief myself, but this one was pure Wharfie.

We met after school, Wharfie, Kenny Fullen, Jimmy Hands and me, and made our way to the Polygon.

It was a warm afternoon in early September, and a blackbird was singing its little heart out in one of the sycamore trees, and ever after I would associate the plangent song of the blackbird with those still evenings in the leafy streets.

We sneaked into the garden through the open gates of the school and, keeping close to the wall, we slid down to the end where the pear trees were. Climbing the trees was easy and in seconds we were up in the branches, filling our jumpers and pockets with pears. Then I looked along the branch I was scrumping and saw, straight ahead of me, a large window and in the room beyond, a group of shawled baby rabbis chanting and bowing in time to their prayers. I froze for a moment, then tried to slither back quietly along the branch but one of the rabbis saw me and seconds later the main door opened and several black-suited figures ran out.

I held on to my branch, the blood leaving my face and draining into my socks. Below us the baby rabbis shouted and waved fists, their pale faces upturned, their locks shaking with anger.

'Bleedin' hell!' Kenny shouted. 'We've had it now.'

'We'll have to give ourselves up,' I said, going the way of damage limitation.

But Wharfie was the boy who had jumped off the garage roof onto the back of Specky Rushton, the ICI policeman, Wharfie was the boy who jumped over the live rail on the Bury to Manchester line, and Wharfie was the boy who had shaved the heads of most of the girls in our street; he was not going quietly into the hands of a lot of baby rabbis.

'Sod off you lot! You killed Christ!' he shouted, and he threw a pear at one of the baby rabbis, hitting him full in the face. I knew then that we were doomed.

Two can play at any game except Solitaire and the ground below the trees was littered with unripe pears. An unripe pear is about as hard as a golf ball and in the hands of a band of angry rabbis they can be terrible weapons. The pears that hit me stung like bees and I know that some hit Wharfie because I could hear him yelping. Kenny and Jimmy had crawled to the end of a branch that overhung the street and had dropped off down into the road. I followed them, shuffling along the branch: it looked a long way to the ground but breaking an ankle was preferable to being peared to death. I took a breath and let go, landing with a thump that knocked all the breath from my body. Wharfie followed me, mistiming his jump and sliding part way down the wall in his hurry. I got up just before he hit the ground and we all set off at a run. A well-aimed pear hit me on the back of the head. The rabbis were out of the gate and on the road behind us. Wharfie copped several more before we turned the corner and shook them off.

When we stopped in the entry near the chippy to get our breath, Wharfie had various lumps on the back of his head and had lost most of the skin from his knees from his slide down the wall. I had an eye that was closing and would be black in the morning, a badly twisted ankle and lots of lumps on the back of my head. Kenny and Jimmy had got away with a couple of angry-looking marks on their legs.

Only Wharfie had any pears left, Kenny and I had dropped ours in the flight. Wharfie showed us his loot, half a dozen pears inside his zipped-up bomber jacket. We bit into them but as our bruises told us, they were rock hard and it was like eating pear-flavoured stones: we spat them out and threw them away. Proverbs 20:17 tells us: 'Stolen bread tastes sweet, but it turns to gravel in the mouth.' Correct, even if the translation from the Hebrew has got it wrong; it's 'pears' not 'bread'.

The Carol Singers

It was Eric Davies' idea. He was in Besses o' th' Barn Boys Brass Band and was a very good tenor horn player. I was a not bad – but also not particularly good – mouth-organ player. On the day we were to break up for the Christmas holidays, Eric, who had been charging down an ice slide we had made in the snowy playground, came up to me with steaming breath and said, 'If you bring your mouth organ and I bring the tenor horn we can go carol singing tonight.'

I thought about it. 'We'll make a load of money,' he added. That was the tipping point, there was no more hesitation – in a moment of greed I said yes to my very first paid gig.

I thought about it some more as I was having my tea. I knew a lot of tunes like 'The Happy Wanderer', 'Danny Boy', 'The Skye Boat Song' and standards like that and I was quite good on the pub songs that we sang on the charabanc outings. I could also play some carols by ear but wasn't quite up to scratch on minor keys, which is awkward for 'We Three Kings' and 'God Rest Ye Merry Gentlemen'. (Or as we had it in a version we claimed was sung outside a German lunatic asylum, 'God Rest Ye Jerry Mental-men'. We were only ten and didn't know what PC meant.)

There was another small problem. My harmonica was in the key of C and Eric's tenor horn was in the key of B flat, which is not the basis of a good musical relationship – unless you are Stockhausen or Philip Glass. We played roughly the same tune but a full tone apart. We did try having a little practice but decided that it sounded so bad we would just have to busk it and hope for the best. This has been my musical philosophy ever since which is possibly how I ended up playing the bones with the Hallé Orchestra (that in fact is true but I'm not telling you about it here).

Of all the boys that promised to come and sing with us only Paul Wysnevsky turned up. We did the playing and he did the singing, with me joining in when some of the parts got too hard for the mouth organ. His croaky voice wavered somewhere between the two keys, shifting from time to time into keys of his own devising so, in fact, we would probably have delighted some modernist music lovers and might even have got an Arts Council grant.

We made a lot of money that night, mostly from people who just wanted us to go away.

It was dark and cold and snow lay on the ground, not crisp and deep and even, but slippy and mushy and wet enough to get through your boots in minutes. We must have tramped the streets of Crumpsall for a good two or three hours, knocking on doors and bursting into 'We Three Kings' or 'Good King Wenceslas' as doors opened and the light and smells of cooking flooded out upon us. One bemused Jewish father appeared in his dressing gown, gave us the incredible sum of ten shillings and told us not unkindly to bugger off because he was 'on earlies and the tea pots (tea pot lids – kids) are in feather (bed)'. After the first hour the soft leather bag that Eric had brought to hold our earnings was already lumpy and fat with sixpences, half crowns, pennies and shillings

We worked all the streets around St Anne's School and made several more pounds, knocking and playing and singing until our hands and feet were frozen. Eric's lips looked as though he'd been smacked in the face with a plank, and Paul's voice was giving out, so that he was no longer singing but shouting in a harsh, high-pitched, tuneless bark that various dogs were taking as a threat. By nine o'clock we decided to call it a night. We looked at the money. There was a lot of it.

'We shouldn't ought to keep this,' Paul said.

Eric and I looked at him in amazement.

'We shouldn't make money from singing hymns. They're holy songs and they belong to God. It's a sin to take money for them. We should give it to the church.'

We weren't sure whether it was a sin or not, and waves of guilt fought with both onsetting hypothermia and greed – and the guilt won. So even though we'd frozen half to death we took a half crown each, reasoning that God wouldn't begrudge us a bag of chips and a bottle of dandelion and burdock, and carried the rest of the money to the presbytery. We walked quietly across the deep snow in the monsignor's garden, stars burning above us, a dog barking streets away and the noise of a steam train shunting in the sidings. Monsignor Aspinall's housekeeper opened the door and light fell onto the snow-covered lawn and onto us three small boys: Eric with his shining brass horn, me with my mouth organ and Paul with the bag of money.

'What d'yez want banging the door at this time of night?' she shouted in a strong Mayo accent, stamping her slippered feet on the cold, salted step. 'Is somebody dying?'

'We're carol singing.'

'Don't ye go starting with yer row here, we don't want no singing here, carols or not, the monsignor is just in bed.'

'We're not singing. We've finished. We've just brought some money for the church.'

She looked suspiciously at the bag in Paul's hand, and for a brief moment the thought that it might just be possible that not all small boys are the spawn of Satan flickered across her mind.

'Hmm. Yez are good lads now.' She took the bag from him.

'Happy Christmas,' we said quietly.

'And a happy Christmas to ye too. Away off home to your mothers and be careful, the roads is awful slippy.'

We felt righteous and holy, but also cold and hungry and with the money we'd kept back we went for a thruppenny bag of chips each from the Clarendon Road chippy. We ate them under a street lamp, warming our frozen hands on the hot greasy parcels, burning our mouths on the scalding chips.

'Shall we do it again tomorrow night?' Eric asked.

The silence from me and Paul was enough and, as the steam from our chips ascended to the sputtering gas mantle of the lamp, the ad hoc trio of Davies, Harding and Wysnevsky broke up tacitly and without acrimony after its first and only gig. From across the snowy streets we heard the sound of the choir of St Mathew's C of E Church, singing 'Silent Night' with harmonies and in tune. It sounded beautiful.

'I bet they don't get paid as much for going away as we did,' Paul said through a mouthful of hot chips.

Can I Do It a Bit and Wear Glasses?

I don't know how it happened though it does seem that the measles were at least partly to blame. It certainly wasn't masturbation: that was years into the future when the warning 'It'll make you go blind' was always followed by, 'Can I do it a bit and wear glasses then?'

Whatever the cause, I do know for certain that my eyesight began to go wrong after a bad bout of measles. In those days you were thrown into a darkened room at the first sign of the disease and kept there, spotty and miserable, for as long as it took to go away.

'He has the spots, Eileen!' my nanna shouted as I sat in the fireside chair one night, exhausted and light-headed and feeling sorry for myself, trying to listen to *Children's Hour*. Larry the Lamb was saying something to Mr Mayor but the world beyond my finger ends had become a faint, fizzy place, the voices seeming to come from inside my head instead of the speaker of the radio. I felt as though I were falling backwards into a lake of cotton wool.

The next thing I remember was waking up in bed with the lights out and a glass of Lucozade at the side of the bed. I knew then that I must be very ill because Lucozadc was too expensive for anything except life-threatening illnesses.

But the lights were out and I needed to read. I need to read like other people need to breathe. Reading has and always will be my life.

So I read: under the covers with a torch at first, then when the batteries failed I pushed the bedroom door open a tad and read by the light that came from the landing. I was in bed for a week or so and must have read a book a day, hiding them quickly under the mattress when I heard feet on the stairs.

Whether this did for my eyes or not I don't know; all I do know is that coming back into the world after the measles everything seemed to be in soft focus. It had been gradual so I hadn't noticed anything particularly strange. Whatever caused it, six months after my little affair with Frau Measles, my eyesight was chronically bad, though so far nobody had discovered this.

One day I was standing with Wharfie on Cheetham Hill Road waiting to cross. Over the road was our goal, the Premier ABC Cinema.

'What's on?' I asked Wharfie.

The letters on the cinema frontage must have been four feet high and only twenty yards away.

'What's on? Can't you read it?'

I shook my head.

'You must be blind,' he said in a matter-of-fact voice as he led me across the road.

Mr Hartnett called me to his desk a few days later.

'Michael Harding, you've made these sums up. You've got them all right but they aren't the ones I wrote on the board. Stand over there. How many fingers have I got up?'

I couldn't even see his hand. I went home with a note from school.

Later that week my mother took me on the number 7 bus up the winding brew of Central Avenue to a large, dark, Victorian house on Rochdale Road where the optician had converted the treacle-painted front room into a consulting room. It was a black, miserable November night with a smoky, greasy drizzle falling on the city, covering everything with a slick, sooty patina.

We knocked on the door and were shown down a dimly lit hall into a dimly lit room by a tall, dimly lit cadaver of a man with sparse hair and long yellow teeth. He motioned for me to sit in a leather and cast-iron chair like that at the barbers, flicked the lights off and asked me to read some letters on a lit-up chart on the other side of the room. I couldn't even read the top row.

He peered into my eyes with a chrome thing, coming so close that I could smell his breath which stank of cigarettes and booze, then he put a wire frame on my head and slotted round lenses into the holder on front. Suddenly the world grew a little sharper and, as he tried lens after lens, the chart and its rows of letters came into crystal focus – all Zeds and Kays and Vees, which I thought (courtesy of Big Lou's Polska paper) were Polish names. By the slotting in of a couple more lenses I was able to read the Polish

My mum, Eileen Pyne, and my dad, Louis 'Curly' Harding, on their wedding day in October 1943. Twelve months later the telegram came, 'missing presumed dead'.

Me and my mum on Aunty Guy's lawn. I'm wearing Daddy Edgar's bowler.

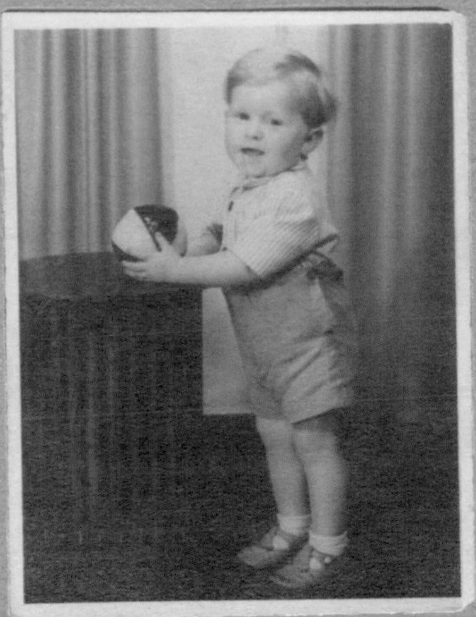

I think I'm using that thing to hold myself up because I ain't too steady – and I hadn't had a drink.

Me sitting on a fence – if you ask me nicely I'll show you where the splinter went.

The handsomest boy in 38 Hall Road at that time.

Aunty Guy on the left and Aunty Cis on the right. Aunty Guy is smiling because she won that day's horse-shit race.

Uncle Harry in the desert near Tobruk, taking a day off from carrying drunk aristocrats to their tents and blowing up German airfields.

Big Lou in the uniform of the Polish Cavalry. From a farm near Warsaw to a wooden hut in Lower Crumpsall, courtesy of Herr Hitler.

Uncle Bernard before he left for India, the Burmese border and a pit full of cobras.

Me with Christina and my Nanna on our back step. It wasn't long after that Nanna killed the coalman for short-bagging her.

My sister Collette on our wall. The corner shop is in the background.

St Anne's Crumpsall, Top Infants. I'm front row, bottom left.

Aunty Julia (left) and my pretend Aunty Jessie, two lovely ladies – picture taken by Uncle Len. I suspect the venue is Grange-over-Sands, where for a bit of excitement the locals come out to watch the traffic lights change.

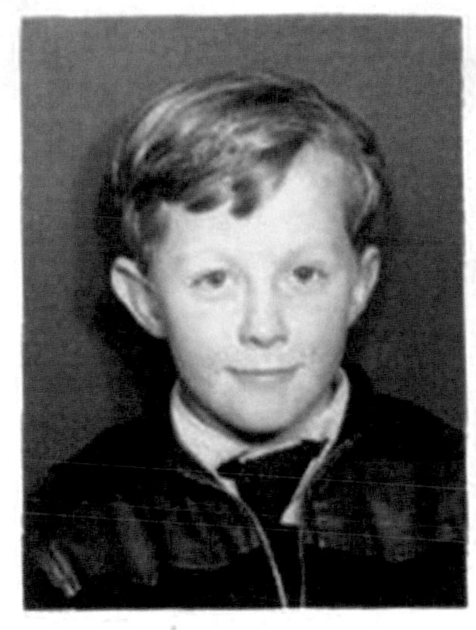

Me about seven years old. I had the makings of a handsome devil – but I lost the makings somewhere along the way.

On my trusty Phillips mangle. A few months later I was off on a sixty-mile run into the wilds of Yorkshire.

Above: Bilko posing by a car we'd hitched a lift in. It was somewhere in Leicestershire. And it was bloody cold.

Left: Bilko without the onions.

Below: The Stylos after Happy had left, l to r, Eric, Roy, me, Tony and Don.

About to be eaten by pigeons in Trafalgar Square. Not a Japanese tourist in sight. They later made a film about this, called *The Birds*.

Hitching a ride to London on a busy A6, aged seventeen.

Attempting to look poetic and interesting but only managing to look dull and confused.

A teenaged Harding winning the 'Flaky Prat in a Photo Booth' competition.

The daughter of the Scouse mother-in-law, looking serene and thoughtful ... unlike the bloke at the top. Picture M. Harding.

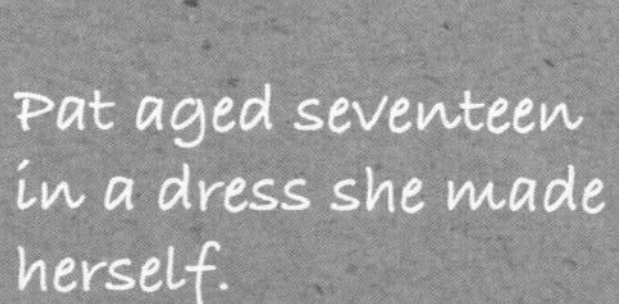

Pat aged seventeen in a dress she made herself.

name on the very tiniest bottom row. He held up a pair of NHS frames with wire ear-pieces and tortoiseshell frames.

'These are the NHS frames for children – anything else you'll have to pay for.'

'We'll have them,' my mum said.

And that was that, from now on I would only be able to see the world through a tunnel of wire and glass. (Mind you, without the NHS I'd have had to do what they did in the Middle Ages and have an even smaller boy walking ahead of me, leading me round.)

The morning after we collected my specs I walked into the school playground to the collective taunt of, 'Specky Four Eyes! Yah! Specky Four Eyes!'

It didn't upset me particularly. I could see clearly for the first time in ever so long and realised now what a misshapen and generally ugly bunch they all were. I stared at them and said, 'So what? At least I can take them off at night. You've got those ugly mugs stuck on forever.'

The only time I really became conscious that lasses generally don't make passes at lads who wear glasses was when I reached puberty and it seemed that, Dr Jekyll-like, I had turned overnight into a dangerous autoclave of hormones ready to erupt at the sight of a swelling bust, a pouty pair of lips or a pair of blue eyes.

I would go with Wharfie and the lads to the local dance hall, Chilton's, which was above the local Liberal Club. The owners specialised in ballroom dancing and took the floor every night in a doomed attempt to get us to follow suit with foxtrots, quicksteps and waltzes. Not a chance. All we wanted was a jive and a snog on the way home. We would have to wait, doing the odd waltz, until the end of the night when they would put a couple of rock records on and stand watching us, tutting and shaking their heads.

Before going to the dance hall we would sneak into the Egerton Arms, a tiny pub run by two old ladies who didn't seem to mind serving under-age drinkers with beer. Two halves of Holts' Bitter later I would have enough courage to launch my sixteen-year-old body into a jive with the best of them. I would study the form from across the floor, stick my glasses in my top pocket and cross the room to ask the object of my desire for a dance. On my way across that sea of maple and French chalk, like a Scud missile whose steering chip has gone wrong, I would lose my way and end up dancing with some of the biggest boilers Chilton's Dance Hall ever held. I had a theory that in the dance halls of those days, when girls always went round in pairs, there was always a good-looking one and a less good-looking to downright ugly one, what was known in dancehall parlance as a 'tug'. The good-looking one reasoned that her plain friend made her look even better and the tug worked it out that, if two lads came up, one of them would fancy her mate and she could have the other one. I think in maritime terms it is what is known as right of salvage. I ended up dancing with so many tugs (courtesy of myopia) that the lads started calling me the Queen Mary.

The Boy Sprouts

We were known as the Boy Sprouts or the Knobbly Knee Brigade – we followers of Baden Powell, we backwoodsmen and survivalists, we helpers of old ladies across busy roads, we boys who knew how to light a fire by rubbing a stick on sand (the sand in this case was sandpaper and the stick had a blob of red phosphorous on the end and was called 'a match').

It was my best pal Pete Gittins who suggested to me that it might be a good idea to join the scouts and at the tender age of almost eleven we took ourselves off to St Clare's Blackley to join the 108th Manchester Scout Troop. There was no Catholic scout group in Crumpsall, possibly because we were not a massive parish, and our mothers would not have allowed us to join a Protestant troop.

So, knobbly knees at the ready, we got on the number 60 bus and presented ourselves in the large hall on the first floor of the St Clare's school. Father Anthony the scoutmaster was a priest in khaki with a dog collar. He looked at our knees, asked us how old we were and told us we were in. First, though, we would be something called 'Tenderfoots' and would have to pass a test before we could become scouts. This seemed fair enough, so armed with our Tenderfoot cards and our copy of *Scouting for Boys*, we sat and watched the lads in khaki shorts and green berets going through their drill. This entailed a lot of saluting and flag unfurling and giving out of notices, most of which was overseen by Mr Debonaire, a tall, thin, lugubrious man with a sandy cowlick. The name Debonaire should really have aroused my suspicion, but at ten I was still a bit gullible and thought that people in authority were pretty much all right. Hah!

Pete and I learned all the Tenderfoot stuff easily and a couple of weeks later we were tested and then enrolled into the troop. I was in the Fox Patrol and our patrol leader at the time was Len Clayton, who had a sister called Rita who I would later fancy the pants off. My friend Kevin Leech was in the scouts too and his big brother Bobby was deputy troop leader to Mr Debonaire's 'Skipper'.

I have to say, hand on heart, that I loved the scouts. I was no great fan of the discipline and I hated the church parades, but camping out and hiking were right up my street, and of course earning badges and stars and thongs appealed to the collector in me, though I never got anywhere near Kevin's collection – he ran out of shirt sleeve for his badges and ended up a Queen's Scout, by which time I had been given my marching orders.

I went to my first camp just a few weeks after passing my Tenderfoot test, at a place called Whittle-le-Woods near Chorley in Lancashire. In those days it was in the countryside, now a combination of the M6, the Mormons – who have built a massive temple there – and various housing developments have made sure that it's a commuter area.

We went to Chorley on the train, then took a bus to Whittle-le-Woods; from there it was just a bit of a walk to the camp site which was in the grounds of an enormous pub called the Howard Arms. Many years later I would play at a folk club there.

Had I been unburdened the walk would have been a doddle, had I been toting one of the framed rucksacks some of the lads were sporting it would still have been a doddle. But we had no money for rucksacks and, just as she had made my uniform, my mum made me a kit bag from khaki canvas. Basically it was a cloth sausage, about as tall as me and about as big. My mum, worried that I might die of Lancashire Summer Hypothermia, had stuffed the sack with most of the contents of my wardrobe together with my washbag, a pair of wellies, an overcoat, two thick blankets and a sleeping bag liner. The whole lot weighed a good bit more than I did. I got off the bus and threw the thing over my shoulder like I'd seen sailors do in films. Putting a lot of kinetic energy into a boy-sized giant erratic cloth sausage is not a good idea and the resulting force shot me back several yards into a hedge. I tried again and concussed the small scout behind me. I tried carrying it before me with my arms around it but couldn't see where I was going and kept wandering into the road, also carrying it that way was exhausting.

A couple of bigger scouts helped me to get the kit bag on my shoulder and, though by now I was at the end of a long crocodile of small boys, I was determined to do what I had read in *Scouting for Boys*, which says as Commandment Eight of the Scout Law: 'A scout smiles and whistles under all circumstances. Scouts never grouse at hardships, nor whine at each other, nor swear when put out.'

The weight of the sack was causing a bit of a nervous tic and rictus in my face so that staggering onwards, cheerfully smiling, twitching and leering, I looked like a young drunken Quasimodo as I lurched down the road in the hot sun whistling badly like an overwrought kettle. I met a few old ladies on the way who crossed the road when they saw me coming.

The camp was already going up on the shores of the lake by the time I stumbled in and I found myself living under canvas for the first time ever, sharing an ex-army ridge tent with seven other lads from the troop. They had sleeping bags, I had two blankets and some blanket pins, the kind of safety pins you see in kilts, with which I was to make my own sleeping bag as per instructions from B-P himself.

I should have known better really. I mean B-P was the man who thought we could learn to track spoor in Crumpsall, B-P was the man who thought we should go round looking at tramps' boots for strange nail patterns in case they were murderers and B-P was the man who thought you could get away without doing laundry if you beat your underpants with a stick. With the aid of the pins I made something that looked like a large woollen envelope; it would have to do.

The first thing we did after the tents were up was rush to the pub to buy provisions, and two bottles of dandelion and burdock and a packet of crisps later I was beginning to feel human again. There were some cock pheasants near the pub that had flown in from a nearby spinney. I had never seen birds as big or as colourful before and wondered what Mushy would have made of them. There were horses up the field, a couple of large white ones and a chestnut one. One of the lads went and snaffled some carrots from the stores to feed them. So this was the countryside, a little different from Besses o' th' Barn with pheasants and horses and a lake. I was beginning to be glad I had come.

The rest of the afternoon was spent collecting wood for the campfire and digging a latrine pit down the bottom of the field. Someone told me that the lake was the fishpond of an old monastery that had once stood where the pub was. You could still see the remains of medieval walls half buried in trees and vegetation.

We ate what Enid Blyton would describe as 'a hearty tea' of sausage, mash and beans and then sat round the campfire as the evening drew on, singing the 'Ging Gang Goolie' song. The song was written by B-P himself and is completely nonsensical, its only merit being that it can be sung by anyone with an IQ slightly higher than that of an amoeba. It does have a downside in that (as explained previously) 'goolies' is Hindi for testicles. Knowing that, we small boy scouts often played havoc with the official lyrics.

So our troop of some twenty scouts sat around the campfire, drinking cocoa singing our way through 'Oh My Darling Clementine', 'Hallelujah I'm A Bum', 'Campfire's Burning' and 'John Brown's Body' – and then somebody suggested ghost stories.

It was getting quite dark now and the shadows beyond the fire seemed to be coming closer. Skipper threw a few more logs on and the sparks flowed into the sky as the fire flared up and made the darkness all around us even more ominous. I had never been away from home before on my own (Aunty Kitty's didn't count) and I wasn't even eleven yet. Skipper told a story about a headless ghost in a Welsh castle that wasn't all that frightening, and then one of the bigger scouts told a story about a screaming skull that was in a big old hall in Lancashire not far from us. It was the skull of a murdered Catholic priest who'd had his head chopped off by Good Queen Bess and it had been put in what the scout said was called a 'niche' in the hall and somebody took it and put it in their room and in the middle of the night as the moon came through the window the skull started screaming and it didn't stop until it had been put back in its niche and by then the person's hair had gone snow white and they were stark staring mad and had to be put in an asylum.

That one frightened the crap out of most of us little ones. Then another big scout said that the grounds of the Howard Arms where we were camping were haunted. He said that the monastery here was raided by King Henry VIII and all the gold chalices and valuable books were taken and when the abbot tried to stop them they killed him by drowning him in the lake. The monks were Cistercians and wore white and, on certain nights, the ghost of the abbot could be seen wandering the grounds where we were camping.

(Before you go zooming off to consult your historical documents can I say that I've found no evidence for this at all, though this being a hotbed of Lancashire Catholicism during the Reformation there may well be some truth in the folklore. In any case, I believed the story in its entirety.)

I woke in the middle of the night shivering with cold and lay there in my pinned blankets realising that the reason I had woken up was because as well as being cold I was dying for a pee; the dandelion and burdock and the campfire cocoa had worked their way down. I desperately needed the loo but I was frightened to go out to the latrines because it was way across the field and it was pitch black and there was a lake to negotiate and there was the ghost of the White Abbot that might get me. From the sounds of gentle breathing in the tent I guessed that I was the only one of the eight of us that was awake. I squeezed my eyes tight shut, crossed my legs and tried to stop shivering but I couldn't get warm. I cursed B-P and his bloody blankets and I cursed God for letting us be too poor to buy me a proper sleeping bag, and then I cursed the daft scout whose idea it had been to tell ghost stories in the first place. I soon realised that if I didn't get up I would pee what passed for my bed. Carefully and quietly, I slid out of the useless blanket bag, stepped carefully over the sleeping forms of the Fox Patrol, unlaced the tent door and stepped out into the night.

A crescent moon was riding the sky behind the clouds, throwing the palest of light on the scene before me. I could make out the edge of the lake and could see that there was a dense mist rising off it that was lingering and swirling gently at about waist height. I reasoned that if I went to the lake's edge I could have a pee in the mist, nobody would see what I was doing and I wouldn't have to go all the way across the meadow to the bogs. I walked into the mist and hurriedly started peeing.

It seemed to go on for an awfully long time, and all the while I was looking around me, my scalp tingling and my whole body shaking with cold and abject fear. There I was, almost eleven years old, having a pee in a haunted ruined monastery grounds dressed only in my vest and underpants. And then I saw it: the unmistakable form of the White Abbot coming towards me through the mist on the lake. I could hear the gentle splashing the ghost made and though I couldn't make it out clearly it had the definite shape of a cowled and tall monk.

My screams woke not just every scout in the camp but everybody in the far-off pub too. Tents emptied as the skipper and assorted scouts piled out, flashing their torches about the scene to find out what was going on.

They found me in underpants and vest by the water's edge, gibbering that there was 'the bloody ghost of the bloody abbot!' and pointing out across the mist. They shone their torches out over the lake and there was indeed something large and mysterious and white. It was one of the white horses; it had heard me peeing and had wandered around the edge of the lake to see if there were any more carrots to be had.

I was not the most popular scout in camp and because I had used the word 'bloody' I had to have a cup of cold water poured down my sleeve; standard punishment for swearing.

The next camp I went to was a fortnight spent at Yelverton, on the edge of Dartmoor and close to Buckfast Abbey, presumably so that Father Anthony could have a dose of monkishness. I remember it for a number of reasons, one of them not good. Early on in our stay I was detailed to cook duties. I had foolishly showed an aptitude for cooking porridge and twists and Skip decided that I was therefore skilled enough to help feed a dozen or so scouts. What happened when Mr Debonaire threw paraffin onto a damp fire to get it going has been worked into a routine I used to do about cub camp but is worth a mention here. Half the paraffin ended up in the dixie full of beans and we were told to stir it in so nobody would notice. A few scouts did notice but most of them were so hungry that they ate the beans (with blackened sausages) anyway. The resulting queues for the latrines were a sight to behold.

Skip also had another brainwave. Buying a large lump of beef from a butcher in Yeoville he put it in a biscuit tin with a little water. The biscuit tin was not one of the piddly little things you get nowadays but a large cube with a lid, about fifteen inches all round. The lump of meat just about fitted in.

'Light a wood fire over there,' Skip ordered, pointing at a low bank. We did and when the wood had burned down to embers, Skip put the biscuit tin in the middle, gathered more embers round it then covered the lot with soil, grass and the hot stones of the fire's edge.

'The wood will go on burning slowly,' Skip said, 'and will cook the beef gently. By the time we get back it will be done to a turn.'

'Get back from where?' somebody asked.

'Dartmoor.'

So over the moor we marched towards one of the tors, smiling and whistling as us scouts were supposed to do, and after a couple of hours we got there and turned back. Skip's map reading was about as good as his paraffin throwing and the return ramble took about five hours and meant that we arrived in camp starving, whimpering and a little delirious. A couple of us set to peeling spuds for dinner while Skip raked away the soil and rocks to get at the roast beef. He lifted the lid off carefully. Inside was a fist-sized lump of charcoal.

It was egg and chips for tea that night.

My last camp with St Clare's Scouts resulted in me being drummed out of the troop. We went to Aylesford Priory near Maidstone in Kent, where we took part in a Catholic jamboree. I have no fond memories of that jamboree: it rained most of the time we were there, all the paths in the site were rivers of white chalky mud, we all got colds and the damp got into our sleeping bags. We began to wonder whether God might not be a Protestant since their jamboree had been sunny and warm.

At the end of a week of coughing and sneezing, saying prayers and ging-gang-goolie-ing we struck camp.

'Any food left over in the stores you can take home for your mothers,' our scoutmaster told us. I selected two tins of cocoa and two packs of butter.

'Harding, you are in charge of the papal flag,' he continued. The papal flag was a gold and white flag with the Keys of Rome crossed upon it and it was very, very important because it had been blessed by the Pope to carry special grace to the jamboree. So, as well as my kitbag, I now had to carry a damn flag case along with a heap of cocoa and butter. Then I had a brainwave: put the food in the flag case. Job sorted.

At Maidstone station we commandeered a couple of baggage trolleys and when the train came we loaded everything on. Everything except the papal flag. In my desire to get home, I struggled to get my giant slug of a kitbag onto the luggage rack and was so relieved when I got it there that I forgot all about the flag.

It was two weeks before it arrived back in Manchester, by which time the lids had come off the cocoa tins and the butter had melted.

Forty-odd scouts stood to attention in the hall at St Clare's as the papal flag was unfurled, only now it was no longer gold and white but brown and orangey-brown like the flag of Lumbago, an obscure African Republic. I didn't wait to be drummed out. I drummed myself out and ended my scouting career for good.

Chilled Blains and Warm Milk

The hot water bottle was cold, my nose was a small cone of ice, my breath steamed in the freezing air of the bedroom and the inside of the window pane was a thick swirl of ice flowers, the outside world muted to a shimmering blur. It was another winter morning and Nanook of Crumpsall was desperately trying to work out an excuse for not going to school. Earache? Toothache? Flu? Leprosy? I knew that none of them would work. Time to get up.

Some winters it was like that for days on end and the ice on the bedroom window grew in a fern-like pattern so thick you could scrape it off with your fingernails; hard white curls of ice, thick as butter balls, dropped onto the windowsill. To look out of the window you had to breathe on the ice and make a round hole with your nails. I didn't want to get up but on schooldays I had to. There was no chance of getting dressed upstairs without dying of hypothermia before I had my socks on so I would grab my clothes and run downstairs to the fire that my mum had lit, hopping from one leg to another as I got dressed.

After breakfast my mum would wrap a scarf around my neck then thread it through the belt on each side of my coat. My balaclava would be jammed on and before she saw me out of the door she would make sure that my mittens were on (threaded through my sleeves on elastic). The fact that I was wearing shorts and my legs were freezing while the wind blew straight up my Khyber Pass never seemed to have occurred to her. All boys wore shorts until they were fourteen or so, and chapped thighs were a constant scourge of icy winters.

The other scourge was chilblains – or, as we pronounced them, 'chilled blains'. Like chimbleys, kekkles and skellingtons (chimneys, kettles and skeletons), we had our very own Shakespearian way of saying things in Crumpsall. Chilled blains hurt like mad and you could get them on your hands or feet. Socks would ride down and end up in the toe section of your wellies and on the worst of days your wellies would fill with snow as you gallivanted about, in which case you were sure to get very chilled blains.

Every winter we prayed for snow or at least a very heavy frost because we could make a slide in the playground and go sledging when we got home from school. The slides in our school playground were made by kids repeatedly slithering on the frost or snow until it turned into a thick skim of ice, several yards long. The game was to run like a demon until you got to the slide, then slither all the way along it. We were allowed to do this for only so long because inevitably one of the teachers or dinner ladies went arse over breakfast on it and then Mrs Barnett the head dinner lady would come out from the kitchen and scatter salt on it to moans and boos from all the kids.

On snowy days the school bell would ring a bit earlier to get us in out of the cold and we'd pile into class, jealous of the kids on the front row who would be nearest the fire (there was no central heating). If you were a milk monitor then you'd have to go and get the milk from where it was dumped down near the bike shed. It would often be frozen and we'd have to carry the crate in with our hands sometimes freezing to the metal of the crate, setting it beside the open fire so that it would melt in time for milk time. It didn't just melt, it warmed up almost to the edge of curdling. We were given straws which we pushed through the centre of the cardboard top and we all sucked like mad; the naughty ones delighted in making gurgling noises.

We made darts from broken nibs, which we stuck in the ends of our milk straws and threw at the necks of boys in front of us. Milk straws were also useful as blowpipes. A small coil of paper dipped in your inkwell could be pushed down the straw and you could blow the inky dart down the neck of the shirt of the kid in front of you. If discovered at any of this sort of malarkey you would be given either a smacked leg, the strap on your hands or the cane across your bum, depending on who the teacher was. Girls got caned across the bum just like boys; equality of the sexes applied to corporal punishment it seemed.

When the big snows did come, and we woke up to find that everything around us was white over, we were in a state of delirious bliss. Snowmen appeared in the middle of the street (much to the chagrin of the milkmen who had to dodge round them in their milk floats); there were snowball fights and home-made sledges made from old fish boxes or sheets of linoleum. One kid had a massive proper sledge that four of us could sit on, with runners and a rope; that sledge went really fast. Duchess Road, the street next to ours, was our sledging street. It had a steep cobbled brew (north country speak for a steep sloping street) and when it was covered with packed, hard snow, it made an Olympic-standard slope – the Cresta Run had nothing on our sledging brew.

There were very few cars on the road in them there days so we had a clear run from top to bottom. The object was to see how far you could get on a single push. Nobody made it to the baker's shop at the far end of the street but most of us could get well past Dolman's corner shop, where the flat stretch began. We would sledge and climb for hours until mothers called us in for tea. Then we would stand before the fire, faces burning as our swollen fingers and toes began to thaw out. Eventually you would return to life again and kneel up on the chair to look out of the window, staring out at the snow as night drew over the blanched street and the gas lamps came on, pouring pools of yellow light onto the snowman we had made.

Jack Frost was lord of all then. The world was locked in ice and we huddled round the fire, with 'sausages' (cotton tubes filled with waste wool) across the door as home-made draught excluders.

Like everybody else in the street we had an outside toilet and in sub-zero temperatures going for a pee was a rushed and frantic affair, while going for a shit was an act of heroism worthy of Captain Oates. If your arse didn't actually freeze to the seat you were eternally grateful and, unlike today, when the centrally heated defecator can linger with a crossword puzzle, we, like bombers over a hostile city, ran down the yard, flew into the bog, dropped our payloads and flew out again, pronto.

And the toilet paper – ah there was the rub! No Labrador puppy tugging a soft cushioning tissue for us. Rabelais' Pantagruel and Gargantua might have found a swan's neck the perfect answer when it came to arsewipe but we had to make do with cut-up squares of the *Manchester Evening News* hanging from a nail on the lavvy door. Newspaper had myriad uses in those days: wrapping chips, cleaning windows (with a little splash of vinegar) and polishing your shoes amongst them. In those pre-Kleenex days my nanna used newspaper instead of a handkerchief whenever she had a cold (which was most winters). By bedtime her nose would be a nice shiny black courtesy of the printer's ink. Using the process of scientific deduction I assume that by using the *Manchester Evening News* as toilet paper we ended up with shiny black arseholes. I often wonder what doctors those days thought when they had to examine the backsides of the poor: presumably they believed the working class of Manchester wiped their bums with lumps of coal.

One snowy winter's day is lodged in my memory forever, a strange day after Christmas and New Year when we were still on holiday and school was looming like the time-devouring monster that it was. I'd been stuck in the house all morning, none of my pals seemed to be about and, as dinnertime came and went, I sat listening to the radio while my nanna told her rosary, my mum got on with some sewing and Christina played with her dolls.

Radio drama with its great narrative force and its sound effects had a way of drawing you in that was really powerful; it still is I think. This early afternoon I was entranced by the play on the BBC Home Service. It was set in Canada and ironically was about a group of passengers in a stranded coach somewhere in the great frozen wastes, hundreds of miles away from any town or city. The wind howled and raged out of the radio's speaker and one by one the passengers began dying. I'm not sure why, perhaps it was because the storytelling was so effective and the sound effects so real, but those fictional deaths entered into me.

When the play finished, I decided to go out and set off for the Hidden Valley to see if anybody else was about. It wasn't snowing but the sky was ashen with the faintest hint of a westering sun, and what snow there was lay thick all about; there were drifts knee-high in some places. There was no sign of any of the other kids, no footsteps, just virgin snow. I walked on, breaking a trail, dropping down the little defile towards the Hidden Valley, noticing the frozen smaller ponds with their thick coating of snow and the frost-rimed branches locked in ice. Coming to the heart of the dell I saw that the big pond was frozen solid and in the still, silent air I stopped and looked out across the ice and blown snow.

I suppose it was a combination of everything: the radio play I'd been listening to, the dead and frozen landscape all around me and the fact that as an eleven-year-old I was beginning to understand a few things about the world, but at that moment, standing there in that secret place, I came to know my own mortality and understood in my own small way the fate that faces us all. It was a chilling thought and I remember that for a brief moment I became terrified by the sense of finality, yet even then as a small boy I knew there was nothing I or anybody else could do about it. I also sensed that everything they taught us in school about God and Jesus and Mary and the saints didn't explain why we were born and why we had to die.

I was standing staring at the icy pond, deep in thought, when I heard a voice and saw a small figure coming out of the gully into the valley. It was Judith Edgar dressed in her new Christmas clothes. She too was bored and had set off looking for somebody to play with and had followed my footprints across the hills. We walked back together, chatting about what presents we'd got but more than half of my mind was still left behind in the frozen wastes.

Eleven-plus What?

You can find out all about the eleven-plus and the grammar and comprehensive school system by reading the thousands of articles, research papers and books written about them and your conclusion will be pretty much determined by what party you vote for: the Tories see the days of the grammar school as the golden days of education, lifting gifted children and setting them on the ladder of success; Labour sees the eleven-plus as a divisive watershed that creamed off the best of the working class and left the rest to fester in failing secondary moderns. There is something of the truth in both views. Unfortunately many working-class children who did make it into the grammar-school system found themselves adrift in a world they didn't understand and, lost and confused, they failed to realise their potential. The eleven-plus tested you on English, arithmetic and non-verbal reasoning and like the modern-day tests conducted by counties like Kent and Trafford, children could be coached to pass.

St Anne's didn't put all the children in for the eleven-plus. It was already decided that some of the poorest kids wouldn't be able to afford to go to grammar school anyway so it was believed there was no point putting their names forward.

There was no way my mum could afford to pay for coaching but she was an intelligent woman who had gone to grammar school herself so she was able to help me. I had no problem with the English or the maths but the non-verbal I found more difficult. There were some questions that edged on the daft. I remember one example.

Q. How many balls of string does it take to reach the moon?

A. One, if it's long enough.

Now that's the kind of joke your granddad would tease you with. It has less than double feck all to do with the intelligence of some poor kid in the slums of Salford who, given a fair deal and a decent teacher, might well have ended up discovering a cure for cancer.

So as that long cold winter staggered on, those of us chosen to sit the eleven-plus got buses into town and waited in the playground of Whitworth Street School in the freezing drizzle. We were called forward by school and went to sit in the big hall where the dice was cast that would determine whether we ended up either wearing overalls and shovelling shit for the rest of our lives or wearing a suit and telling other people to shovel shit.

I sat there all morning, did the tests, had some dinner, did more tests then went home. My mum asked me how I had done, I said I thought I'd done OK then forgot all about it. As the weeks passed and we moved slowly into spring, we had serious work of an agricultural nature to do. And funnily enough, it also involved shovelling shit.

Gardening for Barmpots

One of the skills imparted to us at St Anne's Catholic School was the art of digging manure into a vegetable patch. Whether they imagined that this was good training for any of us who might have been getting ideas above our station and were thinking about doing something like comparative linguistics, brain surgery or particle science I don't know. Perhaps they thought it would be good training for a post-apocalyptic world where we all had to grow our own stuff.

It was the spring of my eleven-plus year when Mr Hartnett said, 'Right – pens down, off to the gardening shed. Let's get your clogs on and have some honest work out of you.'

We had recently had a nature lesson in which he showed us how to mix soil with water in a test tube and watch it settle into different rings – clay, humus, sand etc. It seems that this was preparation for some serious shovel work and, as horny-handed sons of toil, we were led out to the gardening shed where there was an assortment of clogs and tools. The clogs had stiff leather uppers, hardened by countless soakings. They weren't laced but held on by leather straps, which were fastened with glass buttons. It was pot luck what clogs you got and I usually ended up with an odd pair, one foot two sizes bigger than I needed. The leather was so hard and the glass buttons so big that getting the clogs fastened meant ripped nails and bleeding fingers, while shovelling with the forks meant blisters and aching backs – all good preparation for Purgatory.

It was bad enough when all you had to do with the forks was turn over the clods of clayey soil ready for the spuds to be planted. Today was not a 'turning over of the soil' day: today was a 'forking in of the shit' day. Courtesy of some farmer that Monsignor Aspinall knew, a massive consignment of shit was arriving on a big lorry. Not just any old shit – pig shit –rancid, sour, hot and steaming and immensely strong in odour. There may be worse-smelling shit, pterodactyl or hedge fund managers' shit perhaps, but if there is I haven't come across it. The pig muck slid off the lorry in a loud slurp and lay there, a small mountain of it, steaming and stinking, as though some giant pig's arse had just dropped it out of the sky. It was a cold and frosty day with clear icy air, and the assault on our nasal membranes was brutal. Some kids threw up, and those that didn't wished they could.

The girls were inside doing needlework; we were outside shovelling shit. When I asked Mr Hartnett why the girls weren't there as well he said their hands were too soft. I said that mine were too soft, but he pretended not to hear me and I joined the ranks of boys who were lifting, forking in and turning the thick loam of the vegetable garden. I am convinced, to this day, that the vegetables grown there were destined for the monsignor's table and that we, like the lumpen proletariat in the Van Gogh paintings of the potato pickers, were seen merely as agricultural labourers.

Several hours later we struggled out of our shit-caked clogs and went back to writing essays on cocoa beans and deciding which was the odd one out in a bundle of triangles and dots.

That afternoon I walked in the house after school and as the warmth from the coal fire thawed out my wintry clothes, the smell of pig shit from my socks made my nanna's eyes water. My mother made me take my socks off and threw them outside. Before I could be let back in the house I had to stand in the yard in a bowl of warm soapy water to wash the stink from my legs.

'It will make a man of you,' Mr Hughes said in the corner shop when I pushed over my Uncle Joe's Mint Balls money and told him how I had spent the day fertilising the monsignor's potato patch. He was wrong, very very wrong: it didn't make a man of me – it just made me determined that never again would I shovel shit. Since then I have done all I can to avoid anything at all to do with gardening, including looking at seed catalogues.

Losing My Faith

A few weeks later my mum got a letter from St Bede's College, a Catholic grammar school on the other side of Manchester, to say that I had been accepted as a pupil there. With that letter began some of the strangest and most miserable years of my life. But all of that is in the far-off country of Chapter 6.

Once we had passed our eleven-plus there wasn't much for my friend Pete and I to do in school. We were destined to be hawked out and shoved into uniform to travel across town to St Bede's. Our classmates were mostly destined to stay at St Anne's and become the wood hewers and water drawers of Manchester.

It was while I was in my final year at St Anne's that I committed my first big mortal sin and jumped wholeheartedly on the slippery slope to Hell.

There was a girl at St Anne's who was a couple of years older than me who had reached puberty way ahead of the rest of us and at the age of thirteen already had a very large bust. She saw me looking at her bosoms one summer's day just before I left St Anne's for good, and said, 'Come home with me after school and you can see them.' Which seemed a fair offer.

The girl lived near Crumpsall Green and her mum worked at the hospital and wouldn't be home until later. What happened that fateful afternoon was no more than innocent childish exploration; yet somehow, after that, swapping ten *Beanos* for five *Eagle* comics with my friend Eric Davies didn't seem a particularly exciting idea any more.

Walking back home, still dizzy with wonder, I met my mother who was on the way to the shops.

'What are you doing here?' she asked.

My tongue was glued to the roof of my mouth.

'I was just muckin' about with some kids from school.'

'Well, you can muck about with these shopping bags.' And she dragged me with her to the shops.

I knew what I'd done was very wrong in the eyes of the Church and knew also that I wouldn't be able to confess it. It wasn't just that it was a mortal sin, I didn't have the words to describe what I had done. It might have been sinful but it was also wonderful and innocent. But we were made to feel ashamed of our bodies and see them as dirty and sinful. So I went to confession the following Saturday and made up a barrowload of sins about lying and swearing and petty pilfering and left out the big hellfire and damnation sin of touching and feeling.

So I made a bad confession and the next morning my mother took me to church with her and of course, when she went to the altar I had to go with her to take Holy Communion. According to the teachings of Holy Mother Church, to take the body of Christ in a state of mortal sin meant that I was automatically excommunicated, cut off from the Holy Roman Catholic and Apostolic Church for ever without any chance of redemption and automatically doomed to Hell. But that is what I did: rather than not take Holy Communion and risk an inquisition, I took the Body of Christ into my defiled and blackened eleven-year-old temple and damned myself for all eternity. For many a night after I lay awake, terrified, imagining the Day of Judgement when everyone I knew would be stood around as the Archangel Michael, who I was named after, read out how I had done rude things with that girl and how, worse than that, I had eaten Jesus in a state of sin and how he was sorry but there was nothing he personally could do for me because I had damned myself to the fires of Hell. This nightmare rattled on in the attic of my child's mind for years, tormenting and torturing me until, in the end, I convinced myself I was a bad lot and beyond any redemption. Graham Greene couldn't have written a better tale, though he did have a good try in *The Heart of the Matter*.

Excommunicated, damned for all eternity and about to go to St Bede's Catholic College – now there's a good conundrum for you. Kenny and Wharfie and the other lads had no such problems, of course, and got on with their growing sexual awareness without the hump of guilt that the Catholic Church had sewn on my back. Lucky buggers.

If I had problems with God and damnation, my mum and Lou had problems with money, mostly the cost of my uniform. There was a shop in St Anne's Square in the heart of Manchester that sold everything I needed: blazer, grey shorts, grey socks, grey shirts, school tie and cap and the other stuff: gym togs, football togs and cricket flannels. The problem was that we had no money to spare; Julia was gone so there was Lou's small wage and my nanna's pension to clothe and feed five of us as well as pay the rent and keep us warm. Uncle Harry had the solution: the RAF Benevolent Fund; this existed (and still does) to help ex-airmen who have fallen on hard times and the wives and families of those killed in action. My mum was against it, she saw it as taking charity; the race memory of the poorhouse and parish relief was still strong in her genes. Harry snorted, 'That's why we all paid money into the funds during the war. Every one of us – soldiers, sailors, airmen – paid in every week just so people like you and Michael would be looked after.'

So we went, one afternoon, up a staircase in an office somewhere in the city and a man behind a desk, who didn't treat us at all unkindly, gave my mother a cheque to cover the cost of my uniform. I know we had a right to the money but in a way it still felt like charity and I wondered what happened to kids whose parents had no spare money or access to a grant like this. I do think school uniforms are useful, they give children a link with the school, an identity if you like, but I do believe that the State should provide them – that way kids do start with something a little closer to a level playing field. Other things are harder to deal with; the very way middle-class life is structured gives their children an immediate advantage over the equally intelligent children of the poor.

I still find no justification in this. Michael Young's 1958 book, *The Rise of the Meritocracy*, was not an instruction book showing the middle class how to achieve success but a satirical, semi-scholarly look at the way ladders had been built for the children of the middle class to climb while those the working class were offered had greased rungs six feet apart. I soon discovered this once I went to St Bede's, though at the time, lost in a maze of rules, canes and rituals I couldn't have articulated it.

CHAPTER 6

ST BEDE'S GULAG

Almost sixty years on I can still smell the leather of my satchel, still feel my bus pass in my hand and still sense the cool air of that terrazzo-floored corridor and the strong odour of frankincense that was coming from somewhere beyond the great hall. We stood in a long line – grey shorts, grey shirts and socks, dark blue blazers with a cardinal's hat embroidered on the breast pocket and the motto *Nunquam Otio Torpebat*. All these years later and despite the Latin teaching of Bandy Birchall I still haven't a clue what it means; for years I thought it had something to do with nuns and submarines. (It translates as: 'He never relaxed in idleness.')

St Bede's College was founded in 1876 by the Bishop of Salford, Herbert Vaughan, when the Diocese took over what had once been the Manchester Aquarium and turned it into a school. The aquarium was in a terracotta-fronted, Italianate building that was only half finished when the developer ran out of money; so that the great, main door of the building, which should have been the central majestic entrance for an equally majestic Victorian pile, is at one end, and ever since the building has looked slightly at half-cock, symbolic perhaps of many boys' experience of the school itself. Until it was turned into a school for the education, flogging and buggering of Catholic boys the building was full of fish tanks holding strange creatures of the deep. None of the finny and scaly denizens, however, were stranger than the mixed bag of pederasts, sadists, saints, good men and buffoons who went under the guise of masters and priests and who moved into the building once the fish tanks had been drained and taken away.

The best days of your life? As one of my Irish friends says, 'In my bollocks they were.' There are boys who remember their years at

St Bede's as some kind of idyllic, sub-Eton/Rugby version of *Tom Brown's Schooldays*. I have met a handful of them; to them Bede's was everything it set out to be: a nurturing ground for the talented boys of Manchester's Catholic middle class. They played cricket and rugby, took their O levels and A levels and usually did well enough to go into one of the professions that Bede's seemed to channel its boys towards: the law, accountancy, the priesthood and civil engineering.

When I meet them it is as though they went to a school in another parallel universe. These chaps are, on the whole, the ones who fitted in: the obedient, sporty types who believed in playing the game with a straight bat, and who also believed that God was in his (Catholic) Heaven and all was right with the world. Anybody who was slightly different or had a little spirit, particularly those boys who came from poorer, working-class families, found the college a very different place. The collective experience of many of the men I meet now who were at St Bede's in the fifties and sixties is that it was a grim place run mostly on the principle that boys were elementally evil and had to have that evil beaten out of them. It was a school ruled over by a number of damaged men who went on to damage a number of the children in their care, and it was a place where the softening influence of women was several miles away; the only women to be seen anywhere near the place were a legion of whiskery nuns who cleaned and cooked and did the laundry – and there was matron, of course, a large lady of indeterminate sex who gave you aspirin and yellow ointment for everything from earache to leprosy.

The school stands facing Alexandra Park, a fine stretch of civic grass, rhododendrons, stone fountains and a lake – sixth-formers were allowed to walk in the park at lunchtime. Across the park on the other side from the school is Moss Side where nobody walks now unless they are wearing bullet-proof jackets and carrying a Kalashnikov.

Famous alumni (of St Bede's, not Moss Side) include two drummers (Bernie Dwyer of Freddie and the Dreamers and John Maher of the Buzzcocks), one keyboard player (Clint Boon of

Inspiral Carpets), one of our finest poets, Bernard O'Donoghue, the actor Colin Baker, the novelist Edward Docx, the pop singer Peter Noone (Herman's Hermits) and one of our greatest modern playwrights, Trevor Griffiths. Other less stellar Old Baedians include the odd bishop or cardinal, five hundred or so priests, UKIP MEP Steven Woolfe and me.

I was shown the way to school, on my first day at my distinguished Alma Mater, by my good friend Kevin Leech, who had already been there a year and therefore knew most of the ropes. We crossed the city on two buses, together with a mob of shouting and rowdy boys who were going the same way, and went into the school not by the great aquarium door but by the gate at the back of the bike sheds. I lined up with a timid crew of other small boys who only a few weeks before had been cosseted by lady teachers in child-friendly schools where, for the most part, children weren't regarded as the spawn of Satan. We stood there talking quietly, waiting to go into the Academic Hall, a room that I would come to know and loathe. It had originally been the main exhibition room of the aquarium, and it was there that I would, in later years, swing from the wall bars, sit exams and watch Gilbert and Sullivan being massacred by small boys pretending to be girls and big boys pretending to be Beefeaters, Jolly Jack Tars and Japanese Emperors.

As we waited to be summoned into the presence of that cross between Goebbels and the Great Oz, the college rector Monsignor Thomas Duggan, another boy told me that we new pupils were known as 'rookies'. I had no idea what he meant but nodded sagely as though I was completely au fait with everything he was saying. This was only the first taste of what was to become a bewildering new world of meta-language, slang, regulations, protocols and traditions that everybody else seemed to know and which were a complete mystery to me. You may as well have set me down amongst a tribe of Inuit or Bedouin. I had only just about mastered the ropes when I left there seven years later.

Beyond the handful of old boys mentioned above that seemed to have sleepwalked through the brutality and the sexual abuse there are many more that I have met who tell a different story. In the

1980s I was in a bar in Bermuda and I met an Old Baedian there who told me how Duggan had destroyed his life. He had been sexually abused by him for many years and this grown man – a police inspector in his late thirties – wept hot tears as he told me what had happened. Duggan had beaten and fondled him constantly, picking him out as somebody for special attention, until eventually the boy told his father who then went to the bishop. The outcome was that the boy was expelled.

In a pub in Manchester I spent a long night drinking with an old school friend who had trained to be a teacher at the same training college as me – he told the same story of sexual abuse at Duggan's hands, only in his case he never managed to rise above the shame and anger he felt. He ended his days drinking himself into eternity in a crack den in one of the seedy streets of that city.

More than fifty years after leaving Bede's I met another old school friend, a boy who I had admired for his wit and his learning, in a pub in the Ribble Valley. He had been at Bede's as a boarder. He had been bullied and persecuted all of his school life, not by the other boarders (they were as miserable and downtrodden as him) but by the priests. 'They hated me. I was beaten pretty much every day.'

'We survived,' I told him.

'I don't think I did,' was all he said.

But on that first day at Bede's I knew nothing of this, I only knew that this was very different to my cosy primary school, this was a place of dark, marble-floored corridors whose high walls held massive gilt-framed paintings with such subjects as *The Rape of the Sabine Women*, where priests in gowns and mortarboards swept around like great malevolent bats and where, as well as us small and apprehensive rookies, there were sixth-form 'boys' who looked like men in blazers who shaved.

As we stood in line, the boy next to me, who I would later discover was called Frank Ransom (nickname 'Fred'), told me that we were going into the hall for some kind of opening ceremony. I had never heard of opening ceremonies, only 'opening medicine', which my grandmother took regularly for fear that constipation would kill her. Eventually we shuffled down the hall to some spaces that had been kept for us at the front and sat there waiting for whatever happened next.

What happened next was a procession of priests in black soutanes, gowns and mortarboards and laymen in suits, similarly gowned and mortarboarded. Both priests and lay teachers wore what I now know are academic hoods with coloured trims and in some cases furry collars. After they had all assembled on stage, a portly, bald man in a black soutane, his midriff bound in a scarlet silk cummerbund, swept down the aisle towards the front. 'Swept' is the operative word because, like the Mekon in the Dan Dare strip in *The Eagle*, Duggan didn't so much walk as float. I sensed then and I can still feel it to this day, the miasma of fear that rolled over the whole floor of the hall as more than six hundred boys looked ahead and waited. We rookies didn't quite understand that what was rapidly approaching the stage like Yeats' rough beast, its hour come round at last, was a twisted and demonic product of an Irish Catholic upbringing in the slums of Oswaldtwistle. Whatever had happened to that man on his journey from his raggy-arsed beginnings as an Irish immigrant in a Lancashire cotton town to the English College in Rome, it had not given him any grounding in love, sympathy or understanding. He was a monster who should not have been allowed within a nautical mile of children.

So on that day, my first day in the grown-up world of grammar school, Monsignor Thomas Duggan processed towards the stage, all five foot four of him, head tilted up so that he looked towards Heaven, his bald head lightly powdered, his small mean mouth pursed, his pinched nose seeming to sniff the fear in the air with relish.

The masters and priests stood at attention as Duggan made his dramatic entrance and, at a nod from him, sat again.

I remember little of what the Monsignor said that day, but I do remember his eyes. Small as I was I knew that these were the eyes of a dangerous lunatic. I can't remember the exact words but the timbre of his speech was about how lucky we were to be there and how we were all on the verge of a life of glorious Roman Catholic manhood – all of which was of course total bollocks.

After the briefing from the Führer we were marched off to our prospective cells. Fred and I were in Upper Third B. There was a Lower Third B where boys whose parents had more money than sense sent them to be coached for the eleven-plus, paying good money to have their gilded children slide effortlessly into the hands of pederasts and torturers.

I can't remember the name of the master who took us that first morning, only that for the first lesson it was a lay master and not a priest and the lesson was all about giving out jotters and telling us how to put our names in the text books and how we were to cover them with brown paper to save them getting scuffed.

I looked inside the history book I'd been given, noticed that it had originally belonged to three other boys, and then noticed that it fell open at a well-thumbed page where there was a picture of a lady with lots of breasts. This was because she was some Mesopotamian goddess. On the facing page was a picture of some clay tablets with cuneiform letters on them. I don't think that was why it fell open at that section, though; breasts were few and far between in our world and a plenitude of them was not to be laughed at.

After this master had gone, a short, plump, smiley-faced priest called Father Murray came in, gave us all some French textbooks and asked if any of us had ever been to France. One boy put his hand up and said he'd been there on holiday but the rest of us had hardly been further than Blackpool, so he realised pretty early on that he was going to be making bread with some very rough dough indeed.

Jollop

After Father Murray had left to cry and bang his head against the wall, a man walked in who told us he was our form teacher. He was a ragbag of a man in his late fifties (I would guess) who looked like a cross between Mr Pastry and Old Man Steptoe, almost as though he'd been put together from spare parts by God in a drunken moment. I don't know where the name came from (his real name was Mr Ryan) but everybody called him Jollop. 'Jollop', when I looked it up in the dictionary, yielded: 'a strong alcoholic medicine or purgative. Also an urban slang word for semen.' I suspect the first definition is more fitting since Jollop seemed to be either drunk or on some kind of medication much of the time.

He was probably the barmiest, though least harmful, teacher in the school. Permanently shabby, his suit jacket stained with dribble, food and snuff (which he flung up his hairy nostrils constantly), his trousers stained with God only knows what, he stood before us for a whole year and basically just gibbered. From time to time he wrote stuff on the blackboard, and then he gibbered some more. He didn't do us much harm but he probably did us little good. He dribbled rather a lot, perhaps because of his snuff habit, and whenever he got angry and went into a rant he would cover the front four rows with a thick mist of amber spittle.

He lodged just around the corner from school with an Irishwoman who, he told us, used bad language when shouting at her children. One of the lads who had heard her said she used to shout, 'Come 'ere, you bloody bleeding bloody buggerin' buggers.' Which, while not nice, wasn't as bad as the 'F-word' so we didn't know what Jollop was fussing about. He arrived in class every morning always slightly late, looking as though only minutes before he had inadvertently connected with Planet Earth while lying in bed staring at the ceiling and had asked himself, 'What am I doing today?'

To which the ceiling answered, 'Educating thirty-four boys, you dozy old prat.' At which point he hastily pulled his clothes on, threw some breakfast over himself, and shuffle-jogged round the corner to put in another day at the chalk face. Why was he employed by a school that saw itself as one of the premier grammar schools in the north of England? Because he was cheap. The priests were cheap too because their wages were paid to Duggan, who kept the money and gave them spends for things like tobacco and the occasional game of golf.

Jollop told us he was Canadian but I doubt it. He may have spent some time in Canada because his accent hovered somewhere between West Cork and Winnipeg, but whatever schoolmastering he had done must have been with elk or beavers because, as a teacher, he was as much use as a chocolate soldering iron.

He was the intellectual and moral guardian of Upper Third B

and seemed to take us for almost everything except French, PE, and, for some reason, History. I remember very little of anything Jollop taught us except that once, in nature study, he taught us that finches have stubby beaks so they can eat berries. There was no mention of Darwinian evolution or natural adaptation; God had just made them that way: we had heads to stick our school caps on and finches had beaks so they could eat special stuff – that's life, get over it. And then for homework, copy a chaffinch out of a book.

Jollop – wherever you are in the post-death cosmos, if you are reading these words, then know this: that after a whole year of your teaching nothing else remains in my noodle; no great poetry, no wonderful insights into the nature of the world, no understanding of our place in the universe; all that remains in my mind's eye is the image of a badly drawn bird executed in crayon on the living room table after the dishes had been cleared away, for which I got a tick in red ink and a mark of five out of ten. Keith Lawson did a brilliant drawing which got him eight out of ten, but which Jollop drooled over, letting a big glob of dribble fall onto the paper. Keith wiped it off with the sleeve of his blazer. Returning a few minutes later to look at the drawing again, Jollop stared at the picture and pointed at the offending wet patch, which was stained a faint yellow from snuff.

'What's that?'

'Spit, sir.'

'Don't be a pussyfoot, Lawson.'

(We never found out what a pussyfoot was but whatever it was we were not supposed to be one.)

'It is sir, honest, sir.'

'Whose spit is it?'

'Yours, sir.'

'My spit is not that colour,' was the terse reply, followed by a token clout to the back of Lawson's head; token because Jollop, unlike many of the other teachers, didn't seem to get much pleasure from hurting children.

I remember little more of Jollop other than that he came into class regularly with his pyjamas on under his clothes, a result I guess of his sudden conversion every morning from Oblomov to grammar school teacher. He tucked his pyjama bottoms into his socks, but we could still see them when he sat on the desk and his trouser legs rode up. His flies were often unfastened too, and through the gaping maw of his grubby pinstripes we could see his pyjama trousers; the flies of those were also often undone, and through them we could see that which we did not wish to see: a pink slug dozing in an unmade nest.

Life in a Catholic Gulag

Strangely for a Catholic school, Jollop was not a paedophile, just an old man who wouldn't have been a teacher in any normal place of education. But St Bede's was not a normal place of education.

For a start a good number of the pupils there were boarders, most of them from places like Preston and Burnley – too far away for them to go home at nights – and many of the boarders were destined for ordination into the priesthood. Chained up after we day boys had gone home, they had little to do except study, read, play games and be prey to the psychopathic bullies (both priests and boys) and the homosexual advances (from both priests and boys) which it would appear were pretty much *de rigueur* in all boarding schools, Catholic or otherwise, at the time.

Our school dinners were prepared by the nuns and were the best example of grudge cooking I have ever come across: a typical menu would be mystery meat which was mostly lumps of gristle and which we christened 'baboons' arseholes'. This was covered in a kind of gravy ('sludge') and was accompanied by watery mash and cabbage. For afters we would be given something like rice pudding ('dead maggots') or sago pudding ('frogspawn'). This was served in staggered sittings in a large wooden hut near the bike shed (the dining hall wasn't built until later). You need to couple this mental image with the fact that the meat supplier was later taken to court and fined heavily for providing schools with meat unfit for human consumption. I find it diffilcult to look back with fondness to the days I was served broiled baboons' arseholes by whiskery nuns.

It was even worse for the poor bloody boarders. The boarders had the same school dinners as the day boys but all their other meals seemed to be less-than-adequate portions of porridge or bread and jam. My friend Kevin made capital out of their miserable condition as the main purveyor of cold buttered toast to the starving wretches at morning break. Knowing the boarders were starving, Kevin would get his mum to make him a playtime snack of a dozen and a half rounds of toast, thickly buttered.

'I don't know where he puts it all!' Elsie, his mum, said to me one morning as I waited for him in the kitchen; I watched her sweating over a huge mound of Mother's Pride and said nothing. I knew where Kevin put it all: in the boarders, at a penny a slice.

Kevin, later in life, became one of the richest men in England and is (as far as I know) the only man to have floated a company on the London and New York stock exchanges on the same day. At one time his company owned Land's End and John O'Groats – when I heard the news I emailed him to say I was waiting for him to buy the bit in the middle. One couldn't imagine a better example of the parable of the talents: a multi-millionaire's fortune founded on the misery of hungry Catholic schoolboys. (As a footnote I have to point out that the school later opened a tuck shop, selling biscuits and crisps; the market in soggy, cold toast collapsed and Kevin went over to selling the boarders used Dinky cars in the Lady Corridor at break – another enterprise which earned him a schoolboy's fortune.)

The Lady Corridor connected the old school with the covered playground and the day boys' toilets ('the jakes'). It had a terrazzo floor and a strict ordinance that was well in tune with the other mad rules of this half-hinged establishment: NO RUNNING IN THE LADY CORRIDOR!

For this you would be beaten. You would also be beaten for failing to wear your cap outside school or for being found eating chips in the street. One priest, Alf (real name Father Hynes – nicknamed Alf after the famous serial prison escapee of the fifties, Alfie Hynes), was so zealous in his pursuit of chip-eating, non-cap-wearing Bede's boys that he used to borrow the milkman's uniform and milk float, and would drive round the streets at dinner time, disguised as a milkman, trying to catch out boys who were disobeying the rules; if you were *sans* cap but *avec* chips you were in double lumber. It was Alf who used to tell you on a Friday that you were going to get a beating on the following Monday, so that you had all weekend to enjoy the prospect. Playing football in the park on a Sunday afternoon you would pause mid-leap for the ball, struck down by the certain knowledge that at 9.30 the following day, you, a small boy, would be flogged with a leather tawse by a grown man in a dog collar who professed a great love of Christ and His Merciful Mother. For running in the Lady Corridor the punishment was usually six on the hands, often given there and then to save the Prefect of Studies any bother.

In fact being beaten, or the threat of being beaten, was very much the essence of education at St Bede's. *Educare Per Gluteus Maximus* should have been the school motto, not that stuff about torpedoes. Sadism was institutional. There was a regular Latin test each month; the results were given out in the Great Hall on a Monday morning before the whole school. Boys who failed it were flogged there and then on the stage as an example to encourage all the other boys to learn their Latin vocab. I suppose the men of God who did all this had been treated pretty much the same way and thought that, if it had been bad enough for them, it was bad enough for the boys in their care.

I was spared the Latin test because, at the end of my first year, I went up into the Moderns where you didn't do Latin. Bandy Birchall must have decided, after a year of trying to teach me eight ways of talking to and about a table and failing, that I was a hopeless case. In fact, talking of cases, I still have no idea what they are, I wouldn't know an ablative case if it bit me on the gluteus maximus. And let's face it, if Latin is all that good why does nobody speak it any more?

The only Latin I remember from Bede's is in the shape of schoolboy jokes, my favourite being:

Caesar et sum jam forte
Brutus et erat
Caesar sic in omnibus
Brutus sic in at.

Bandy Birchall, our Übergrupenlatinmeister, was a rotund man with a bald head and round glasses who insisted that the Romans pronounced 'V' as 'vee' and not, as some scholars maintained, as 'wee'. His sole evidence for this (since nobody alive knew how the *civitas Romanus* pronounced their words) was that a brave conqueror like Caesar would never have stood on the prow of his trireme as he landed on the southern shores of Britain shouting the slightly limp, '*Weeni, weedy, weecum.*' Instead, Bandy asserted, he would have screeched the much more manly '*Veni, vide, vecum.*' I can still hear him telling us all this in his high-pitched, thin voice, his lower lip fat and wet, drawing the words in the air with a piece of chalk. Not a bad man, just another pre-war teacher who was being engulfed by the helter-skelter of the post-war years.

It was Bandy who was the victim of one of my more imaginative April Fool's jokes; for which I ought to feel ashamed but don't. I bought a pair of kippers on the way to school that morning and tied them on the bulb of the board light. First lesson was Latin and as Bandy stood at the wall-mounted blackboard writing Roman gibberish in scrawly chalk letters, the kippers began to cook quite nicely on the hundred-watt bulb.

Bandy sniffed, shook his head, then sniffed some more.

'Somebody', he said in a rising voice with a note of incredulity or perhaps desperation in it, 'is cooking kippers in this classroom.' His face had a look on it that I find hard to describe – perhaps 'at the end of its tether' would do.

We stared at him in feigned innocence, though a few boys were struggling hard not to collapse in smothered hysteria.

'I can't smell anything, sir,' one boy volunteered, perfectly straight-faced.

Bandy turned back to the blackboard muttering something under his breath. He scrawled some more. The smell of grilled kippers grew stronger. He turned to face the class again.

'I know it's April Fool's Day, and I also know that somebody in this class is cooking kippers. Lift up your desk lids!' He made a tour of the classroom, sticking his head inside each desk, but not one single boy had a primus stove and frying pan working away there amongst the jotters, chemistry stencils, broken protractors, *Eagle* comics, conkers, cats' eyes that had been prised out of the road and smelly gym togs.

He stood back at the blackboard, defeated, and glared at us.

'I know that you're all in this together, and I will stand here until I find out what is going on.'

At that point a large glob of scalding-hot kipper fat slid sizzling off the lightbulb and onto Bandy's bald head. There was a cry of 'Oh my God!' and Bandy whirled round, clutching his blistered bonce, his master's gown flying round like a whirling dervish's skirt as the rows of small boys fell about laughing hysterically.

It was well worth getting twelve for that, and I'm not sure that that April Fool's joke didn't have a good deal to do with my move to the Moderns and my shunning of Latin in favour of 'stinks' (chemistry) and 'joggers' (geography). I have no regrets. A knowledge of Latin might have been nice; had I 'the Latin' I could have gone on to Oxford or Cambridge and now be a retired don, sitting in my book-lined study with my pipe and a glass of fine wine reading Virgil in the original; instead of which I am a part-time comedian and broadcaster sitting in front of my AppleMac with a glass of Talisker.

Playing tricks on priests and masters was something we did well. Just as they mostly regarded us as spawn of Satan, we regarded them as gaolers and the worst of them as dangerous lunatics. As I grew older and more covertly rebellious, the tricks I played became more serious.

One involved our French teacher, Tojo. His real name was Father Grourke but because he had an uncanny resemblance to the late Japanese Emperor it was inevitable that he should end up with that nickname. He was quite a decent bloke in most respects but a pretty useless teacher. The jape against him was simple but not one to try at home. I bought some stink bombs from a joke shop in town and laid three of them along the inside edge of the master's desk, lowering the lid very carefully so as not to crack them. Tojo waltzed in with a stack of textbooks under his chin and dropped them soundly on the desk. Five minutes later we were evacuating the classroom in a fairly disorderly fashion, claiming innocence and blaming the navvies nearby who were working on the new annex Bede's was building. 'They must have hit the sewer, Father.' A lame excuse but it did work. As I remember it, nobody was nobbled for that one.

Not all the teachers were monsters. In the Lower Fourth Modern, geography was in the hands of Bill Whalley. His nickname was 'Wild Bill' Whalley but a gentler, less wild, man never existed. Short and slightly plump, he was a man of infinite patience, and cared about his subject so much that he stayed behind after school every Friday to run the Geographical Society, of which I was a member. In one of the great gloomy rooms off the main corridor, he would crank up the old school projector to show us films about the world outside Manchester. They were mostly black and white and ranged from the great documentary films of Robert J. Flaherty – *Louisiana Story*, *Man of Aran* and *Nanook of the North* – to Auden and Britten's *Night Mail*, together with a great body of films made by the GPO film unit to cheer up wartime and post-war Britain. Many of them were no more than propaganda films but we lapped them up. They showed images of ploughmen shot against cloud-roiled skies and boats fishing for herring off the Norfolk coast and were film versions of the paintings of Eric Ravilious or Batsford's British Rail posters. They spoke of an England that had already begun to vanish before the war. Teams of shire horses nodded as they dragged the harvest home, jolly Cockneys on stilts gathered the hops in the Kent fields and postmen trundled round Cotswold villages on cranky bikes, as music by Vaughan Williams or Elgar accompanied the warm, sure tones of Alvar Liddell.

We in the Geographical Society loved those Friday evenings, particularly the boarders to whom it was a respite from the dark dorm, the gloomy prep-room and the predatory groping priests, and was instead a glimpse into that other world out there from which their parents had banished them. The films had a deep and lasting effect on me also. That lost world of pre-war England seemed to have more than romance about it; it seemed more real somehow, more rooted and in tune with what was right and what should be. Perhaps this was because the only countryside I knew was either bounded by iron railings in the Manchester Corporation parks or was polluted by the mills and factories of the Irk Valley. Also, I suspect that it was the films Wild Bill showed us in that cold, old room that left me with a profound and lasting love of the English modern classical composers. Give me a T-shirt with 'Romantic Old Fool' on it or 'Vaughan Williams Does It for Me!' and I will wear it gladly.

When I failed O level joggers I was as sad for Bill's sake as I was my own. I loved physical geography and knew all there was to know about ox-bow lakes, hanging valleys and karst landscapes but, try as I would, I could not cram the major exports and imports of the Canadian Shield into my bonce. Learning facts by rote so I could spew them back out again in a three-hour exam might seem like a good education to people like Michael Gove but I look at such benighted views in the same way Dickens did in *Hard Times*.

One of the most interesting teachers of my early years was a fairly new addition to the teaching staff; his name was Daniel (Danny) Gleeson. He was a thick-set, handsome Geordie with dark Gypsy looks and long hair swept back and reaching to his collar. Think Tarzan and Heathcliffe in a grammar-school master's gown and you won't go far wrong. Rumour had it that he once played in goal for Gateshead, which meant a great deal to the footie fanatics in the school but not me; I was far more impressed by the way he swept through the school, eyes bright and gown flapping behind him, in what I can only describe as a 'fuck it' walk. He gave off an air of dangerous anarchy, but probably confounded Monsignor Duggan because, as a Catholic father of many children who also painted murals for churches and was quite an authority on the early Christian church in Northumbria, he must have seemed the ideal schoolmaster. He was perfect, as far as I was concerned, because he loved art and literature and life and didn't give a flying fuck about the rest. As a child of the working-class north-east he was also no great fan of the Tory party. He seemed very grown-up to my thirteen-year-old eyes yet, thinking about it, he was probably then only in his early twenties.

Danny Gleeson had been appointed as an art teacher but also

took the lower forms for English. It was through him that I came to know the poets of the First World War and visionary poets like Manley Hopkins. It was also through him that I came to read Leo Walmsley, Joyce Carey and William Golding, none of whom were on the syllabus.

Mr Nat Parker was the head of art and, according to what Dan Gleeson told me many years later, was the only man in St Bede's who was not afraid of Monsignor Duggan.

'Nat Parker just ignored Duggan and got on with what he wanted to get on with,' Dan said over a glass of Merlot in a pub in Rochdale thirty years later. 'For some reason Duggan left him alone; he knew he couldn't bully him.'

Nat Parker was close to retiring age when I started at St Bede's but he was a gentle man who rarely raised his voice and who treated boys decently and did his best to teach us art with the school's meagre provisions. Danny Gleeson also told me in that Rochdale pub how Nat had once gone to see Duggan to ask for more money for the department.

'Art', Duggan told him, 'is a Cinderella subject.' Which is a monsignorial way of saying, 'Feck off.'

So our art classes were mostly spent trying to make silk purses out of pigs' arses. With the best will in the world there isn't much you can do with powder paints, jam jars of water and sheets of rough, porous sugar paper. There are only so many times that you can start out to paint a rose and end up with something that looks like a haggis on a foggy highland moor without becoming despondent.

When Danny Gleeson took over things looked up a little and we managed to get some pencils so we could sketch a thing or two, but by then the damage had been done and we were all convinced we couldn't paint or draw. A pity really because there may well have been some amongst us who had the potential to enjoy art – or perhaps even become artists? But Cinderellas could feck off as far as T. D. was concerned.

The first day that Dan Gleeson took us for art he told us all to take out our pencils and draw a lamppost; when we'd done that he left enough of a pause for comic effect and then told us to draw a dog. This Zen-Dada comment on Monsignor Duggan's attitude to art might have gone over the heads of some of the budding Hockneys in the Lower Fourth Modern but it hit me between the eyes like a can of Warhol soup.

Danny was a brilliant calligrapher: he had a beautiful italic hand and taught us, amongst other things, how to construct the Versal alphabet. I can still do much of it from memory.

But it is his English lessons I remember most of all. He read Wilfrid Owen's 'Exposure' to us in his soft Geordie accent, and, as I was listening, I left the classroom and shivered and despaired, hovering over the trenches like some kind of revenant seeing everything as Owen had seen it. He read us *Foreigners* by Leo Walmsley and I fell in love with the book immediately. It is one of the neglected classics of children's literature, though I believe that it has recently been brought back into print. The book opens with a little boy whose nickname is 'Worms' lying in bed on a freezing cold morning, terrified of going to his school because he knows that the school bully, Grab Fosdyk, is going to beat the living bejasus out of him. He wishes that God would strike Fosdyk dead, then realises that God doesn't do things like that. His mother shouts for him to get up and Worms rattles his boots around the bedroom floor with the help of a long stick as he lies there in his misery. Every child I have read that opening chapter to has been as affixed on the book as I was when Danny Gleeson read it to us half a century ago.

I didn't see Danny Gleeson for a long time after leaving St Bede's: my sister-in-law used to babysit for him when he became head of art at De La Salle, a Catholic teacher training college near Rochdale, so I kept tabs on him. Later on he became head of art education in the Rochdale area and asked me to open an exhibition of his work in a gallery in the town. I have two pieces of his work that he gave me that night: one is a pencil and ink drawing of a street in Rochdale showing O'Brien's chippy, the other a beautiful piece of calligraphy – Tennyson's 'The Eagle' with a pen and ink illustration of an eagle at its head. We had a few drinks together after the opening and gnawed the lard more than somewhat about St Bede's, like two escapees from a POW camp. The last I heard of him he was living in the south of France, drinking fine wines and painting full time.

Daniel Gleeson was a teacher of rare talent who treated the boys under him with humanity, wit and warmth; Father William Coulthard, on the other hand, was a sadist of the first order. I note now that St Bede's awards a Father Coulthard Cup every year; I hope it commemorates a different Father Coulthard to the one I knew. The priest of that name that I remember once lifted a boy from the floor by his ears and smashed his face against the blackboard for getting a sum wrong. The boy was called Riley and was sitting next to me in class. His front teeth had been chipped in an accident when he was small and his dentist had covered them with tin caps, waiting until Riley had finished growing before finally capping them with ceramic. As Coulthard pushed Riley's face into the glass of the board (Bede's had frosted glass blackboards fixed to the wall), the tin caps on the lad's teeth were pushed in against the nerve and he fainted. Coulthard kicked him a couple of times as he lay there, telling him to get up, then when Riley came to he was dragged to his seat where he eventually recovered.

Coulthard was a short, thick-set man with thin lips and dark, hard eyes. I think a psychiatrist would have described him, without a second thought, as a psychopath. This may have been familial because his sister taught at Loreto Convent down the road from Bede's and, according to my wife, Pat, who was a pupil there at the same time that I was trying to tunnel out of Stalag St Bede's, Miss Coulthard was every bit as cruel and sadistic as her brother.

'Willie' Coulthard was sports master and had been, for some time, coach to various Manchester Catholic pole vaulters. I had no interest in team games at all and in either a rugby scrum or in wicket I was as much use as balls on a nun. Running, however, was something I was quite good at. One day Coulthard introduced us to the starting block.

Now, going off like a shot from the starting block is a fairly subtle art. You only have to watch Olympic sprinters ballsing it up time after time to realise how delicate it is. I wasn't very good at getting my balance right and knowing that Coulthard was watching me made me even clumsier. His idea of coaching me on a sprint start was quite interesting. He stood on the back of my hands in spiked running shoes and pressed down hard while telling me not to be a 'bleddy fool' and to get it right. A couple of days later I was one of the altar boys serving mass for him in the college chapel. He saw the marks on the back of my hand as I held the cruets of wine and water for him, but his face showed not a single trace of emotion.

He also took us for gym where his favourite punishment was making boys hang from the wall bars. The slightest offence would find you hanging from the topmost bars for ten or twenty minutes, heels well away from any support. After a few minutes it felt as though your arms were about to come out of their sockets; a burning pain would spread from your neck along your arms to your wrists and back up again. If your heels touched the lower bars for respite he kicked them off again with a sadistic snarl and if you dropped off the bars, you were made to get back on and do your time all over again. It was on such an occasion that Tony Green, a dark-haired imp of a boy and a natural comedian, found himself suspended between two others. After ten minutes of agony he turned to one of the flanking boys and said, 'This day thou shalt be with me in Paradise,' the words Christ uttered to one of the robbers crucified with him on Golgotha. All three boys howled with glee and fell off. Luckily the Man of God never found out the root cause of the hysteria and simply thrashed them and made them get back on the bars again, but Tony Green's wall-bar wit entered our canon – he quite rightly became a school legend.

Monsignor Duggan, while being as sick as Coulthard in his own peculiar way, was much more subtle. He was known as a fumbler of boys and as somebody who took great delight in getting boys to bend over while he beat their bare arses.

Nowadays St Bede's is another country: a co-ed school with girls, computers, compassion and bright lights – and flogging is verboten. In the foggy, inky-fingered 1950s, however, flogging, like physics and Greek, was regarded as an essential part of the curriculum and ranged from getting the standard six on the hand with the tawse to being forced to bend over the settee in the rector's study, trousers and underpants round the ankles, and take several on the bare backside. After the beating Duggan would stroke the victim's buttocks and rub himself up against him, telling him to be good in future. The beatings in themselves were rarely more painful than the lashings we got on our hands from the Prefect of Studies but the humiliation, the debasement and the feelings of violation of trust were terrible. When boys came out of the rector's study crying, it was often tears of shame and despair they were shedding rather than tears of physical pain.

I thought that he stopped short of buggering the boys in his study but there are court cases pending at the time of writing that indicate that this may not be true. If there is a Hell then I hope that Thomas Duggan, who preached so righteously and pompously what he never practised, is rotting in it. I have met a few evil people in my life, the truly evil I can count on the fingers of one hand. Duggan was one of them. If there had been any way in those far-off 1950s of measuring terror then the emotions boiling in that small corner of Manchester would have swung the needle off the dial.

Duggan left Bede's in a sudden rush (if not a cloud) long after I'd escaped his clutches. The story I heard was that he accused a boy of being a homosexual but picked the wrong lad; his father was a barrister, and a mover and shaker in the Knights of St Columba, the Catholic Mafia. Within days Duggan was slopping around in Langho, a parish in North Lancashire on the furthest extremes of the Salford diocese. When I confronted the safeguarding officer of the diocese with the story years later and asked him why Duggan had been put out to grass so quickly I was told it was due to 'ill health', which like 'wanting to spend more time with my family' ranks as one of the great excuses of all time. From head of one of the major Catholic colleges in the country to parish priest of a village most people haven't heard of seems a strange move, particularly when he would have been closer to medical treatment in Manchester than he would have been up there in Ribblesdale. The diocese handily keeps no records so, as Bishop Holland who made the decision is now dead, and since the truth seems to be well hidden, it's possible that we will never know the exact reason why the Scarlet Pimp from Hell so suddenly flew Bede's coop to a parish where (so I heard) the parishioners hated him.

I have tried to understand what drove Duggan but as yet I haven't reached either understanding or forgiveness. I don't believe people are born bad; something happened to Duggan that turned him into the man he was. But I only know the bare bones of his story: that he came from a traditional Lancashire-Irish Catholic family, went into the priesthood and after years of study at the English College in Rome was ordained and became a teaching priest. From there he seems to have taken various leaps up the clerical ladder to become first a monsignor and second a 'Prelate of the Domestic Household', a position of immense power. He did, however, teach me one thing, and that inadvertently: that most people in a position of authority or power are up to no good. Think about it: Jesus Christ said a great many wise things mostly while living the life of the people he moved amongst. The popes, cardinals, bishops and monsignors of the Catholic Church dress in the most extraordinary clothes, embroidered with gold thread and encrusted with precious stones, and live apart from the common herd. What this has to do with Jesus and his teachings is still completely beyond me.

I often wonder what some of the masters thought of it all. They came into the asylum each morning and were able to leave it each afternoon to go home to their families or their bedsits or whatever. Did they ever wonder at the lunacy of a man like Duggan being allowed to run a school? I suppose that Duggan had the whip hand (no pun) and that if he sacked them they would have had trouble finding another job.

Rhinemaidens and Irish Buglers

Monsignor Duggan was a martinet, oblivious to the real needs of the pupils in a rapidly changing post-war world. Latin and Greek were the bedrock of the syllabus and he ran the place like a minor public school at a time when the world had no more need of a school like that than a duck needs a handkerchief. French was the only foreign language offered (German was offered in the sixth form for scientists – Germany was going great guns in chemistry in them there days), while art and music were limited to one period of each a week and weren't offered to examination standard.

Music was even more neglected than art. Again the teacher, Gordon Frost, was a good and talented man, but all he did with our one hour of music a week was sit us in his dark old music room and play us stuff until the bell rang. He was a small, rounded man, not unlike Gerard Hoffnung to look at, and was a well-respected organist; but he had a jaded and slightly zany take on the affairs of St Bede's and, realising that having us forty boys for sixty minutes a week was not much grist to his musical mill, he gave up and either entertained us by bravely attacking a potentially explosive piano or tested us on the spelling of words like 'fugue', 'baroque' and 'rococo'. He had a high squeaky voice and an arid sense of humour and, being small, was all but invisible behind an enormous square grand piano, which he claimed had come off a ship and which had been made square to fit. He swore it was so overstrung that, 'it could explode at any time, catapulting me out of this classroom into Alexandra Park lake'.

For five years we boys waited for this to happen: for an almighty bang to send Mr Frost heavenwards in a shower-shroud of ivory, ebony keys and brass-wound piano strings. It never happened and as far as I know the square piano is still there, waiting to launch itself into eternity. When I was in the sixth form, Frosty took us for aesthetics and logic which were supposed to develop our minds but didn't do very much, though I can still remember the syllogism, 'All horses have four legs, a dog has four legs, therefore a dog is a horse.' Which is the kind of argument most politicians use when talking at us. I'm sure that like a lot of the masters he was driven slightly mad by the school which really had no place for Frosty other than as an accompanist.

Sadly I can only remember learning two pieces of music from Frosty and of those two things not much remains: one is a phrase from a German lieder called 'Die Laurelie' which is all about river maidens, or freshwater mermaids as biologists call them – sirens of the Rhine who used to sit half naked singing their songs and enticing German sailors to their deaths.

The other is a poem by Alfred Lord Tennyson, called 'The Splendour Falls', which Frosty set to music. The poem has some lines in it about a bugle being blown and echoing around some crags; it is a small part of *The Princess*, a long, rambling blank verse epic about a women's university where men have been forbidden to enter. I tried reading the whole thing but gave up. Life is too short. Years later, I interviewed John B. Keane, the Irish playwright and novelist, for the BBC and we got to talking about English writers who had been influenced by their travels in Ireland. He told me the poem was inspired by Moll's Gap in Killarney and that the bugle in the poem was a real one. During the Victorian era when English tourists visited Killarney for the 'picturesque and the sublime', they would take a pony and trap to Moll's Gap, that narrow defile in the mountains where the beetling crags no doubt brought on 'the vapours' amongst the ladies. There was a hovel in the gap which housed a local peasant who would come out, touch his cap respectfully and blow his bugle, sending multiple echoes bouncing round the crags in order to extract a few coppers from his audience. Apparently Tennyson had spent some time in Killarney and had witnessed the phenomenon.

I can still sing these lines for you if you meet me in the street. But that's all; five years of music with Frosty and all I've got for it is a verse about an Irish bugler and a few lines of a bloody German *volkslieder*. As somebody who would have loved to learn to read music I am more than a little miffed at the fact that St Bede's didn't have an orchestra and didn't offer tuition on any instrument – us potential musicians could obviously feck off, too. I've managed to teach myself to play a few instruments but I can't read music; to me the tadpoles on the wires are just that and only by dint of plod and determination can I begin to decipher them. Like art, music was treated as a Cinderella subject – until it came to the light operas of Gilbert and Sullivan or the warblings that went on to accompany school speech day.

Ah, those speech days! One of Frosty's tasks was to prepare a choir of young boys whose voices hadn't yet broken to sing at the speech day at Manchester's Free Trade Hall. He got us all to stand and sing 'We Three Kings' while he walked up and down between the desks listening to our voices. The tone deaf and the 'growlers' whose voices had well broken were tapped lightly on the shoulder as he walked by and all those thus marked sat out the choir practice reading comics instead of the set texts for English literature while the others got on with learning songs. And so every speech day, after the prizes had been handed out and the proud parents had clapped their little meritocrats, the boy sopranos sitting on the orchestra stalls would sing about freshwater mermaids and dying echoes as Duggan sat there smirking like a scarlet-bellied toad.

Rock and Roll Man!

My formal musical education had gone down the pan but informally I had begun taking a few baby steps. I listened to my first Lonnie Donegan records while playing snooker with my pal Kevin on a mini table next to the room where the dead bodies were laid out in his dad Bob's funeral parlour, and I knew immediately that this music was for me. *The Billy Cotton Band Show* went out of the window and 'Rock Island Line' came in. I turned into an active skiffler when Jimmy Hands loaned me his guitar and I discovered that I could play three chords on it fairly easily: C, F and G.

After a lot of mithering I got my mum and dad to go on the Saturday before my birthday to a music shop on Cheetham Hill Road to look at the guitars. It was a foul, rainy afternoon and the shop was just about to shut. The only guitar which was anything close to what I wanted was a Framus acoustic jazz-style guitar with 'F' holes like a fiddle instead of an 'O' hole in the middle; and that's what I ended up with. The guitar cost more than £14 and was roughly what Lou was earning per week at the time, something which has crossed my mind ever since on many an occasion.

The action (the height of the strings above the fingerboard) was too high and the strings were a heavy gauge but I persevered and with finger ends red raw I worked my way through the first few pages of the Bert Weedon *Play in a Day* book. Reading music was beyond me but I could cope with chord shapes and my ear told me what was right. My mum was really pleased when, after a day or two, I could mumble and play my way through 'Molly Malone' and 'Home on the Range'. She was a great fan of cowboy songs which, to be fair, did have good melodies and (added advantage to me) could mostly be accompanied using only three chords. I've spent most of my musical life reducing songs to three-chord versions and so far it seems to have worked. I was more than pleased when I came across the phrase 'three chords and the truth' and have used that as an excuse for my limited musical vocabulary ever since.

Fingers ragged and tonsils scarred, I persevered, practising for hours in our cold front room until I had three songs off by heart: 'Tom Dooley', 'Rock Island Line' and 'It Takes a Worried Man'. Jim Hands and Kenny Fullen could also knock a few chords out and from somewhere out of thin air they conjured up a very tall lad whose nickname was 'Ladybird' who could play the tea-chest bass. We never got to world-class standard but the Irk Valley Stompers did play at least one gig at a local youth club. We weren't very good but we weren't very bad either and I do remember that afterwards girls wanted to talk to us, which seemed to me a very good reason to keep on practising.

One of my favourite skiffle groups at that time was the Vipers, who had a big hit with 'Don't You Rock Me Daddy-O'. Little did I know it then, gentle reader, but many years later I would become great friends with Wally Whyton, lead singer of the Vipers, who was one of the best and kindest men I've met, and John Pilgrim, the washboard player anarchist and jazz authority who probably has more stories about the jazz and blues world than anybody I've ever known.

However, by the time I'd learned a fourth chord and all the words to 'Puttin' on the Style', skiffle was being pushed out of the nest by another cuckoo – rock and roll.

Rock Around the Clock was on at the Fourways Cinema in Moston and together with Pete Murphy, a school friend, I went to watch a middle-aged man with a kiss curl play rockabilly while his bass player lay on his bass fiddle and a saxophonist played a snorting riff lying on his back and, somewhere on the backline, a Hawaiian guitarist played an early version of a pedal steel guitar. Bill Haley and his Comets (I'm sure the Haley's Comet connection would have been lost on Middle America) were what passed for Alice Cooper in those days. There had been riots in some cinemas when Teddy Boys decided to dance in the aisles of the picture houses and met up with opposition from the men in uniform. In one cinema in Manchester, Teddy Boys turned fire hoses on the killjoy commissionaires and police, which must be the first time rioters have ever turned water cannons on the Law.

There were no riots in the Fourways; a couple of Teds did get up to dance with their birds but they sat down again when the usherette shone her torch on them and told them to stop it or their mothers would find out. But in spite of the lack of riots, Pete and I were both thrilled by the film and agreed that rock and roll was where we were headed. Interestingly, the song itself almost never was: history tells us that Bill and his boys set off for the recording session and got stuck on a sandbar when the ferry that was taking them to New York ran aground. If they'd been stuck for a few hours longer the song would never have been recorded and the world might have been a different place.

Ironically, while searching the music archives for my internet folk show recently I came across an American CD called Yodelin' Crazy, dedicated entirely to yodelling songs (don't ask – I just do these things) and discovered that, before he became a famous rockabilly singer, our Bill made a bid for fame as a yodeller and has two tracks on the compilation: 'Yodel Your Blues Away' and the even more unlikely 'Yodeler's Lullaby'.

A Priest in a Bubble Car

But rock and roll was only a distant distraction from the daily terrors of St Bede's. I am often asked why sadists and perverts like Duggan and Coulthard weren't reported, why children didn't tell their parents that a priest had felt them up or slapped them in the face so hard that their nose had bled. The answer, I suppose, is that we regarded it as normal; without anybody to tell us otherwise we assumed that grown-ups could pretty much do what they liked to you. Another reason is that children, in those days, didn't tell. I suppose we felt that they wouldn't believe us if we told them about the sexual abuse, and as for the physical abuse – it was assumed at home that, if you got a whack, you probably deserved it and more likely than not your dad would give you another hiding for getting a hiding. So children tended to suffer in silence, hardly finding the terror and the shame and the unhappiness in the least bit remarkable.

There were exceptions of course; there were gentle priests who genuinely cared about the boys and who did see them as children of God. Father O'Connor (Coco) was one such, a gentle but firm man who was sincere and caring in all his dealings with the boys; Father Rigby was another, a handsome young man with a crew-cut who I believe had a genuine affection for the boys and who loved teaching. And then there was 'Pag' – Father Pasagno. He came from Manchester's Italian community; the family sold ice cream from brightly painted horse-drawn carts and Pag had the easy, affectionate and slightly fatalistic temperament of his Mediterranean forebears. I was once sent to him for a beating for something really evil I had done (failing to produce my homework on time or some such). I knocked on the door of the Prefect of Studies room (the Prefect of Studies' main job was beating boys – Pag covered for him on a Monday).

'Come in.'

I did. Pag was reading a confiscated *Wizard* comic. Without looking up he asked, 'What are you here for, Harding?' I told him.

'How many were you told to ask for?'

'Six, Father.'

'Hold out your hand.'

I did. He opened the drawer and, still reading the comic, took out the leather tawse (they were still in school supply catalogues in the 1970s). Then, without looking up, he gave the desk six very hard lashes and said, 'Go back and tell him it hurt.'

My hero.

Other priests who strutted and fretted their hours upon the stage of our boyhoods were Father Riley (nickname Eggo – with his long neck and bald head he looked a little like the ostrich of that name in the *Beano*) who was an ex-Church of England vicar, and Father Hamilton (Hambone), who taught us English for a term. There was Father Hanlon, a gentle priest who took us occasionally for English and his best friend, a man who more than anybody else was responsible for me becoming a writer, Father Augustus Reynolds (nickname 'Foxy' – Reynolds = Reynard = fox). I will speak more of him later.

I mentioned Father (Alfie) Hynes earlier. He was a character, too, in his own strange way. He took us for physics up to O level and was a good teacher, even if he did have the unwholesome habit of whacking any boy who didn't know his Boyle's Law from his Wheatstone bridge with a length of rubber bunsen burner tubing. He also liked to make such boys kneel up on the lab benches while he stood behind them and pressed down on their heels, thus bringing their shins into contact with the hard edge of the bench. While hardly rating alongside the stuff doled out in Abu Ghraib or Guantanamo it still isn't quite the sort of thing an ordained priest should get up to and I was not surprised to hear, a few years later, that he had left the priesthood, got married and was teaching at a non-Catholic grammar school north of the city.

During his time at Bede's he did get up the noses of a few of the older lads, particularly the boarders who bridled at his unsportsmanlike use of disguise (milkman, baker, postman etc) to catch them in wrongdoing while out of school. When he couldn't borrow the milkman's float, Alf often cruised the streets in his bubble car. I think it was a Heinkel (Father Hynes' Heinkel does have a certain ring to it) but it might have been a Messerschmitt; whatever it was, one night it was lifted from its parking spot by eight big lads from the College First Fifteen and was carried out of school and across the shallow waters of the lake in Alexandra Park to the island and dumped there. Apparently it was one of the masters in the Senior Common Room who noticed it the next morning. Coffee in one hand, cigarette in the other, he looked out of the window and across the lake and commented idly to the other masters, 'You know, that looks like Father Hynes' bubble car over there in the lake.' The car was brought back, but only with some difficulty. *Sic transit carrus magister.*

The Isle of Levant

By the time I was fourteen my faith was going down the plughole faster than a baby's bathwater. Innocent heavy petting sessions with various girls had laid more black sins down on my soul, which in any case was already damned after my earlier bad confession. Although half of me (the half below the navel) didn't believe God would damn me for all eternity if he really knew the circumstances.

I was palling out at the time with a lad called Lawrence Wood who lived in one of the big houses on Crescent Road near St Anne's church. I loved going to his house because they had a huge AGA stove in the kitchen and his mum and dad made real coffee and big pans of delicious stew. Lawrence's mum was a teacher while his dad was something in insurance and was one of the most interesting men I've ever met. He had a photographic memory; you could take down any book from the shelves in his library, open it at random, read the opening line and he would carry on reciting the rest of the text from memory.

The family were all talented musicians (in fact Lawrence and his brother Chris went on to play in the Hallé Orchestra) and they decamped to Scotland every summer to one of the western isles, Rùm I think it was, driving all the way in Mr Wood's battered old car. I loved the faint whiff of eccentricity in the Wood's house and I liked it that they accepted me for what I was. I suppose they were middle class but not in a stuffy 'Little Englander' way, they were too Bohemian for that.

Lawrence and I were going around with a couple of girls from North Manchester Girls' School, we were still far from going the whole way but were getting further than we did with the girls from Notre Dame. Snogging and light to heavy petting in the ABC Cinema was about the length of it. My girlfriend wore circle-stitched bras and seemed quite well busted until one night when we were snogging I found a loose bit of cotton which I pulled and which turned into a long string of cotton wool. Collapse of bra was followed by slap to side of my head.

It was not long after that incident that Lawrence and I saw our first nudist film. I assume we lied about our age to get in. The film was an X certificate, which, from 1951 until 1970, meant that you had to be over sixteen to watch it. Since both of us were fourteen and strangers to the razor, I reckon we only got away with it because the people who owned the Globe Cinema needed all the money they could get and weren't bothered whether we were six, sixteen or sixty-six just so long as we shoved our ninepence under the glass and didn't set fire to the seats, as some of the clientele were wont to do when they got bored. However it was, we found ourselves walking out of a miserable late winter's night into the smoky, damp fug of a cinema that tonight was filled only with men. Every one of them had queued up, bought Murray mints and Woodbines and were now waiting for the reels to roll of what was probably one of the worst films ever made. It had no plot to speak of, wooden acting, bad camera work and even worse directing. Its sole redeeming feature was that it was full of naked women.

As far as we were concerned it could have been a film about yak herding in Outer Mongolia or wooden spoon carving on Benbecula; providing it had bare-naked ladies in it, Lawrence and I would have been there with our tanners melting in our grubby hot teenage mitts. Neither of us had ever seen a real bare-naked lady before, and since school rumour had it that the film was full of them, we were in like Flynn.

To the old blokes there it must have been as much an act of remembering as anything else: the firm young bodies, the large breasts, the slim bellies, all that nubile nakedness – who knows what memories the film was stirring in the flat-capped fraternity behind us. To me and Lawrence, however, this was no journey into the remote past but a voyage into a Terra Completely Incognita. The groans of lust and the rustling of macs that filled the cinema were not echoed by the two virgins on the front row who were speechless and, at least in my case, turgid and half-unconscious with lust.

The plot was flimsy and centered, if I remember it right, round two pretty girls going to a nudist camp on an island for the first time. They were shy at first (of course) but rapidly got into the swing of things (of course) and were soon bouncing beach balls about and skinny-dipping with the best of them. There were plenty of bosoms but no fuzz (fuzz was banned by the Lord Chancellor) but for two boys who could still go dizzy looking at pictures of women modelling bras in the Littlewoods Catalogue, *The Isle of Levant* was Eldorado.

Even now I can remember the feeling of total disbelief when the girls arrived on the island, went into their chalet and simply took their clothes off before the camera. They slipped off their tops and bottoms and, while we were still catching our breath at the sight of them in their underwear, took off the rest of their kit. And there they stood, towels folded over their arms but with their firm jaunty breasts jiggling firmly and jauntily with every movement. (We didn't know that breasts jiggled.)

Was it as simple as that, we wondered? Women just took their clothes off? They didn't always do a strip tease? For the last tumescent months of our raging puberty we had all been convinced that only marriage, a lot of money or a state of temporary lunacy would induce a girl to show you her bits, and there they were getting them out as though they were going down the greengrocer's for five pounds of spuds. These feelings of amazement lasted at least a tenth of a nanosecond before being replaced by feelings of rabid lust, and soon our fourteen-year-old lungs were wheezing as noisily as those of all the old codgers in the raincoats that filled the darkness behind us.

There were groans coming from somewhere in the heart of that darkness, pitiful inhuman sounds conjured up from some primordial night and probably akin to that uttered by Neanderthal Man during the rutting season. It wasn't me or Lawrence; we were too busy trying to remember how to breathe. I was not to hear that noise again until years later on the night boat from Liverpool to Dublin. There were a number of heifers below deck, destined for the abattoir, and, as the ship tossed and pitched in the middle of the Irish Sea, the sea-sick heifers started to lament. It was an echo of those macintoshed Neanderthals in the Cheetham Hill bug hut.

To kids growing up today, this would all seem fairly strange. In a world where near nudity is pretty normal both on TV and the beach, and where no road digger's tea break is complete without Page 3 of the *Sun* being passed around for aesthetic appraisal, the thought of two raddled, angst-ridden Catholic boys wriggling in tormented lust at the sight of a few pairs of jiggling bosoms must seem very odd. But let me tell you, in a world where liberty bodices and cardigans were *de rigueur* and where girls, on the eleventy-ninth date, might just let you touch them 'on top and outside', the Globe Cinema on that glum winter's night was our Garden of Earthly Delights. In fact, some of the old geezers behind us would not have looked out of place in a Hieronymus Bosch triptych.

Film over, we shuffled out with the raincoat brigade, nobody making eye contact, and with slowly subsiding erections Lawrence and I somehow managed to walk as far as the Clarendon Road chippy where we bought chips to take our minds off those acres of naked flesh. The chippy was run by a gay couple who always seemed jolly and homely and were as camp as a jamboree. One was tall with glasses and thinning hair combed across his dome, the other shorter with a round smiley face. The short one seemed to do most of the running about: chipping the potatoes, bringing in the lard and making the batter. They kept up a constant stream of witty banter both between themselves and their customers.

'Ooh! Look what the cat's dragged in,' as we walked in the door.

'I'll shoot that cat if he keeps bringing in stuff like that.'

'What you 'avin', gentlemen?'

'Bag of chips twice, please.'

'I heard you the first time.'

'Where've you been tonight then? Tripping the light fantastic at the Palais de Dance?'

'No, we've been to the Bug Hut.'

'Oooh! You pair of rips. Eee, they've been to see that naughty nudist film!'

'I'd rather watch paint dry. Some things are better covered up.'

I have tried since to find that film (purely in the spirit of research you understand) and have failed. I believe however that it was made by Edward Craven Walker, a World War Two Squadron Commander and brave flying ace who flew sorties in unarmed Mosquitoes, taking aerial reconnaissance photographs over Germany. A lifelong naturist who was married four times, Walker also invented the lava lamp. His films were the first nudist films to be shown in British cinemas, mostly because he managed to avoid showing any pubic hair. He is no longer with us but if he was I would tell him that I got far more out of watching his film than I ever got out of watching a lava lamp.

Gilbert and Sullivan

Don't tell me that they wrote good melodies and clever lyrics, don't tell me that they are the finest examples of English light operetta – I would rather be chased by a randy cardinal round the Vatican for a year and a day than have to listen to a single note of those damn D'Oyly Carte/Savoy Opera offerings ever again. According to Wikipedia, Giblets and Solomon created a world where '… fairies rub elbows with British lords, flirting is a capital offence, gondoliers ascend to the monarchy, and pirates turn out to be noblemen who have gone wrong.' Well, we had no pirates or fairies in St Bede's (as far as I know) but the topsy-turvy world the operettas were supposed to represent might indeed have been seen as a twisted metaphor for the lunatic, non-singing and very un-comic parallel universe we inhabited.

Once a year in the lunatic asylum that was Bede's gulag, the school put on a performance of something by Gilbert and Sullivan. Thankfully my voice, though it was deep, wasn't tuneful enough for any of the male parts nor was I pretty enough for any of the female parts so I was excluded from performing. We were, however, expected to turn up as the paying audience and a dim view was taken of any boy that didn't buy at least one ticket. By the time I was sixteen I had worked out that by buying my mum a ticket, taking her to her seat then telling her I'd go and sit with my mates, I could slip out the back, go to the pub, down a couple of pints and be back for the final curtain.

Unfortunately it took me five years to work out that particular scam so I had to endure five of the Savoy Opera's finest offerings. I can only remember four of them: *Iolanthe*, *The Yeomen of the Guard*, *The Pirates of Penzance* and *The Mikado* so perhaps I got out of the fifth (*The Gondoliers*?) by shooting myself in the foot or arranging for a gang of hoodlums to kidnap me: I don't remember.

But how I hated the whole damn performance. Unlike some of my friends, I took no pleasure in laughing at our schoolmates in frocks, I just regarded the whole thing as a charade, as some kind of strange Catholic torture even worse than high mass or benediction.

Who were these people that guffawed and clapped and cheered such rubbish? Why did they applaud that dismal and inept bunch of gauche actors who staggered their way through three hours of Victorian yo ho ho? The answer I suppose must be twofold: firstly, their beloveds were often in it (since Gilbert and Sullivan allows you to fill the stage with lots of singing extras, a good lump of the school was up there, powdered, wigged and prancing) and secondly, at a time when *Chips with Everything*, *The Quare Fellow* and *Look Back in Anger* were taking the West End by the scruff of the neck and giving it a well-deserved kicking, it was nice to know that there was something safe and jolly and wholesome on offer at the former Manchester Aquarium.

The priests loved it, of course, because whether they fancied young boys or young girls their tastes were well catered for – well, sort of.

The smallest and youngest of the boys were dressed as girls and, with cotton-wool bosoms and a thick crust of Leichner No 7 stage make-up, they primped and pranced, yodelled and tra la la-ed their way across the stage, looking as though they wouldn't be out of place in Hogarth's *The Rake's Progress*.

As if being dressed as a girl or a fairy wasn't bad enough, they were then made to sing such gems as 'Tripping Hither, Tripping Thither' or were dressed in kimonos, given names like Yum-Yum, Peep-Bo, Pitti-Sing and expected to sing songs like 'Three Little Maids from School Are We'. One such unfortunate (though I think he quite enjoyed it at the time) was Colin Baker, who went on to become the sixth incarnation of The Doctor in the long-running science fiction television series, *Doctor Who*. I remember him very well from my school years; he was a year older than me and seemed to spend much of his time swanning round the school in a very thespian manner. It was obvious even then he had talent in spades.

The scenery was painted by the groundsman who looked after our playing fields and was the most impressive thing about the performances. With a few pots of paint and a damn good eye, the man who drove the mower and linseed-oiled the cricket bats managed to turn flat canvases and paint into Cornwall, the Tower of London, Titipu and Fairyland. The lights weren't bad either so I have to concede that in terms of staging the school did well. The 'orchestra', however, was Frosty on an upright piano.

Let me take you to one special night in operatic life of St Bede's. We have all been ushered in, it is a full house and we are sitting on hard seats waiting for the show to begin. Frosty is at the piano playing the overture; there are the assembled parents and dutiful siblings and there, sitting in row three, is a very pretty girl called Sheila.

I have got over it now, but there was a period when I thought Sheila was the most beautiful girl in the world. She went to Loreto and took the same bus home as me: the 62 to Heaton Park. She was very pretty, with a thick pigtail and a bosom. My chatting-up routine was pretty bad and I don't think she was inspired much by my pulling her pigtail as a kind of foreplay. However, her brother was at Bede's in the year above me, and one day he told me that

Sheila and their parents were coming with him to the opera. I girded my loins, gritted my teeth, sponged the mud and sago off my school uniform and, with a ticket in my hand and a few bob in my pocket, I set off for the aquarium. I didn't actually manage to sit with Sheila but I did talk to her in the interval and ask her if I could get her anything by way of refreshment.

Yes, she said, she would like some Turkish Delight.

That box of Turkish Delight cost me everything I had, she ate it all without offering me a single piece and, as I began my long walk home through the drizzly night, she and her parents passed me in their warm car heading homewards; they could have dropped me off en route but I expect the thought never crossed their mind.

I could wring more pathos out of this by telling you that their limousine went through a puddle and the bow wave drenched me but it wouldn't be true. However, I did have to walk home through the rain for two hours and the soaking I got that night, the spurned love and the bloody jangly piano, together with the caterwauling and braying parents, may have played some part in steering me away from Gilbert and Sullivan towards Lonnie Donegan, Little Richard and Chuck Berry. You can stuff your Titipu and Yum Yum, give me 'Memphis, Tennessee' and 'Long Tall Sally' any old day.

The Genius in the Attic

It was about this time that I began to pal out with a boy who was in the year above me at Bede's called David Doyle. We chatted one morning on the bus and had found that, as well as both playing the guitar, we were both interested in building radios and messing with stuff. He had a twin brother called Peter who went on to become a lecturer in Russian at Manchester University, and an older brother called Bernard who ended up as treasurer for the SDP. Their mum was the headmistress of a secondary school in Salford and their dad, like Lol Wood's father, was something to do with insurance. They lived in one of the fine, tall Edwardian buildings along Oak Road and I have two vivid mental images of this house: one is a typical frosty morning when I called for Dave on our way to school and stood in the kitchen while he got his stuff together, subliminally registering the smells of coffee and toast and the sound of Jack de Manio on the radio. I can still clearly picture Mrs Doyle, 'Marsie' or 'the Old Trout' the boys called her, making sure Dave had everything for the day. Memory is a strange thing.

The second thing I remember about that big old house is Dave's attic room. It was under the rafters, had one window and a sloping roof and always smelt of flux and hot wax from the solder and the radio sets he built. We would sit there for hours nattering away, but we didn't just talk diodes and superhets like the boffins we were, we also talked about books we had both read and it was Dave who first introduced me to the short stories of H. G. Wells and the adventures of Sherlock Holmes. We also talked about girls because both of us had begun to take a real interest in the local lasses who gathered in Crumpsall Park of an evening after school.

When the spring finally arrived, our young men's fancies turned and we began to spend more time in the park and less time bent over melting solder, because some of the girls there were far more interesting than microfarads and ferrite rods.

As the evenings grew longer and summer finally came, we got our bikes out after school and cycled away from Crumpsall out into what was left of the Lancashire countryside beyond Heaton Park. Then the land between Heaton Park and Heywood was beautiful, unspoiled, rolling countryside with small dairy farms, hedges, brooks, wooden fences and quiet country lanes. We would take art pads and pencils with us and sketch anything that took our fancy and we would leave our bikes outside the Three Arrows pub while Dave, who looked older than me, would go in and buy us an underage half of bitter shandy each. If Marsie had found out he would have been unable to sit on his bike saddle for some time to come.

It was hard to believe that we were only a few miles from the city centre with the smell of summer grass and flowers, the wide, open country and the ancient farms. I remember us stopping on more than a few occasions at a farm somewhere in the middle of all this where the farmer's wife would sell us a glass of warm milk, fresh from the cow, for threepence.

I was fourteen and Dave was fifteen the summer we went off on our bikes on a cycling holiday, youth hostelling in the Yorkshire Dales. I had never had a family holiday and apart from camping trips with the boy scouts had never been further than Blackpool or Llandudno; now I was off on an adventure to the wilds of that there Yorkshire.

Dave had a Dawes Lincoln Imp bike with ten-speed derailleur gears, I had a Phillips bike, made in Birmingham, all my mum and Lou could afford. It had been converted from a sensible sit-up and beg affair to a 'racer' when the man at the shop, at my asking, put a pair of drop handlebars on it to try to make it look more like a sporting model. It fooled nobody. It was heavy and sluggish with a three-speed Sturmey Archer hub and riding it was like pedalling a clothes mangle. We had no panniers and somehow managed to pack everything we needed for our ten days away into our saddle bags and so, with a couple of one-inch Ordnance Survey maps, enough money for our hostel fees and just a bit more to feed ourselves, we set off.

We cycled north through a cool summer morning through Prestwich and Whitefield to Bury where it was Wakes Week, the annual cotton town holiday. Wakes happened all over Lancashire during the summer months. Everything would shut and everybody went to Blackpool so the mill boilers could be serviced and scaled, and the weavers and spinners could get enough fresh air to keep them going for another year without 'popping their clogs'. We stopped in Bury to fill our water bottles at a civic fountain. I had never seen a cotton town during a Wakes Week before; it was so still and empty that I expected tumbleweed to roll through the streets and saloon doors to swing in the breeze; the only moving things were the hands on the floral clock.

From Bury we headed north through Haslingden and Accrington, two more of King Cotton's towns, then climbed the Whalley road over the flanks of Pendle Hill to wheel down into the Ribble Valley, heading for Long Preston via Clitheroe and Gisburn. The sun shone, our wheels whirred, and beyond Long Preston the verges were full of butterbur and cow parsley. I remember us stopping in Settle for a drink from our water bottles. It was late afternoon by now and the local girls' grammar school was turning out. We sat on the bridge over the Ribble, slack-mouthed at the stream of fine Yorkshire lasses who went past us, laughing and swinging their schoolbags. I know that we were easily impressed but there was something about that constant stream of good-looking girls that seemed extraordinary. Afterwards we cycled on in a more reflective mood towards our bed for the night at Stainforth Youth Hostel.

The hostel had once been an old country manor house called Taitlands, square-fronted and built in the Greek Revival style by a wealthy local, Thomas Joseph Redmayne. It smelt of Calor gas from the kitchens, Dubbin from the hikers' boots and sweat from the cyclists. Dave and I were in a bunk room with iron bedsteads and nothing but a couple of wool blankets to sleep under. We had brought sheet sleeping bags (as per the YHA rules) and after we'd set our beds up we went to the kitchen to cook our food. We had called at the post office in Stainforth and found enough cheap food to keep two Manchester schoolboys alive for a few days. We bought skinless sausages, margarine, eggs, bread and a thing called Sunny Spread, which was supposed to have been a kind of ersatz honey. We reckoned that it was nothing but sugar, water, thickener and bee farts.

The ten days we spent cycling around the Dales were amongst the best days of my teenage years. It rained for just one day, when we were heading over to Thorpe and got there drenched even though we were wearing capes. The rest of the time the sun shone, we climbed the hills, swam in the rivers and chatted up the local girls.

This didn't always go well. In fact on the day we climbed Pen-y-ghent I came close to murder. We cycled from Stainforth to Helwith Bridge, left our bikes at the roadside and followed the bridleway of Long Lane to the hill's flanks. The scramble up the 'neb end' was great fun in the hot sunshine and we were soon over the summit and looking for somewhere to eat our sandwiches before the descent by the old miners' track. On the edge of the gritstone cliffs we saw two girls sitting eating their lunch and, thinking they might be in need of the company of two of Crumpsall's finest, we walked to the cliff edge and sat beside them. They had new Black's framed rucksacks and proper hiking boots. Dave had his big brother's old boots and I had a pair of army boots Uncle Len had found in his garage. They had proper hiking shorts and shirts; we had gym shorts and T-shirts. They had packed lunches from the Crown at Horton, consisting of chicken legs, Mars bars, apples, cheese sandwiches and bottles of ginger beer – the whole Enid Blyton Famous Five picnic lunch. We had Sunny Spread bee-fart sandwiches (Captain Bee Fart – what a great name for a rock singer!) and watery lemon squash. We munched our way in silence through the bee farts and white sliced bread while they chewed on their big chicken drumsticks and took great slurps of ginger beer. I have never come so close to pushing somebody off a cliff.

That afternoon we joined a gang of locals about our own age who were jumping off the riverbank into Stainforth Foss. There were some really good-looking girls in amongst them so donning our swimming togs we joined in. I go fishing there now and, looking at the drop and the savage waterfall of the foss, often think that testosterone must have rendered us slightly mad.

From Stainforth we went to Aysgarth, where we chuckled at the gravestone of Fanny Botting, then on to Kettlewell where we swam in the river and chatted up some local lasses until their red-faced tree-stump-fisted boyfriends arrived, then eventually – days later – we spent our last night at Burley Woodhead YHA. The next day we made it back to Manchester in one long push and the morning after that I was back on my paper round morning and evening and delivering groceries on a butcher's bike for the Maypole Dairy in between.

Dave was a bit of a genius, of that I have not the slightest doubt. He had a brain as big as a city and could do almost anything, it seemed. His little workshop in the attic at the top of the house smelt of meths and steam as well as flux because – not content with having his own radio lab – he had also made a working steam engine with a boiler and pistons that could drive a stationary power wheel. He had bought all the pipes and brassware and had cut and filed and soldered everything himself, building the whole thing from the ground up.

While I was still struggling with the idea of how diodes and ferrite rods worked to transmute the gibberish of the airwaves into something that emerged in our headphones as The Goons and Radio Luxembourg, he had already moved on to transistors and was making portable radios that could actually fit in your pocket. He was also making valve amplifiers, buying aluminium chassis and drilling them out to take all the gubbins needed to make something that would mean that our guitars could play proper rock and roll. The amps he built worked really well and he even managed to get hold of a circuit diagram for an amp that incorporated a tremolo effect. This was *de rigueur* for the 'big guitars from Texas' sound that we need for Duane Eddy tunes like 'Forty Miles of Bad Road', 'Shazam!', 'Ghostrider' and 'Three-30 Blues', all of which were in our repertoire.

Armed with one of Dave's amps, we got ourselves a booking at Crumpsall Tennis Club. I don't remember much about that booking; we had no bass and drums so it was just Dave on rhythm and me on lead and we belted out what Shadows, Duane Eddy and Lonnie Donegan stuff we knew while some girls in dirndl skirts jived to the music. I don't remember us getting paid but I do remember getting a snog on the way home from one of the girls so I saw that there might be a future after all in three chords and an attitude. We were promised a repeat gig by the spotty herbert who had booked us. I'm still waiting.

CHAPTER 7

THE BEAT GROUP NAMED AFTER A SHOE SHOP

Somehow, word had spread around the local rock groups about Dave Doyle, the electronics boffin who could make and repair radios and guitar amps, and Dave soon found himself fixing amplifiers for some of the local guitarists.

One of the bands he did this for was a Crumpsall group called the Stylos. Their lead guitarist had left and they were looking for a replacement; Dave told them that I played a bit and not long after our glorious triumph at the Crumpsall Tennis Club I was at home one summer evening when my mother told me there was somebody at the door who wanted to see me. A slim lad a bit older than me sporting a large quiff and wearing a Gurney Slade raincoat was stood outside in the sunshine.

He said his name was Tony Lowe and that he was in a rock and roll band that was looking for a lead guitarist. Would I be interested in joining?

I said yes, but quietly so my mum didn't hear. I had O levels coming up and rock and roll and exams never have and never will be good bedfellows.

That evening I went round to a semi-detached house in Balliol Street, a small cul-de-sac near Cheetham Hill, knocked on the door and walked into the world of rock and roll.

My mum had made me a canvas carrying case for the guitar I had then: a Hofner Colorama, a truly horrible guitar but the only one my folks could afford. It was covered in gold plastic so it looked like a piece of one of those glitzy corner bars that people used to put in their homes in those days complete with bullfighting poster and straw-covered bottle of Chianti. It sounded like a corner bar, too.

I'd managed to make myself a tremolo bar from an old Morse

tapper and though it looked ridiculous it did work and on a fair day, with a passing wind, I could play a version of Duane Eddy's 'Three-30 Blues' that didn't sound too bad. At the time I had no amplifier and while practising at home had to plug the guitar into the back of the radio using the gramophone socket. The result wasn't good and every so often the Light Service would break through, and 'Rebel Rouser' would segue into *Journey into Space*, but for rough workouts of tunes it was just passable.

In Tony's front room I plugged into his amp and with him playing rhythm guitar on a Guyatone (collectors' items nowadays, folks!), I went through my repertoire of Duane Eddy and Shadows imitations. The audition/practice was watched over by Tony's older brother, Roy, bass player in the group, and after a couple of songs, having proved I knew at least four chords, could keep reasonable time and could rock a bit, I was accepted as a probationary member of Cheetham Hill's finest rock and roll band, the Stylos. The group was named after a shoe shop (good job they hadn't picked Freeman, Hardy and Willis) and was becoming quite popular in the area.

Tony worked as a carpet fitter, Roy was a clerk in a firm called Jabez Clegg which I think had something to do with cotton – if it didn't, with a name like that it should have. Tony was a year older than me at sixteen and Roy was a year or two older again.

After the audition their mum, Jean, came in with a plate of sandwiches and a pot of tea. The sandwiches were magnificent: thick brown bread and ham and tomatoes with plenty of butter. Then their dad, Joe, came in. He was the man for whom the word 'dapper' was invented. Always smart-looking and always full of fun he was a travelling salesman for Masco Felts, a big manufacturer in Bury, and like all travelling salesmen in those days he had a fund of jokes which he added to every time he went away. When firms had travelling salesmen out on the road they would put them up each night in a commercial hotel and the salesmen used to meet each other in the bar after dinner and tell jokes. A daft story could be invented in Inverness on a Monday and be in St Ives by the Friday. I can still remember one of his jokes; in fact I used it on stage for a while because it is so beautifully daft.

Two snakes in Belle Vue Zoo, Jim and Fred, are talking one day and Jim asks Fred:

'Fred, are we them kind of snakes what if you bite somebody they go purple then black and fall over, or are we them other types what wrap themselves round someone and squeeze them and squeeze them 'till their eyes pop out?'

And Fred says, 'I don't know, why?'

And Jim says, 'I've just bit me tongue.'

The Stylos had a residency in a pub called the Dover Castle in a small side street off Waterloo Road, close enough to the Salford border to be in bandit country.

That first Saturday, on my first paid gig, I took the number 7 bus to Hightown on a warm, late summer evening, still hot from the day of sun; children were playing in the street, old men sat out on chairs smoking pipes and women sat on doorsteps gossiping. The Dover Castle was a traditional Edwardian pub, quite small but with a loyal local clientele. I walked through the door and into the lounge. Roy and Tony were there setting up the gear and with them were the two other members of the band: Les (Happy) Harris, the drummer, about my height and wearing thick black glasses, and Dicky Dobbs, the singer, tall and skinny with slightly buck teeth and a Tony Curtis haircut.

Les was a curly-haired lad about sixteen years old from the council flats near Strangeways Prison. He was an optical mechanic and one of the first things he did was turn my NHS goggles into a pair of Buddy Holly black-rimmed specs. Happy was a forthright lad whose catchphrases ranged from 'Stroll on!' (said when amazed) to 'Fucking stroll on!' and who gave me my nickname after he saw me puffing away on a ten and sixpenny pipe.

I had decided that if I was going to be a real intellectual I had to smoke a pipe. Not just any old straight pipe like my Uncle Bobby smoked, I wanted a long curly pipe like all intellectuals smoked. Hughie Jones, my trombone-playing school pal, smoked a pipe and I partly blame him for my making such a prat of myself. I was hoping to get a Peterson of Dublin 'Bent' but they were far too expensive so I got a long weird curly pipe and the cheapest of the thick twist tobaccos they had. I knew my mother would kill me if she thought I smoked (even though our house had always been filled with a cloud of tobacco smoke from her and Lou and Aunty Julia's constant sucking at their 'coffin nails'), so I decided to go for a walk and fire my pipe up away from the house where nobody would see me. After my tea I chopped up the twist, grinding it in the palm of my hand just like I'd seen the old-timers do at the bowling green in the park, and set off for the hospital fields. Once away from the house I struck a match and lit the pipe. In my school blazer, looking every inch the arse I was, I puffed earnestly away at the thick twist, sucking in great clouds of tobacco smoke.

The dizziness hit me first followed very closely by nausea. Luckily there were some rhododendron bushes at the roadside. Any passers by would have seen a schoolboy with his head stuck in the bushes emitting low moans as he said a second hello to his cold tripe salad.

A couple of days later I got a small tin of Balkan Sobranie which was nowhere near as toxic and managed to take small puffs of that without falling down. When I lit my pipe in the Dover Castle that Saturday, Happy nearly fell off his drumstool laughing.

'Bloody stroll on – it's Sherlock Holmes!'

The nickname 'Sherlock' stuck with me for a good few years after.

Dicky Dobbs, our singer, was a skinny gangly lad but he could sing like a demon. He had to be careful when he was singing though because his top two front teeth were on a plate, and when he got excited, as he often did when he was giving a song some welly, his teeth would launch themselves into the audience. It wasn't too bad if they landed in somebody's lap or in the ashtray but on the odd occasion when they landed in somebody's beer we would find ourselves in trouble. Beer was serious stuff in Salford.

The story was told of a bloke in Salford who had a glass eye that he used to leave in his pint when he went for a Jimmy Riddle to put off any potential beer bandits. One night while he was in the khazi, a local beer heister downed his pint in one, swallowing the glass eye with it. The glass eye caused a blockage and after a few weeks of constipation the beer thief went to see his doctor who told him to drop his strides and bend over.

The doctor took his speculum, switched on his headlamp and, peering up the gentleman's anus, saw an eye staring back at him.

'We really are going to have to learn to trust one another,' the doctor said.

Actually, thinking about it, I heard that tale from Joe Lowe so it may well be apocryphal.

Dicky was a great fan of Emile Ford and The Checkmates and knew all his stuff: 'That Lucky Old Sun', 'On a Slow Boat to China', 'What Do You Want to Make Those Eyes at Me for?' and normally when singing these his teeth would stay in position. Chuck Berry and Little Richard were a different kettle of fish, though, and 'Good Golly Miss Molly' or 'Johnny B Goode' would often be accompanied by the flight of the dentures.

There was no podium or bandstand in the Dover Castle. Happy's kit was set up in the corner and the amps stacked behind, leaving just enough room for the four of us to back up Dicky as he strutted his stuff. The summer's evening was winding down and the pub took on a golden glow, the etched glass, Britannia tables and long mahogany bar all typical of a northern pub of its day. As we waited for the punters to arrive, Roy went to the bar to get the drinks. I was only fifteen and beyond a nip of sherry at family parties had little experience of alcohol. Roy put a half of Wilson's bitter in front of me. At the age of fifteen I was now a real rock and roller.

Fortunately for me, the landlady, Mrs Dwyer, turned a blind eye for once. Strong Irishwomen (most of them are) have featured large in my life; my Aunty Kitty was a feisty woman with her own views on everything, and my nanna was probably one of the strongest people I had ever met – but they paled alongside Mrs Dwyer. Mrs D was a tall, flame-haired, well-boned lady, not fat but what an old Irish navvy I once knew called 'a fine big agricultural girl'. If she were your friend she would defend you to the death but if you crossed her – well, several perfect Acts of Contrition might be needed. She ran a great pub, and could pull pints, order her staff around, watch the till and bar people without moving or getting out of breath.

She liked the band and secretly, down in the cellar after the gig each Saturday night, she paid us all ten shillings each, but before last orders she would take a pint pot round the room collecting money from the punters, telling them that the band weren't paid and that donations were therefore needed to keep us from starvation.

'It's for the lads now, they're only playing for what's in the hat.'

With the top-up from the collection we often took home the best part of a pound each – which is about forty quid in today's money. Not bad for a fifteen-year-old schoolboy's spends.

That Saturday night was my induction into the world of rock and roll – now I was part of a real band, playing real music. Amongst others, we played 'Forty Miles of Bad Road', 'Somebody's Diggin' My Potatoes' and 'Walking to New Orleans' and it can't have been that bad because the audience cheered and clapped after every number. My guitar solos were derivative and my version of 'Apache' was a slavish copy of Hank Marvin's but the audience loved us – especially Popeye and the Teddy Boy.

Popeye was a strange wee chap, early middle age I'd guess, slight and nervous with a bad combover. We called him 'Popeye' because each Saturday he would get pissed and just before closing time he would come up and ask for the microphone and sing 'Popeye the Sailor Man' several times through.

This could go on for some time because the rest of the punters would encourage him by stamping and clapping and joining in with the song's final 'poop poops'. We'd play faster and faster, trying to get the damn thing over with, and Happy would bring the debacle to a climax with what seemed less like a drum roll than somebody trying to trash his kit before it was repossessed.

Now the really strange thing about Popeye was not that he only sang one song, and that only when he was off his crust with northern bitter, but that when we met him in the street during the week, he was a completely different person. He wore a dark overcoat and a bowler and carried a brolly like a city gent. I think he was a rent collector or insurance man or some such. When we met him in his other life we would always say, 'Great singing in the pub on Saturday,' and he would always say, 'I don't know what you're talking about!' And I think it was true, I really believe that he got so pissed that he had no idea he was in a pub up the road from Strangeways Prison singing a daft song. He probably arrived home every Saturday night convinced he'd been abducted by aliens.

The Teddy Boy was a little bloke, in his late thirties I'd guess, with the most amazing haircut. His hair was prematurely grey but there was a lot of it and it was shaped perfectly into a quiff that was like the prow of a ship at the front and a perfect DA (duck's arse) at the back – grown long with the two sides combed so that the wings swept back but never quite met. He was very proud of his hair and took great care of it. He wore a fairly conservative version of a Ted's clobber, with drainpipe trousers, a drape jacket and crepe-soled shoes, but his gear was toned down to a modest sugar bag-blue with little in the way of gilt or leopard-skin waistcoats. His girlfriend had a huge bouffant hair do and wore many paper nylon underskirts. They were a really nice couple, working class to the core and just enjoying their Saturday nights out down the pub listening to the band after a hard week's graft. Towards the end of the night they would get up and dance the odd number but mostly they just sat and listened because Mrs Dwyer wasn't licensed for dancing and would rush in waving her hands if it looked like dancing was on the menu.

What was unusual about the Teddy Boy was that inside this short, mild man there lived a fierce tiger. At the slightest sign of trouble or disrespect, this five-foot four, grey-haired rocker would cross the pub and simply lay the offender out, either with a punch or more often than not a well-aimed head butt. After giving somebody a 'Salford kiss', he would carefully comb his hair back into place, sit down and carry on as though he had just been for a pee.

Mrs Dwyer ran a good house; it was clean and bright and orderly, very unusual for pubs around Hightown. Being close to Strangeways Prison and the grim tenements of Derby Street it attracted its fair share of hard men and women. Fights broke out occasionally and if real trouble erupted Mrs Dwyer would pile in herself and sort it out with her version of kung fu, which involved a heavy metal beer tray. In those days men didn't hit women, which gave Mrs Dwyer a distinct advantage when it came to punch-ups.

In her hands, the tin tray broke noses and cracked heads as she waded in, whacking anybody and everybody involved in the fight, while telling us to 'Keep playing, you lads!' – the theory being that the band noise would cover the sounds of punching, kicking, chair throwing and tin tray whacking, so that any passing bobbies would think all was well at the Dover Castle. I used Mrs Dwyer as a character in my play *One Night Stand* just as she was, large as life. I suppose she's long gone now up to that great taproom in the sky and is probably laying about her with a heavenly tin tray giving errant angels a good whacking.

The Dover Castle was our regular Saturday night gig; Fridays we played for free at the Trinity Church Hall on Cheetham Hill Road where Roy was part of the youth club and was going out with a girl called Beatrice who always seemed to have a smile on her face and was probably the main reason Roy was a member of the club because I don't remember him being very religious.

We played the Trinity Hall as a kind of live practice and soon found that we were getting bookings from other places too, and not just youth clubs and rowdy pubs. Manchester – and the north-west in general – was going through a boom in clubs. As variety clubs went into the doldrums, old cinemas and billiard halls across the region were turned into private members' clubs, one step removed from working mens' clubs and probably more than one step up. They sold cheap beer and easily prepared food like scampi and chips in a basket; on the whole these clubs booked the acts that were falling off the bottom rungs of the variety ladder.

The members of both the variety clubs and the social clubs (variety clubs were run for profit, social clubs were run as mutuals with a committee and a chairman) paid a membership fee, drank lots of beer and filled the club every night so that some of these little places became quite successful. Some became so wealthy they could book star names. The Batley Variety Club, for example, could seat 1600 people and over the course of its lifetime booked acts like Shirley Bassey, Roy Orbison, Eartha Kitt, Tom Jones and Louis Armstrong. All of that in a town famous for making shoddy, a cheap material produced from minced-up woollen cloth.

So Batley booked the Bee Gees and Dusty Springfield; others, like the Ramsbottom Dyers and Spinners Club, booked groups like us.

The main problem was that the concert secretaries of most of these working men's clubs were moulders, riveters and spinners during the day and comperes and booking agents at night. Unlike the variety clubs, which paid comperes and were run for profit and therefore a bit more glitzy, the WMCs were often run by blokes who deeply resented the fact that 'the turn' was getting a week's wages for one night's work. It never occurred to them that 'the turns' had spent years learning their craft, had no pension fund, didn't have a gig every night of the week, were running a car, paying for the fuel, buying expensive stage gear and instruments and divvying up the money afterwards between a group of five or six, all of which meant that they were probably on a level footing with the con sec. Some of the introductions we got were classic.

'We've gorra rock 'n' roll band on now. I don't like 'um but t'committee's overruled me. They say we 'ave to 'ave stuff like this fer t'younger members. Well, I think younger members should learn to like what we like – not us 'avin' ter get with it! Anyway you're payin' 'em – so ye can mek yer own minds up – 'ere they are – the Stylos.'

Many of the clubs had a blackboard near the entrance with the names of the acts appearing there chalked on it; top of the bill had their names in coloured chalk.

Some of the WMCs were dire but some of the privately run variety clubs were worse. The Stylos once played a week at one variety club and when we went for the money on the Sunday night we were thrown out by the bouncers without our wages. No reason was given, we were just told we weren't getting paid and five minutes later we were out on the steps. So much for the private sector being better than the public.

I did the Batley Variety Club a couple of times in my later career as a folkie stand-up comedian, but as a rock and roller I never made it down the plush carpet. We played clubs like the Southern Sporting Club, Leigh Road Empire, the Devonshire Sporting Club and the Domino Club. My memories of those clubs are of dark, damp places with glitzy stages, cold dressing rooms and outside toilets, and the thing I remember most about them is that they stank of chicken in the basket (the Matterhorn of sophistication in them there days), stale cigarette smoke and even staler beer.

I remember years later doing stand-up in a massive club in Lancashire that was paying London money and had all the pretensions of a Batley Variety Club. The club was owned by a shady local character who had a couple of second-hand car dealerships. He and his wife were dressed very expensively in Torremolinos chic, but I couldn't help noticing that his wife's hands were covered in diamonds and ingrained dirt in equal measure. As my granddad used to say, 'You can't polish a turd.'

The Stylos didn't have a group van; when he wasn't in Ecclefechan or Dudley telling jokes and selling felt, Joe would take us to gigs, other times we used to get lifts in the Lowes' Uncle Ken's Morris Minor Traveller, which was a sort of Elizabethan half-timbered bijou dwelling on wheels. I never quite understood the half-timbering of the Traveller. Perhaps it was a nostalgic hankering back to an imagined bucolic past when men wore codpieces and women were buxom, or perhaps it was simply a natural expression of the English love of suburbia – in which case the car should have had a garden gnome on the bonnet like the flying lady on the Rolls-Royce. Whatever it was, ours died, in the end, not from engine failure but from deathwatch beetle. Many's the mile I travelled lying on blankets in the back of the Traveller on top of three amps and a drum kit as Uncle Ken drove round the backstreets of Salford or Oldham, teeth clamped on his pipe, nose to the wheel, looking for the gig.

I remember working a club called Johnny's Spot in a place called Milnrow, on the extreme edge of the then known world. Beyond there were dragons, Yorkshire ones. It was at Johnny's Spot that we witnessed at first hand a phenomenon that many other musicians and singers experienced all across northern clubland: 'The Coming of the Pies'. Not all clubs had kitchens where they could cook scampi and chips in the basket and those that didn't, in an attempt to lend their gaffs an air of sophistication, would have outside caterers coming in. In the most basic cases this would be a bloke going round with a tray of pork scratchings; higher up the food chain came the hot pies, heated up somewhere near and rushed round piping hot. When they arrived everything stopped because, of course, the pies had to be eaten while they were still warm.

On our first gig at Johnny's Spot we were half way through 'Man of Mystery' when the power went off on stage, everything stopped and the house lights came on.

'Bloody stroll on! What's bloody happening?' Happy shouted into the wings. The compere walked on, took the mic out of Dicky Dobbs' hand and shouted, 'Pies 'ave cum!' We looked out to see three blokes with trays held above their heads wending their way through the audience. Everybody stood up and rushed to the back of the club where the pies lay steaming in a row on the bar. We gave up and joined the queue ourselves: the pies, after all, had to be eaten hot. And they smelled delicious.

Everything stopped for pie and peas and everything stopped for bingo, which was more like a religion than a game. Mess up the bingo and you stood a fair chance of being torn limb from limb by the beehive-haired harpies with their halves of lager and lime on the front row.

And so we went on, me revising for my O levels, Tony fitting carpets, Roy selling cotton and Happy making specs. Dicky seemed to have a variety of different jobs and a complicated love life to boot. I remember him having a particularly stunning girlfriend who looked half Spanish but who insisted on bringing her mother with her on dates. Since the mother seemed to be able to consume endless shots of Cherry B, Dicky used most of his gig money filling his future ma-in-law up.

Dicky left the group to get married and was replaced by a butcher called Don Sands, who sang like Frank Ifield. It must have worked because after a short audition we became the resident rock and roll band at Bernard Manning's World Famous Embassy Club and also a few weeks later at his equally famous Palladium Club.

For any guitar freaks who might be reading this, until the latter end of my time with the Stylos we were still playing the amps that Dave Doyle had made; Happy had a Premier drum kit with a couple of skull blocks he had got off a 1930s dance band kit; Tony was still playing his Guyatone Japanese plank, Roy his Framus bass and I had graduated from a Colorama to a Hofner V3, a German-made attempt at a rock and roll guitar and about as exciting as a wet November Thursday in Dortmund. I wanted an American Fender Stratocaster as played by Hank Marvin but there was no way Lou and my mum could have afforded one.

Most of the Manchester beat groups of the time wore toned-down versions of the Teds' outfits and straddled a sartorial line somewhere between lounge lizard and rebel. Think Buddy Holly and the Crickets and you'll get the idea.

Girls wore tight sweaters, circle-stitched bras that stayed in when you pressed them and dirndl skirts with lots of paper nylon underskirts which they stiffened by immersing in the bath in a thick sugar solution. The underskirts acted as an early warning system and any attempt to move your hands up a girl's thigh was accompanied by the crackling sounds of an Australian bush fire while blue sparks from the static generated by your bri-nylon shirt, the nylon underskirts and the friction of your two bodies rubbing together meant that heavy petting (or even light petting) was sometimes almost as dangerous as touching un-earthed club microphones.

Beehive hairdos – back-combed, stacked up and heavily lacquered – often made a girl another eighteen inches taller and were a fire hazard when cigarettes were being lit in crowded clubs. The hairdos coupled with big heels meant you would often take a girl home and find that when she kicked her heels off she suddenly sank six inches and you'd be kissing a large Brillo pad. Some girls used so much lacquer that the assembled blonde busby was hard enough to give you concussion.

Stockings and suspenders, and the feel of the cool skin of a girl's thigh during a quick snog between sets at the Jungfrau, were pretty damn exciting and often made playing the second half a bit of a hit and miss affair as testosterone fought a winning battle with my recollection of the chords. The thick part at the head of the stockings where the suspenders were fastened was called 'the giggle band' because 'if you got past that you were laughing'.

Hair was the big thing though and, in a time when people often only had weekly baths, hair washing was a weekly ritual too and usually involved two or more girls getting together for the event.

'Can't come out with you Wednesday/Friday [whenever], I'm washing my hair' was a common cry – sometimes it was the truth but often it was a great excuse not to have to go to the local bug-hut to eat Spangles and watch Vincent Price slicing somebody in two, while fighting off a sweating and persistent acned octopus.

Buckets of Blue Steam and Sparks for the Grinder

Something truly strange happened in the summer of my fifteenth year. Not only had I become a rock and roll guitarist doing a bad Hank Marvin impression, I had found myself a summer job and turned into a teenager with money to spend and a bit of freedom to do it in.

The job was with a firm of ball bearing suppliers in Manchester called Apex Bearings. There still is a firm of that name in Manchester but I doubt it has any connection with the place I worked at. I got the job through Don at the corner shop. Don was a freemason, and the managing director of Apex was an ex military man, tall and mustachioed and officer class. He was also a Mason; Don had a word and bingo, I had a summer job. I know little about Masonic beliefs but I do know that Hiram Abiff, the First Grand Master and central figure in Freemasonry, is the 'Widow's Son' and that Masons do look after widows' children; being the son of an RAF war widow may have tipped things in my favour.

Apex Bearings was in an old Victorian building close to London Road not far from what is now Piccadilly Station, and when I went for my interview on the Saturday morning after I finished school the boss, Mr Head, told me I would be paid five pounds a week and would be expected to work five full days Monday to Friday with a non-optional half day on Saturday. I would be there seven weeks and my job was helping with packing ball bearings and anything else Frank, the foreman, wanted me to do.

Frank the foreman was a bluff northerner who called a spade a shovel. I liked him because, even though he was gruff and shouted a bit, he was fair and knew full well that I knew bugger nothing about ball bearings and even less about packing and despatching them.

The bearings we sold were highly specialised: roller bearings, needle bearings and ball bearings encased in races and made by firms like Timken and SKF – they were, I think, super precision races used in special machine tool applications.

Frank didn't mind too much what I did just so long as I turned up on time, brewed a good jug of tea and kept quiet while he listened to Test Match Special on the radio. All that long, hot summer it seemed that there was cricket on the radio, Frank's mind's eye decoding John Arlott's commentary with amazing precision. I hadn't a clue what Arlott was talking about with silly mid off, short leg, square leg and so on but Frank could picture every move, every stroke and every run. I used to marvel at his ability to transfer himself, courtesy of the radio magic carpet, to the Oval, Headingley or Old Trafford as he sat there with a pencil stuck behind his ear, sorting dockets and pulling bearings off their shelves. I was in that place for almost two months and at the end of it still hadn't a clue what innings were and why you declared when you hadn't finished. I still haven't. I like to go and watch Yorkshire village cricket on a summer Sunday afternoon, sitting with a pint in the sun watching the lads enjoying themselves – but I still don't understand what's going on.

As well as selling ball bearing races, Apex also reconditioned them, which mostly involved taking out all the gunk and old grease, cleaning them up and re-packing them with nice new grease. On the ground floor of the works was a large vat full of warm carbon tetrachloride, into which the bearings were dipped. The chap who did the dipping was a chirpy, happy bloke whose name I think was Bill and who I'm sure was chirpy and happy because he was high most of the time on the 'carbon tet' that he was breathing in. He never used a face mask and spent most of his working day leaning over the vat. I took a whiff of it once and was slightly high for a while after. It is no longer used in the cleaning industries because it causes liver and kidney damage. I hope Bill still has his liver and kidneys.

Rites of passage are pretty primitive things but they are an essential part of much tribal life. Workplace initiation ceremonies are tribal too, in their own way. At Apex Bearings they didn't circumcise you with a sharpened seashell while you chewed on a coca leaf but they did play the usual workplace tricks on this particular greenhorn. I was sent to the stores for a bucket of blue steam, some sparks for the grinder, and a replacement bubble for the spirit level. The storesman was not a happy chap with all the daft things I kept asking him for and when they sent me to ask him for a long stand he just smiled and said, 'OK, son, just wait over there.' A quarter of an hour later he said, 'Been standin' there long enough?' I nodded. 'Well, you can go back and tell 'em you've had a long stand.' Oh, how I laughed.

The trick that put the tin hat on it though happened on my first day at Apex and was my first brew of tea. The brew served the whole workforce and was made in a huge enameled metal jug that contained the best part of three quarters of a gallon of tea and it took a good half packet of leaf tea to get anything like a decent brew. I was there nice and early on my first Monday, Frank and Bill and some of the other packers were already there. The office staff and Mr Head would arrive later.

'You can go and brew up, young 'un. The tea and sugar and the boiler's over there,' Frank said, handing me the jug which was half filled with the dregs of the previous Saturday's tea leaves.

'Where shall I tip these?' I asked innocently.

'Up the stairs. Door marked office. Through there to the end. Door marked 'Head'. In there there's another door – that's the toilet. Dump it there.'

The brown warehouseman's coat I'd been given on my arrival to protect my clothes from oil and grease was one of Bill's old ones, far too long for me, and I had to hitch it up as I climbed the stairs. When I got to the toilet door, however, I needed a free hand to turn the knob so I dropped the hem. I opened the door, tripped on the hem and launched the best part of a quart of soggy swollen tea leaves all over the managing director's toilet, cistern and washbasin. I cleaned the place up as best I could with toilet paper and paper towels then scooted downstairs to brew the tea.

I sat drinking the strong sweet tea with the rest of the lads and half way through our break Mr Head and the office girls arrived and went upstairs.

A short while later Mr Head came down.

'Who brewed up this morning?'

The lads all looked at me but said nothing.

'I did, sir.'

There was a moment's silence, which seemed far longer than a moment.

'Well, don't empty the tea leaves down the director's khazi, there's a good lad. You could read me fortune off me arse.'

And with that he turned and strode smartly back upstairs.

Tommy the Tray

In the late fifties and early sixties, variety, the natural daughter of music hall, found itself in terminal decline. Television, the working men's clubs and the epidemic of cabaret clubs that seemed to be raging through the north west like a form of showbiz measles meant that theatres that had once been 'palaces of varieties' were now struggling. Some of them gave up the fight and turned themselves into bingo halls, those that carried on – mostly the big-city Empires and Palaces – still managed to pay a bill-topper like Ruby Murray or Michael Holliday, a couple of comedians, a musical act like the Morton Fraser Harmonica Gang, a soubrette or two and several speciality acts – 'speshes' as they were known in 'the business'. These could be anything: tumbling dwarves, fire-eaters, knife throwers, mind readers, animal acts, ventriloquists, jugglers, unicycling balloon modellers and, further down the scale, odds and sods like Tommy the Tray, Ricker George and Wu Lu Chan – the World's Strongest Man.

As more and more variety theatres began to kneel to the inevitable and turn themselves into bingo halls, the spesh acts moved into the cabaret clubs, and for a number of years a rock and roll band like the Stylos would often find itself following a vent or a paper tearer or worse. Perhaps because they were cheap, Bernard Manning seemed to book a fair number of these often dire spesh acts at the Embassy.

One night an act called Tommy the Tray went on before us and brought the house down. His act was a simple one, probably devised one night at a drunken family party in an inspired fit of lunacy. Tommy came on in cowboy costume – not the handsome Gene Autry variety, but an exaggerated Sons of the Pioneers rig: boots and spurs, wide, shaggy sheepskin chaps, a leather waistcoat full of chrome studs and rhinestones, a red bandana and the biggest ten gallon hat possible. Since he was only about five foot tall the effect was comic rather than romantic. As he walked on stage to a taped recording of 'The Mexican Hat Dance', Tommy threw his hat on the stage and went into the first part of his act: a mock flamenco-style caper round the brim, complete with exaggerated hand movements and hip twitches so that he looked, at the end of the dance, like somebody who was trying to get out of his clothes without touching them. All this was done with a completely straight face, which, of course, made it even funnier.

The taped music began to speed up, getting faster and faster and, now dancing like an epileptic dervish with impacted haemorrhoids, Tommy would completely trash the hat. At that point there would be a couple of seconds' silence as Tommy stared at the ruins of his ten gallon titfer, then the first bars of Frankie Laine singing 'Mule Train' would blare out of the speakers with their dum diddy, dum, diddy, dum diddy dum intro, at which point Tommy would pick up a thin aluminium beer tray and, at the beat in the song where the whiplash comes, he would bring the tray down very hard and loudly on his head.

'Mule trainnnnnnn (CRACK), clippity clop clippity clop.

'Mule trainnnnnnn (CRACK).'

As in the hat dance, the music would speed up, the tray would crash on his head more and more frenetically until, as the song spiralled off into a vortex of musical gibberish, Tommy would stagger off as though about to collapse to rapturous and clamorous applause. Not much of an act, I admit, but it went down tremendously well.

Ricker George was a strange man from Bolton who came on stage in full evening dress, a full head of long, lank hair and an old-fashioned wind-up gramophone under his arm. He would place the gramophone very carefully on a chair centre stage, wind it up, put the needle in the groove and, as the first bars of the 'William Tell Overture' rang out, would take two pairs of 'rickers' or bones out of the pocket of his jacket and step into the limelight. Very seriously and very competently, he would accompany the record, playing along straight-faced, tossing his lank hair back from his brow at the end of each phrase of music like a crazed Polish violinist. After half a minute of this, the spring in the gramophone would wind down, and the record would begin to slow, grinding its way downwards in both tempo and pitch in a groaning rallentendo. With a nervous flicker on his face, Ricker George would dash back to the gramophone, give it a few quick turns until it hit speed then sprint back to the microphone. This would be repeated over and over: play – dash – wind, play – dash – wind, until huge chunks of the audience lay on the floor, ill with laughter.

It might not seem funny now, but these were simple days when we took our pleasures where we could.

Deaf and Dumb Chinese

Chinese strongman acts weren't very common, even in the clubs of the north, so Wu Lu Chan the World's Strongest Man was something of an oddity. We worked with him at the Luxor Club in Hulme, a former cinema once resplendent in faux Egyptian temple decor, now covered in hardboard, plastic and glitter in an attempt to make it look like an American speakeasy. It didn't really work; the hardboard was swollen with damp and the place smelled of cooking fat and cat pee. The compere, Ronnie Mack, was a short sparky bloke with a head of bleached blond curls and a penchant for minstrel show songs like 'Toot Toot Tootsie', 'Chattanooga Choo Choo' and 'Who Were You With Last Night?' He would do these as a medley to open the night, getting the punters to sing along as he strode the stage in straw boater and striped blazer, a huge grin on his face, singing along to the organ and drums. Sometimes they would clap and sing along madly, other nights they'd carry on rabbiting, ignoring his Swanee

Medley. On those nights, as he skipped smiling into the wings to the last cymbal crash from the Eddie Ward Duo (we christened them the Very Bored Duo), he'd squeeze past us, the smiley mask gone, his parting quip: 'They're fuckin' crap tonight – must've been drinking fuckin' cement.'

We'd go on stage and play our way through our set of Shadows' hits, following them note for note and even doing the famous Shadows walk. I cringe now when I think of it – but we were young and no doubt the Beatles and the Rolling Stones started off the same way. The only trouble is we were still doing it years later while they were writing their own stuff, becoming world-famous rock gods and doing peculiar things with Mars Bars.

Wu Lu Chan, the spesh act on at the Luxor with us one unforgettable night, was about five feet four inches tall and a little more than that wide, with thick black hair cut in a pudding bowl crop. He was naked except for a pair of wrestler's trunks and the muscles of his oiled and glistening body were truly massive. He was a sort of muscular Chinese version of the Michelin Man.

We hadn't had chance to meet him backstage because he'd arrived from working another club half way through our first set, so the first we saw of him was when Ronnie Mack introduced him as '... a victim of the Japanese concentration camps, ladies and gentlemen. They tore his tongue out with red-hot pliers and beat him up so badly he is now as mute and deaf as that wall. Please welcome …' There was a good deal of sympathetic clapping at this and Wu Lu Chan, his inscrutable eastern face betraying no emotion at all, began to rip up telephone directories, bang six-inch nails into wood with his bare hands, and lift four men above his head on chairs fastened to a plank. The highlight of his act came when he coiled a rope round his neck and got three strong men either side to try and strangle him. For several minutes he dragged them round the stage as the Very Bored Duo made 'effort and struggle' noises on organ and drums. Finally, defeated, the men left the stage to more chords and cymbal crashes and Wu Lu bowed unsmilingly and inscrutably and exited to the sounds of 'Chinatown' on the organ and wild applause from the punters.

After our second spot we went backstage and walked into the

dressing room only to find Wu Lu Chan naked and kneeling before the sofa. On the sofa, also naked, her legs wrapped round his massive back, was the pretty blonde lady who had opened the second act with a selection of torch songs. Wu Lu looked up and, without breaking tempo, said in a broad Scouse accent, 'Shut the fucken' door, lads, she'll catch 'er death o' cold.'

'I knew he wasn't a real Chinese,' was all Happy said later.

I must explain that there was a lot of nudity or semi-nudity backstage in the clubs. We often shared dressing rooms with dancers and strippers who thought nothing of sticking their tassles on while downing a Babycham, smoking a fag and telling the other strippers what they'd cooked their husbands for their tea; we in the meantime would be trying to tune up while trying not to look interested. As a fifteen-year-old Catholic schoolboy who next morning would be sitting in class taking lessons on the Revocation of the Edict of Nantes from a cassocked priest, the two worlds couldn't have seemed further apart and my mind would often drift from Huguenot silk weavers settling in London to the bosoms and bums and long legs of the night before.

The Greek Group

One of the regular gigs the Stylos played was a youth club in a dark, damp church hall close by Strangeways Prison, in the shadow of the warders' houses. It was the kind of soot-encrusted gothic pile you see in the early scenes of the film *A Taste of Honey* and, when I watch that film now, it reminds me how much of the world seemed to be in black and white in those days. Most of the civic buildings were a deep black, their yellow millstone grit having been coked by hundreds of years of industrial smog.

The youth club gig had been organised by our drummer Happy, mostly I think because it was so close to his home that he could walk there in five minutes after his tea. We played each week to thirty or so kids of various ages from twelve to eighteen. It was hardly showbiz but it meant we could work new songs into the act and not worry too much if they were crap. The interval refreshments were pop and biscuits dished out by the caretaker. I don't remember much about the nights there except that we seemed to attract a few of the local girls – which was probably not far from Happy's mind either when he negotiated our next-to-nothing fee.

One of the girls drawn to us by the fact that, outside the Belisha beacons across the road, we were the only moving thing for miles, was a dark-haired, full-busted lass called Sheila. She seemed to take a fancy (or perhaps a pity) to me and let me take her home and take liberties with her standing against the wall in somewhere called Chimney Pot Park – named that because it was on a hill looking down on acres of blue-slated house roofs. I used the name years later in a children's play I wrote called *The Witch that Nicked Christmas*. It was an attempt at a traditional panto with daft songs and a perilous quest. One Christmas there were two theatre groups performing it: one in Bury, Lancashire, the other in Hong Kong.

One night, before we left for our fumble in Chimney Pot Park, Sheila and I had a dress rehearsal in a meeting room behind the stage under the watchful eye of a long-dead minister painted in treacley Victorian colours. I noticed as we stopped for breath that there was an old cabinet in the corner, inside which was a twelve-inch Electrovox speaker. It seemed to be in good nick and when I asked the caretaker if I could have it he nodded and said between spasmodic coughs and drags on his Park Drive that it would only get broken anyway left there.

I took the speaker to my mate Dave Doyle. He pronounced it good and for a few quid made me an amp to go with it. The speaker and amp were in heavy unvarnished plywood cabinets so, one Saturday, Tony and I went down town to the fabric shops on Shudehill and got a few yards of red Rexine plastic cloth. We stuck the cloth on with dobs of Copydex carpet adhesive and put metal corner protectors on. To try and make it look more professional and less Heath Robinson we bought some white plastic letters from Woolworths – popular for making up house names at the time – and screwed them on to the front so that the amp proclaimed 'The Stylos' to the world.

Dragging it in and out of Joe Lowe's Minor Traveller didn't do it any favours and after a few weeks the letter 'L' lost its horizontal line. One Friday night we were at Bernard Manning's World Famous Embassy Club, waiting in the wings to follow the comedian Eddy Grant. Eddy looked like Fyfe Robertson, the 1960s Scots TV personality, and was one of the funniest men I've ever seen. He seemed to have no fear and once took Manning's piano to pieces and threw it across the dance floor in the middle of his act because he said Manning was a cheapskate who owed him money. Manning tried to make light of it by coming on stage and throwing fivers at Eddy but Eddy carried on until he saw there was enough money scattered round then, mic in hand and still cracking gags, he gathered up the loot before exiting with the words, 'We've noticed that people have been going out of this club and pissing in the car park. We don't park our cars in your shithouse – please don't piss in our car park. Goodnight.' As good an exit as any I have seen.

This particular night, as we waited to launch into 'Man of Mystery', Grant noticed the disfigured name on my amp. He stared at it for a while then said, 'Sty-ios? Must be one of them Greek groups.'

Manning had his own distinct way of running his clubs. Having been a greengrocer as a lad and being well used to getting up at sparrowfart to go to market, he got to his club each morning at dawn and set about bottling up and making sure the cleaners did their job. He also carried his greengrocer's expertise on into his booking policy. He might not have liked grapefruit himself but they were popular with the punters. He didn't like rock and roll either, but it was popular with the punters. We were booked as the resident band at the Embassy and Palladium clubs because we played rock and roll and because we did it quietly. Manning's theory was that if people were listening or dancing they weren't drinking and the clanging of the tills was the only kind of music he liked. He was right, we were a quiet group – what he didn't know was that the reason we were quiet was because we couldn't afford loud amps and Happy, being a good drummer, whacked the skins a lot quieter than he would have done had we been kitted out with VOX AC30s or other such backline sound gear instead of home-grown boffin-made jobs with Greek names.

As an aside here, can I explain that Happy was called that because he was a trifle grumpy at times and that this seems to be most drummers' dominant mood. This I think is because they have more gear to carry than anybody else, nobody helps them, they have to set up all that complicated ironwork on their own; then they have to sit at the back staring at the backsides of four blokes who are getting all the glory. You rarely heard girls boasting, 'I got off with the drummer,' just as nowadays on the folk scene you rarely hear girls telling their friends that they have scored with the banjo player.

One night during our residency at the Palladium we arrived to set up and found the stage full of amps and drums and feathered headdresses. When we asked the barman what was going on he said that the main act that night was an American band called the Cherokees. They were a college band, an eleven-piece outfit with a big horn section who had a minor hit record in the US and somehow Manning had got them cheap. They took up the whole stage and the entire dressing room and we were expected to work around them. Happy used their drum kit and we perched our amps on chairs in front of their massive backline. We had never seen so many amps outside of Barratt's music shop in town. We watched them getting ready in the dressing room; eleven crew-cut, white college boys stripped off, donned buckskin pants, moccasins and leather waistcoats, covered themselves in bronze make-up, painted war stripes on their faces and then put on their feathered headdresses.

The club filled up with punters and Manning stood at the back, smiling. It was going to be a good night. The compere introduced us, we did our bit, got a half-decent round of applause and walked off, taking our amps with us.

Following us was a girl singer who did Shirley Bassey songs to a backing tape then there were a few moments turn around when the stage went dark and the roadies got the stage ready (yes, the Cherokees had roadies! We didn't even know what the word meant). By now we were at the back of the club, standing next to Manning at the bar. The house lights went down and we saw figures going onstage in the gloom; the sound of tribal tom-toms began to fill the air. An ochre light slowly suffused the stage and revealed, ranked across it, eleven 'Indians', most of whom were probably Mormons. There were two tom-tom players, a drummer sat waiting behind his kit, a guy on Fender bass, another on a Telecaster and another on a Stratocaster, the brass section was two sax players on tenor and baritone and three lads on horns. The pounding of the tom toms grew louder, the braves began to utter war cries and to jig from leg to leg. Then, right on cue, a bomb went off: it was actually a marine maroon (an exploding firework, used to warn ships in fog) in a metal drum, standard panto gear for the time but it didn't half make a racket in a club. Dust and dead pigeons fell from the roof onto the punters and a white-faced Bernard Manning muttered a dazed, 'Fuck me.'

As the smoke began to clear, the Cherokees hit the room with everything they'd got, and they'd got a lot. They were singing something about a running bear on the banks of a river while belabouring the club with the biggest noise since the Blitz. There were nosebleeds on thc front row and one old-age pensioner's hearing aid melted. A waitress dropped a tray of drinks and fled back to the bar. The noise grew louder still as the brass section got into a groove and fought the guitarists and the drummers for the highest decibel count.

It was then that Manning moved. On normal occasions you wouldn't have seen him as a contender for the hundred yards dash but this was no normal occasion; he was on the stage faster than a rat up a drainpipe and with one yank had pulled the plug on the band. There was a small deafening silence, then as the last dead pigeon fell onto the stage the lead singer in the band shouted, 'Man, you can't do that!'

'Why not?' Manning asked.

With every word enunciated as though he was addressing an idiot, the singer told Manning, 'Because We Are The Cherokees.'

With the rapier wit and command of language for which Bernard Manning was celebrated, he told them, 'Well, you can fuck off! Custer's coming back.'

Manning paid the band off, we went on and did another set, the pies came and life as we knew it in clubland went on.

Sadly, the imminent threat of O levels was rearing its ugly head and trying to be Hank Marvin while writing essays on the War of Jenkins'

Ear was like juggling with loose soot. Something had to go and with a couple of months in which to catch up on five years' schooling I resigned my position as lead guitar and occasional backing singer with the Stylos and got my head down.

Spike Martin, our history teacher, told me later that the teachers thought I would fail everything. I didn't. Half way through the summer holidays I went and stood in the Lady Corridor on the edge of a scrum of boys who were struggling to look at the GCE results posted up on the wall. When I eventually got to the front I found that I'd got six decent grades and had only failed geography and French, which didn't matter really, unless somebody was to ask me what the major exports of French Guiana were. A few days later, while I was at work at my summer job digging holes in the road, my mother got a letter from St Bede's telling her that I had a place in the sixth form. Since I had nothing better to do at the time, I took up their offer.

I Got the Sixth-Form Blues

Going back to school after the summer holidays I found that as well as being able to buy and wear a sixth-form scarf, which marked us out as serious chaps destined for serious things, we were studying a smaller list of subjects in more depth and were in much smaller-sized classes. What had been the old tuck shop was now a sixth-form common room where we could smoke and play cards and we were now treated like semi-intelligent human beings instead of Satan's spawn. We no longer had our old school satchels but toted our stuff in leather briefcases. All of this came as a bit of a shock to my system, this sudden change coming at a time when I had lost my faith completely, discovered girls completely and found my salvation in poetry and books. Not only would I never be the same again but many years later I still remain seventeen years old at heart – though outside I am fooling no one.

Our English teacher was Father Foxy Reynolds, the priest who had been an inspiration and a comfort during my early years at

Bede's. I loved studying E. Lit under him. John Donne, Milton, *King Lear*, *The Tempest*, George Eliot – reading was no imposition and I found the fact that Foxy actually listened to our ideas quite amazing. He didn't see education as a way of pouring stuff down a funnel into our heads, he saw it as enabling, as a process.

History was taught by Father Burke, who later went on to become Auxiliary Bishop of Salford. He was an intelligent man but unfortunately believed in rote learning. He was Jesuit-educated and was still fighting the Reformation. From him I learned that Henry VIII had a syphilitic ulcer on his leg and that Elizabeth I had to be buried in a lead coffin because she stank so much. This reinforced my generally jaded view of kingship. He did, however, set us all the task of giving a lesson ourselves once a week which we were expected to research, write and deliver, on subjects such as, in my case, Luther, Machiavelli and the Tichborne claimant. I quite enjoyed this and actually won the public speaking prize that year.

French was taught by Mr Ganley; I resat and passed the O level but since my grounding in the language had been at the hands of Tojo it was pretty much next to minimal, and I was at a loss with things like the subjunctive and the past historic. The texts we studied were Molière's *Le Malade Imaginaire* and Racine's *Andromaque*. I didn't mind the Molière because that was supposed to be a comedy (though I didn't find a lot of chuckles in it) but I hated Racine. I could never understand why people went on about him, I found the plays turgid and completely artificial, pretty much like French society at the time. I was destined to fail French from the very start.

It was Mr Ganley, a good and kind man, who wrote on one of my French essays, 'Alas, the wasted years.' Mr Ganley was nicknamed 'Prune' after Pilot Officer Prune, a fictional wartime RAF character. I think it was Tony Green who wrote, to the tune 'All Things Bright and Beautiful':

The crumbling towers of St Bede's stood,
The walls were falling down,
A sign outside on a piece of wood:
'For Sale, Half A Crown'.

I saw a figure in the ruins
It was a shape most manly,
Standing faithful to the last
I saw 'twas Corporal Ganley.

Making Rain in a Panel Van

There was a knock on the door one Sunday and when I went to open it there was a lad standing outside in a jacket, tight trousers and white winkle-picker shoes. In a repeat performance of the Tony/Stylos recruitment scenario he said his name was Pete and did I want to join a rock band. Simple as that. I'd been away from playing for a while and with no thought at all of the A levels that would loom up sometime in the not-so-far future I said yes.

The band was called the Manchester Rainmakers. This was to distinguish us from another group on the scene at the time called the Warrington Rainmakers (and, I suppose, any other Rainmakers that might have been knocking round the northern rock and roll world of the sixties: the Giggleswick Rainmakers? The Oswaldtwistle Rainmakers?). The name came from a 1956 film called *The Rainmaker*, which told the story of a spinster in a drought-stricken, American small town who falls in love with a charlatan who claims he can make it rain. Naturally it all ends terribly. She should have moved to Manchester; there the people have webbed feet and the buses give lifeboat drill before setting off.

I suppose somebody must have thought that the Rainmakers was a striking name for a band that came from the Rainy City, and I suppose that same somebody thought it was a good idea to have the band photographed holding umbrellas. I have to admit that, in those days, I was a callow youth and was so in awe of rock and roll that I would have joined any band, even if it had been called the Eccles Existentialists, and would have posed standing on my head in a bucket of treacle if they'd asked me.

The Stylos were probably the better band, but the Rainmakers had a proper van: a VW Transporter, almost new, and in one of VW's standard liveries – sealing-wax red. Two of us came from Crumpsall, north of the city: myself (lead guitar and backing vocals) and Pete (rhythm guitar, backing vocals and owner of the van). The drummer Dave, bass player Terry and our Scouse lead singer Ricky came from south of the city so they mostly arrived at gigs separately in Ricky's works van. He was a chirpy bread delivery-man during the day and a tight-trousered rock and roll sex bomb at night. At the end of his working day he emptied out half a ton of Wonderloafs, sliced Hovis and Milkloafs and replaced them with Terry and Dave. They usually arrived at the gigs covered in crumbs and smelling delicious, and girls followed them round for the smell of fresh bread alone.

Our VW had no seats in the back so on the odd occasion when the van was carrying more than us two Crumpsalites one of us had to lie flat out on the gear as the bus rattled its way over the Pennines to Cleckheaton and Milnrow, or back along the A roads from Blackpool, Matlock, Bolton, Buxton or Leek, all regular gigging towns for us. The neddy in the back was usually me. But mostly it was just the two of us; Pete driving and me beside him, dozing off after a hard day of A level history, and an even harder night of rock and roll. It was not a very successful spinning of plates, and most of the time I was only half awake, both on stage and in class where the doings of Luther, Calvin and Zwingli would spool around my head in a dark soup as I tried to focus on a wobbling blackboard while the chord sequences of 'I'm a Hog for You Baby' ran along as a soundtrack.

At nights I occasionally broke nasal inhalers open and swallowed the impregnated cotton-wool insides because, according to the jazzers and bluesers I knew, they contained Benzedrine and would keep you awake. They didn't keep me awake, they just gave me a terrible case of heartburn – which did, in fact, keep me awake, so I suppose they worked in a way.

From time to time on those long, tedious journeys back from gigs, I would be brought out of my exhausted, catatonic slumbers by Pete screaming, 'Talk to me! Talk to me! I'm falling asleep at the bleedin' wheel!' in a voice that almost shattered the windows and certainly didn't do much for my nerves. There wasn't anything like the amount of traffic you find on the roads today so it was quite easy to nod off as the six-volt van with lights as powerful as two jam-jars full of glowworms trundled along on deserted moorland roads at fifty miles an hour.

One summer, towards the end of the season, we found ourselves working the North Pier Blackpool every Sunday night. Our drummer, a good-looking blond lad who later went on to become a successful local radio jockey, had formed an attachment to one of the lady fish fryers from Pablo's chippy – 'The Biggest Fish and Chip Shop in the World' – just down the prom from the Tower. She was about our age and spent all her days shovelling chips, fish and mushy peas into the open maws of Lancashire millworkers on Wakes Week and Glaswegian shipyard workers down in Blackpool for 'Glasgow Fortnight'. She was an attractive girl with an untroubled sexuality and a good sense of fun and would give the drummer a quick knee trembler against the pier railings in the moonlight then any of those who wanted it a quick hand job in a spirit of absolute generosity. You were grateful for what you got in those days.

One night Pete and I came out of the stage door to find a couple of girls waiting for us. They were from Manchester and were over in Blackpool for a night out. We offered to take them back to town but explained that we wouldn't be leaving until the morning. We were going to sleep in the van.

They said that was fine by them and so Pete drove through the suburbs of Blackpool and out into the countryside looking for a field to park in. Behind the façade, Blackpool truly is a depressing place, and street after street of dim terraces with houses called Shangri-la or Dungraftin carrying cardboard signs in their windows reading 'Vacancies' sailed past.

At last we parked outside the town in a field well off the road and managed somehow to all get down on the mattresses in the back of the van. We had a bottle of whisky with us and set about it with a will, and as George Formby once said it 'turned out fine again'.

I woke, with a girl's head on my long dead arm, my head hammering. Suddenly I heard the sound of an engine. A lorry or something big was coming towards the van, and it was showing no sign of stopping. In fact it seemed as though it were coming right at us. I shouted and the other three woke up in time to hear the lorry, its engine roaring, come crashing towards us then go right over the top of the van.

Pete wiped the steamed-up windows and peered out, red-eyed and hungover.

'Fuck me!' he said quietly. 'We're parked on the fucking airport.'

Not just on the airport but on the end of the runway and planes were landing and taking off over us, their wheels a few metres over the van roof.

We left, dry-mouthed, and headed for Manchester, the two bedraggled and befuddled girls sitting in the back.

Cleckheaton Town Hall

For some unknown reason we suddenly started working a lot outside Manchester in places like Staffordshire, Nottinghamshire and Yorkshire. The Manchester scene had become almost as important as the Liverpool scene and bands like the Hollies, Freddie and the Dreamers, Wayne Fontana and the Mindbenders, Johnny Peters and the Crestas were all making waves in the rock and roll world. We weren't making any waves, though we did manage to get our photograph on the front of a northern rock scene magazine, all wearing those high-necked jackets and Ben Sherman shirts with pin-through collars that were the fashion amongst the young bloods of the day. I suppose that, though we weren't in the same league as the Hollies, we were cheap, and the cover versions we played were pretty true to the originals, plus we did have a real live Scouser as lead singer.

We worked Leek Town Hall on a number of occasions. Our changing room was the Lord Mayor's parlour on the next floor up from the ballroom. The great staircase that led up to the parlour had long windows that were covered with thick curtains. Girls used to sneak in and hide behind the curtains and grab unsuspecting rock stars as they went past. I didn't mind.

Cleckheaton in Yorkshire became a regular Sunday-night gig for us. The first time we did it we arrived in town mid afternoon, hoping that the hall would be open and we could set up the gear and go and get a coke and a Wimpy burger before the gig. Nobody but the old now will remember those northern Sundays when everything closed, when it seemed that all human life had been sucked out of those soot-blackened towns. Manchester was bad enough on a Sunday, but the mill towns of Yorkshire, dominated by Methodism, were true ghost towns on the Sabbath. Nothing moved but the odd empty bus, nothing was open, nobody walked the streets. The sole sign of life was the odd scrawny dog scuttling down silent deserted streets; it would sense you watching and look furtively back before disappearing again up some ginnel or back entry. The only sounds came from dour chapels where people were singing about shining cities on shining hills while the world outside was soot black.

We rolled into town and pulled up at the town hall. It was locked. Not a soul about, we knocked on the back door near the boiler house, hoping to rouse the typical grumpy town hall caretaker. Nothing happened. We stood looking around us. Every shop closed. Mills and civic buildings loomed, black and grim.

'Fuck me,' Terry said. 'They must have dropped the fuckin' atom bomb.'

It was a lovely late summer day, sun toasting the dark gritstone walls of the town, heat coming back at us from the great Yorkshire stone flags. In the far distance we saw a movement. A human being was coming towards us. As it got closer I saw that it was a bandy-legged little bloke in a cloth cap and tweed jacket with a gaberdine over his arm and buckled leather casings covering his legs from knee to ankle. They are called 'Yorks' in England and 'Nicky Tams' in Scotland; they were standard wear for farm workers then and were for keeping muck from your trouser bottoms. We thought he was a local but it turned out that he'd come into town from further up country in the Yorkshire Dales and had brought some pigs down to the slaughterhouse.

'It dun't oppen till termorrer but I'm stoppin' in town terneet, tha' knaws, ready for first thing in't morn. Aw've a few gradely porkers in t'wagin ready for t'mart.'

I understood what he was saying but Ricky the Scouse singer stood there open of mouth and blank of face ('Worra woollyback! I thorr 'ee was fucken' Polish,' he said later).

'D'you know where we can get something to eat?' I asked.

'Aye.' The farmer nodded. 'Dus'ta like pie and peas?'

We agreed that we did indeed like pie and peas.

'Good, 'cos that's all she sells.'

And he led us on foot away from the town hall, five rock and rollers in their stage suits and Teddy Boy quiffs following a bandy-legged Dales pig farmer. On and on and up and up we walked through a maze of steep cobbled streets, all with their identical scrumbled doors and lace-curtained windows until we came to a high part of the town and a small, stone, terraced cottage with its door open.

'Cum in,' he said and led us into the front room of the house. The only furniture was a number of plain wooden benches and similar wooden tables. The room could sit at most a dozen people.

'These yur lads want pie and peas,' he said to a short skinny lady who had appeared, wiping her hands on an apron; then he vanished somewhere out the back.

Within minutes there were mugs of tea and plates of hot pies and steaming mushy peas in front of us then, without a word to any of us, the woman disappeared in the same direction as the pigman. We ate the grub, which by the way was delicious, supped the tea and waited for someone to come and take our money.

Nothing happened.

Then nothing happened again.

After nothing happened some more, we coughed and whistled and Ricky called a tentative hello, then Terry placed a shilling on the table, said, 'Fuck it, I'm off!' and walked out. It seemed a fair price so we all did the same and followed him.

Years later, post 'Rochdale Cowboy', while on the road in a series of one-night stands, I worked the Victoria Hall, Halifax. It was a sell-out gig and the two lads who ran the theatre very kindly presented me with an engraved glass tankard. As we were having a drink, the name Cleckheaton somehow came up and I told them the story of that strange little farmer and the pie and peas shop.

'Oh that was Mrs So and So's,' said one of the managers, Les. 'It was a brothel. She used to see to all the old farmers when they came into town. The pie and peas were a sideline.'

I have never been to a brothel, but had always imagined them cosy affairs with Tiffany lamps, comfy sofas, voluptuous half-naked girls and a wise old concert pianist whose career had been ruined by drink playing cool jazz in a corner. A brothel-cum-pie-and-peas-shop took a bit of thinking about.

When we weren't eating pie and peas in Yorkshire brothels we ate the usual muso's diet of transport caff nosh while on the way to the gig and, afterwards, usually ended up in the only late-night places still open: the Indian or Chinese restaurants that were starting to appear in the back streets. Transport caff food is still pretty dire; then it was guaranteed to kill you. Standard fare was sausage, egg and chips with loads of brown sauce, mugs of tea and bread and margarine. You could feel the lumps of fat coursing round your arteries like manic slugs as you were eating it and the tea was so strong you could have served it in slices. (Lorry drivers liked tea you could 'trot a mouse across'.) Since these were the only places open on the main routes we were forced to eat there, but opening the door on a rainy day and walking into a fog of cigarette smoke, chip fat vapour and the steam from wet overalls was not my idea of the rock and roll life.

The Indian and Chinese cafés were much better places and by the time we got to them on our way back from the gigs they were usually empty. There was an Indian restaurant opposite Strangeways Prison that served plain but good curries and we worked our way through the menu. Until then my understanding of curries had been the abysmal stuff served up by Vesta.

Our favourite late-night eating place was a restaurant in a street off Ardwick Green that served authentic Chinese food. The cook/manager was a friendly Hong Kong Chinese woman who taught us how to eat using chopsticks and who, after the first few times we went there, told us to ignore the menu as she would do something different every time we came. We made that our main stopping point post gigs and over the months we got to know and appreciate the great variety of Chinese food. I drew the line at the duck's webs in ginger and garlic, though.

CHAPTER 8

THE COFFEE BAR COWBOY

There are some books which change you, which take you by the hand and lead you into another place, another country that is entirely different and once you have been there you can never be the same again: *1984*, *Animal Farm*, *Brave New World*, *Lord of the Flies* – they all had a great effect upon my understanding of the world. But the book that really brought about a sea change in the way I saw 'Life, the World, the Universe' was *On the Road*, Kerouac's bible of the Beat Generation. Just at the time when I was most Bolshie, most attracted to the beatnik way of life and most anti the Establishment in all its forms, I came across it, read it in one hit and then went back to the library and got *The Dharma Bums*, which I thought was even better. I wanted more than anything else to be Japhy Ryder wearing a lumberjack's shirt, old denims and hiking boots, sipping China tea and reading wise old Buddhist texts. The excitement, the sheer heady lunatic excitement I felt in those days has stayed with me to some extent ever since. I had come upon another way of being and thinking that didn't mean being tied to the machine; a way of looking at the world that was not through Vatican-tinted goggles. I saw that there were other truths beyond the kind of serfdom that was on offer via St Bede's and Monsignor Duggan's career plans.

The sixties was a heady decade, a time when we believed all things were possible. It was a time when four lads from Liverpool could change the face of popular music, and playwrights like John Arden and John Osborne could give the Lord Chancellor blood pressure. It was a time of novels like *Billy Liar* and *Room at the Top* and of films like *Saturday Night and Sunday Morning*, *This Sporting Life* and *A Taste of Honey*. To be alive and a teenager in those days was exciting enough; to be a lapsed Catholic, potential Buddhist, guitar-playing raver and wannabe poet was potentially dangerous.

All of this was underscored by my belief that poetry, like music, could carry essential unspoken truths. I had heard Eliot's phrase, 'Genuine poetry can communicate before it is understood,' I had read Dylan Thomas and *The Waste Land* and had started scribbling my own verse. Most of it was very bad stuff and, drawing on the industrial wasteland that was all about me, was full of images of dripping chemical pipes, rusting boilers and toxic dumps as well as, of course, moons and mythical creatures.

I had no doubt that I would be a writer – all I needed to do, I reckoned, was keep writing and one day my genius would be discovered and I would be up there with T. S. Eliot and Dylan Thomas. Luckily I didn't share these thoughts with anybody at the time.

One of my poems, 'The Mouse', found its way into the school magazine, *The Baeda*. I also sent some of my poems off to William Empson, who I admired at the time. He wrote back to me saying he'd enjoyed reading them and that one of the lines in particular was 'Websterian'. My mum was very impressed. My favourite book of poems then (I was just finding my way to Larkin, Heaney and Hughes) was the *Penguin Book of Chinese Poetry* translated by Arthur Waley. I loved the mysticism and the sparseness of the poems, in particular the poems of Li Po. I used to recite one of them nonstop and bored the backsides (though not the knickers) off most of the girls I went out with. John Donne was another great love.

Books are dangerous things – look how they have been banned and burned over the years. If Thatcher had not read Hayek's *The Road to Serfdom*, that blinkered diatribe against society, we might never have ended up in the mess we're in now. However, I digress.

Having fallen upon Kerouac I now knew exactly what I wanted to be: a Dharma Bum who travelled constantly in search of the Truth. Rock and roll wasn't doing it for me any more. I still loved Chuck Berry and the early rock and blues musicians, but the more recent home-grown crop like Cliff Richard, Marty Wilde and Adam Faith just seemed Tin Pan Alley constructs. I dabbled with the blues, turning in my old tremolo harmonica to get a blues harp, and I started learning a few blues licks. Sonny Terry and Brownie McGhee were my mentors but I hadn't yet discovered Folk, so musically I was pretty much adrift. Poetry and the novel were now filling the gap left by rock and roll. I had stumbled on the Beats and been converted and like all converts to a new religion I took on all of its creed. I bought a US Army combat jacket from an ex-army store in Manchester and started hanging out around the coffee bars in town. Fired by stories I heard from other Manchester 'Beats', I began hitch-hiking to the Smoke, as us hipsters called London. We were convinced that stuff was going on down there that was far superior to the stuff that was going on in Manchester. We were wrong, of course, but didn't know it at the time. London may have ended up swinging but most of the push that swung it came from the provinces and much of it from the north.

The first time I hitched to London was with Pete Gittins during the spring half-term. On a cold but sunny day with rucksacks on our backs, we took a bus to the other side of Stockport, got off somewhere on the old A6 and stood at the roadside with our thumbs out. Within a few minutes a lorry had picked us up and we were off on our travels. The only thing that might have told people we weren't real Beats was the lack of beards and the sixth-form scarves wound round our necks. It took us about eight hours and a couple of rides to make it to Mill Hill in north London, from there we got a bus into the centre.

We stayed at a youth hostel on that trip though on later trips I would end up sleeping in doorways or in parks. I still have photographs of that first journey to the Smoke: one shows me sat on the monument facing Buck House, another shows Pete with an armful of pigeons in Trafalgar Square. Hopes that we would meet a couple of mysterious older beatnik women who would lead us into temptation came to nothing and we were back in the hostel in time for cocoa every night. Most of the other people at the YHA were students or travellers in London on their way somewhere else, but there was one man who seemed to be a long-term resident, which was odd as, according to the rules, you weren't supposed to stop in a YHA hostel for more than three nights. He was a short, muscular, crop-haired guy in his late twenties called Tony who wore blue jeans, workman's boots and old navy sweaters and was more like Sal Paradise, the narrator of *On the Road*, than anybody I had ever met. He cooked spaghetti – then unknown beyond the stuff you got in tins – and told us he was a writer who worked as a navvy on building sites during the day and wrote at night and had already had one novel published. I was in thrall. I wrote his name down and when we got home a few days later I checked at the library but no such author existed. I wasn't put off by this, though, and started to branch out in my own writing; as well as writing poems of teenage doom and despair set in an industrial wasteland, I began writing short prose pieces, sketches almost, and I never went anywhere without a notebook. Of course, I had the thumb out whenever I could, too; sometimes the lifts came easy, other times I'd end up sitting in a motorway services nursing a cold cup of tea hoping they wouldn't chuck me out. Kerouac in *The Dharma Bums* followed his cosmic wheel, his circular pilgrimage going from New York to San Francisco; my less adventurous route went from Manchester to Stockport then on to Leicester and sometimes London.

I wasn't on the road all the time, I was only a weekend Beat; the rest of the time I was supposed to be studying for my A levels. It is hard enough that these take place at the very time of life you should be out and about finding yourself but to make matters doubly worse the exams always take place in the best summer weeks when you should be lying on the grass watching clouds sail by on high like stately galleons instead of being stuck in the gym waiting for a master to tell you that 'you may now turn your papers over'.

My mother wasn't happy about me turning into a Beat but since we had a new baby in the family – called Collette – she had her hands full. But she was more concerned about me kicking the Catholic Church into touch.

Losing my faith left a vacuum that has really never been filled, since the sureties of the Bible fairy stories had in my case not been replaced by anything but doubt. Which is fine, I can live with that; as Iris DeMent says in her great song, 'I think I'll just let the mystery be.' But for a considerable time, after I had decided that it was all hokum, I was left with a residue of guilt. The sound of bells ringing on a Sunday afternoon can still cast a shadow on a sunny day.

There were times, too, when being a teenager sometimes became too much and adrenalin mixed with whatever changes were happening in my body wired me to the moon and it was all I could do to stay in the house. It was particularly hard on hot summer nights, when day after day of sun had soaked into the red-brick houses and the granite cobbles of the city, and Crumpsall was almost as sultry as a Barcelona barrio, but with fewer burglars. The city acted like a giant storage radiator, taking heat in during the day then, at night, sending it out again in waves so that, even with the windows wide open, there would be no relief. With the temperature high and with testosterone and poetry raging through my veins like molten lava rising up the vents of Vesuvius there was no way on this earth that I was going to get to sleep.

On such nights I would lie on my bed beside the open window staring out at the star-spattered sky stretching in a caul over the city. I would watch the moon rising over the houses across the back entry, silvering the slates, and listen to the sounds of the night: the hospital bell mournfully sounding the hours, perfectly matching my angst-ridden, doomed, pain-in-the-arse, poetic persona. To make it even more perfect, most nights you could also hear the clanking of shunting trains in the ICI sidings, and the sirens from the ocean-going ships in Salford Docks. On Fridays and Saturdays this would usually be accompanied by the singing of Reg the Drunk as he crooned his way unsteadily up our street after the last bus had dropped him off.

On some summer nights, when it was obvious that there was no way at all that I would get off to sleep, I got up, dressed, climbed over the windowsill and slid down the coal shed roof to the ground. I would let myself out by the back-yard gate and set off walking the four miles to the city centre. In those days there weren't all that many cars on the road and I would go through deserted and silent streets towards an empty town where yellow-pink shop window dummies stared out blankly and where the only living things were the occasional drunk or a helmeted bobby checking shop doors.

Manchester was dead as Dixie's dog, the pubs (apart from any late drinking dens where curtains were drawn and lights and voices were low) were all shut, the clubs had finished and the butty van on Cannon Street, where you could get a sausage sandwich and a mug of tea for a bob, had shut up shop.

There was always one place that was open 24/7 though: Nick the Greek's, a.k.a. the Oxford Snack Bar on Oxford Road. Run by a Cypriot family who seemed to have endless patience with all the drunks and druggies that ended up there, Nick's was the refuge of pimps, pushers, prostitutes, bouncers, transvestites, taxi-drivers, print workers, musos and a few criminals who weren't so small-time. On nights like these it was a haven for a bespectacled, hormonally disturbed poet to whom Nick the Greek's was Hemingway's Deux Magots and Keroac's Vesuvio Café all in one. I would sit there all night over a cup of tea and a slice of toast, people-watching, fascinated by all the stories that came in from the dark town beyond the steamy windows.

That guy over there was a pusher selling drugs to the dribble of people who came to his table, sat down with a coffee and went out again with something that had been passed over the sugar. Those two girls over there with all the hair and make-up and the short skirts and gold anklets were a couple of prostitutes taking a break from their beat. Those two lads in the corner were Donovan and Gypsy Dave and they'd just finished work at the Twisted Wheel, while that old man in the window in the old overcoat and worn-down shoes I would meet again in Ralph McTell's song 'Streets of London'. More than once I watched a couple across the room, he with a quiff and a sharp face and she brassy with blonde, back-combed hair. I watched them looking about, staring at people. They caught my eye and I looked away; there was something about them I didn't like. They were regulars in Nick's.

As dawn broke over the city rooftops I would start my trek home through town, along Red Bank and Angel Meadow, past the plague burial ground, following the Irk to Smedley where the air from Queen's Park would have more than a hint of open country in it, then it was back along Smedley Vale to Lower Crumpsall, up the hill to our street, over the coalshed roof and into bed in time to be shouted up for my paper round and school, my head still spinning and two or three new poems in my pocket.

Years later when I read the reports on the Moors Murderers, Ian Brady and Myra Hindley, I realised I recognised the man with the quiff and the woman with the beehive hair staring up from the newspaper photographs from Nick the Greeks. It has crossed my mind more than once how close I might have come to ending up on Saddleworth Moor in a shallow peat grave.

The Sovereign

Central Manchester in the sixties before the developers got at it would have been familiar to any Edwardian resurrected, Lazarus-like, and dropped in the heart of the city. Courtesy of Adolf there were a few bomb sites, but there were still some medieval buildings and the great edifices of Cottonopolis were still there: Albert Square with its neo-gothic town hall which at one time the city planners wanted to knock down, the old Midland Hotel, King Street with its great rows of banks, John Street with its Georgian terraces, which was and is Manchester's Harley Street. The great medieval cathedral was badly damaged during the Manchester Blitz but it had been rebuilt pretty much as it once was. The area up from the cathedral around Cross Street and Cannon Street was a great mix of old buildings, some of them medieval, most of them Victorian. There were model shops with fabulous working steam trains, fishing tackle shops where Arthur Ransome bought his rods and flies, milk bars, a music hall, a Kardomah coffee house and the offices of one of the world's greatest newspapers, the *Manchester Guardian*.

The town hall did more damage than the Luftwaffe and most of that area was trashed completely when a young council planning officer sanctioned the building of the Arndale Centre, a tile-covered monument to Brutalism which I christened the largest urinal in Europe. The IRA blew it up in 1996 but unfortunately the council rebuilt it.

Since then, year on year, the city has become more of a Euroville with architects outdoing each other in an attempt to design the ugliest building. Winner so far is the Beetham Tower, a 171-metre high glass tent peg with a superstructure on the roof which makes a howling noise like a regiment of banshees whenever the wind gets into a certain quarter. There are those who think that it is a classic of modern architecture; I'm not one of them.

Before the planners turned it into the bus station for the Arndale Centre, the Shudehill area of the city was still much as it had been when the gallows were up on nearby Hanging Ditch. The Sugar Loaf pub was still there, an old, low building that had a sugar loaf on the bar counter; it was the favourite boozer of the journalists and printers from the nearby Kemsley House where my Aunty Maire worked. There was a bird market that sold pigeons that would fly off back to the birdman if you weren't careful, and there were radio spares shops where I had bought all the stuff for my crystal sets. Slightly up the hill and reached by a flight of gloomy wooden stairs was the Sovereign Coffee Bar, which was basically nothing more than one long room with bookshelves covering most of the walls, a handful of rickety tables and a simple wooden bar that served coffee and tea, beans on toast and buns. It was a second-hand bookshop with sex and drugs and beans optional, and an office at the back where the owner, Tony, answered the phone and where a bit of hanky panky would happen from time to time. The drugs were pretty tame – Benzedrine and hash mostly – and the dealers were hollow-eyed skinny drifters with long greasy hair and army greatcoats. You could spend hours in the Sovereign over a single cup of coffee and a bun (and I did) reading the books, perhaps buying one or two, and watching the beatniks and musos come and go.

It was in the Sovereign that I had witnessed the death of rock and roll as we then understood it. Tony brought in a new album which he put on the record player. It was rock and roll, but nothing like Chuck Berry, Jerry Lee Lewis or Little Richard; it wasn't even any of that terrible anodyne rubbish like Bobby Vee with his bloody awful 'Rubber Ball'. No, the music Tony put on that day was rocky but very melodic and very English and very different.

I went over to the counter where the Dansette player was blasting out the music and looked at the cover. Four lads with haircuts like Larry out of the Three Stooges were looking down over the railings of what looked like the stairwell of a block of flats. The album was called *Please Please Me* and the group were called the Beatles and they came from the other end of the East Lancashire Road in Liverpool. It was obvious that they had something extremely rare and extremely good. The record was played endlessly in the Sovereign and later, having heard it at least five times through, end to end, I knew that these Scouse gits playing more than three chords and doing it all brilliantly would do for us all – they were in a league of their own. The three-chord trick, drainpipe trousers and Teddy Boy sneers were not going to cut it now. At the next rehearsal we learned 'I Saw Her Standing There' and 'Love Me Do', on which my mouth-organ playing came in handy.

People fall out about the relative merits of the Stones and the Beatles – to me the Stones were never much more than middle-class white boys trying to be black; like Bryan Ferry it all seemed so much more like an art school pose than real music. But the Fab Four didn't try to pose, they were Scousers with attitude, they were on a ride and they loved that ride and they took a big chunk of the world with them. The fact that they left the rest of us three-chord chancers behind at the bus stop is something I'm still trying to learn to live with, but even then, in that smoky, book-lined room in Shude Hill, it was obvious that something of great import was happening.

The Sovereign was a fairly anarchic place and some of its clients were 'well lary'. Tony had a policy of letting anybody in unless they caused trouble or dealt hard drugs – then they were out, and he was tough enough to put them out. He looked a little like Acker Bilk, and, like him, wore a bowler hat. He was generous too and if he saw you were brassic (boracic lint = skint) he would stand you a plate of beans on toast and a mug of tea. He also booked folkie musicians from time to time. I saw Donovan do an all-night gig there with Gypsy Dave and remember him singing the line about how he and the gypsy boy's ages together came to thirty, and I realised with a shock that they probably did. Donovan looked about fourteen at any rate. They slept on the floor in the office that night.

It was a wild and interesting time to be a teenager. We were the first generation of Welfare State kids, there was full employment and free education, and unlike our parents we didn't have to leave school and get a job in a non-unionised sweatshop. We could stay on at school and go to university or we could get an apprenticeship; there were real choices. When I finally left Bede's and ended up doing a variety of manual jobs you could jack one job on a Friday and walk into another on a Monday – providing you weren't too choosy.

It's difficult to picture now the definite air of hope and optimism among young people in the early sixties. We thought anything was possible. If a group of working-class lads from Liverpool could succeed then so could we, and if working-class writers like Alan Sillitoe could get published then so could we. *Coronation Street* first screened in 1960 and became within its first year the most watched programme on British television. If you watch the earliest episodes you will see carefully crafted, character-driven dramas, gritty and real and played out in what was then a recognisable urban landscape. Coronation Street was a mirror of the street I was born and brought up in; Hall Road had its Ena Sharples, its Elsie Tanners and its Albert Tatlocks. My street has changed now – the corner shops have gone and most of the families I knew have moved away – but then, in the sixties, there was still a community and though my old gang were all working while I was still at school (which did seem strange) we were still all part of the street.

I was reading three or four books a week – Huxley, Waugh, Wells, Orwell, Steinbeck, Hemingway, Greene, Kafka, Camus, Sartre. I was also reading (or trying to read) books like Colin Wilson's *The Outsider* and August Renan's *Life of Jesus*, and it was books like these that turned me into an argumentative agnostic.

Before class every morning there would be a full-scale row raging across the desks as I rubbished yet another aspect of Catholic doctrine and found that I was pretty much a one-man atheist band. Lads that I thought had intellectual depth were still accepting things like Infallibility and Transubstantiation. Once I came across the vegetation myths and realised that Christ's journey was just one among many other death and resurrection legends, I was on my way out of the Church for good.

Adam and Eve's belly buttons were what finally did it for me, though. We were looking at some sixteenth-century Italian paintings in general studies one morning when I noticed that Adam and Eve were both depicted with belly buttons. I pointed this out to Father Fay (aka 'Fudge') and asked him the question that had been noodling away in my brainbox for some time now.

'Father, we now accept that evolution is a fact and that, rather than God making the world in six days, it evolved gradually. If that's right, then there was no Garden of Eden and no Adam and Eve. And if there was no Adam and Eve then there was no Original Sin and no need for God to turn himself into his own son and come down to be nailed to a tree so that he could redeem us. Right?'

Fudge was an intelligent man who had studied at Oxford; he nodded and agreed that the story of the garden was a fable but said that our fallen natures came from another elemental fault and that he would lend me a book on it and could we now get back to Titian.

The other boys thought I was bonkers, of course, and dangerous bonkers, too. I don't think it was one of the lads in my form but it was certainly a devout member of the Church of Rome who, later that year, shopped me to Duggan and got me thrown out of Bede's.

One half term I hitchhiked to Leicester with my pal Barry Soylan. Kath Shirt, an old girlfriend of mine (in that she was a girl and a friend), was there at university reading philosophy. It was Rag Week and we aimed to get us some beer and some women in no particular order. Kath had got us beds in a student house where some friends of hers were living. The Rag Ball was at the De Montfort Hall, a civic hall of considerable size and by the time we got there the main hall was already full of sweaty dancers and the floor was a shallow lake of spilled beer and fag ends. We joined in and gradually anaesthetised ourselves with bitter beer while trying to chat up some of Kath's friends who, being undergrads, didn't think much of the idea of a couple of northern sixth-formers getting into their pants. We danced a bit and drank some more, then Barry wandered off with some woman he had met and there was a changeover of the bands and things began to go strangely out of focus.

Time suddenly jumped and I found myself standing in front of the stage watching a tubby bloke in a suit who looked slightly deranged. He was holding onto the microphone stand as though it were all that was holding him up, belting out something about being a ding dong daddy while the band behind him played up a storm. People were dancing to the music, that strange kind of half jitterbug, half beatnik hopping and swinging routine that us Beats favoured. I was far too drunk to dance and held onto the stage staring up at this strange vocalist who – while smoking a fag and gripping the mic stand and a glass of brandy – was still able to belt out terrific songs. His collar was askew, his suit looked as though he'd been swimming in it and a cowlick fell across his forehead. He sang 'Frankie and Johnny' like I have never heard it done before or since, hugged himself and kissed the air in the first verse and when it came to the shooting the drummer hit four rim shots and the singer threw himself flat down in a spectacular pratfall. The whole thing was a performance that turned the song into a drama with a bit of singing.

Many years later, while working for the BBC, I was to photograph the singer sitting on a park bench in Sefton Park, Liverpool and also having a pee in the wonderful gents' toilet at the Philharmonic Hall. He was George Melly and we became friends, though strangely, when we met, I always forgot to tell him about that night and now it's too late.

After the ball, as the crowds were leaving, Barry and I found our student hosts and followed them back to their house. It was one of the worst night's sleeps I'd ever had. A bed for the night was right – but nobody had mentioned sheets and blankets. They had assumed we had sleeping bags; we had assumed that we would be sleeping in proper beds with pillows and stuff to keep you warm. Wrong on all counts. There were no sheets, pillows or blankets, just bare mattresses. It was midwinter in Leicester, not one of the warmest places on the globe. I shivered, fully clothed on top of the mattress for a while then gave up and got underneath it. That was not much better, in fact it was worse because the mattress didn't cover me and the fact that I'd nothing underneath meant that the cold struck up from below. Hungover, ragged from lack of sleep and without breakfast we hitched our way home in a stream of fits and starts via a bus ride from Batley – how the hell we ended up in Batley I'll never know. When getting undressed for bed that night I notice the diamond shape pattern of bedsprings across my bum.

Bilko

One afternoon I was sitting in the Sovereign, reading more scurrilous and dangerous literature, when I met a lad who was to become the Sancho Panchez to my Quixote – or perhaps it was the other way round and I was the Robin to his Batman? There used to be a section in the *Reader's Digest* magazine entitled something like, 'My Most Unforgettable Character'. If I had been asked to write that column I would have been fairly spoilt for choice since there are a number of people I can't easily forget but Bilko would have been up there on the top table because he was one of the most interesting, exciting, crazy-good people I have ever come across. In Tibet he would have been revered as a holy shaman and garlanded with marigolds; the problem was that he wasn't in Tibet, he was in Manchester.

His real name was Geoffrey Silver, he was a year or two older than me and he was a Jewish lad whose parents ran a newsagent in the Hightown area of Manchester. He was nicknamed Bilko after the Phil Silvers' character – like him, he was a ducker and diver who sailed close to the wind.

I had wagged off school that day and was sitting in the Sovereign trying to read a much-handled Everyman Library edition of the *Bhagavad Gita* when I noticed that I was being watched by a strange character sitting across the room. How do I describe him? At one time there were a fair number of 'Johnny Onions' running round England; they came here from Brittany on heavily loaded bicycles and travelled from town to town, selling strings of their pink-tinted onions door to door. They had just about gone by the sixties but all the photographs show them as short of stature, quite plump and sporting berets and black beards with strings of onions round their necks.

Staring at me across the Sovereign Coffee Bar that morning was a Johnny Onion, complete with a beret, a sparse black beard and dark Latin eyes but without the onion necklace. He stood up and, as he approached, I noticed that he was wearing an open-neck shirt with a red neckerchief, black slacks and leather sandals without socks. I also noticed that the expensive-looking suede jacket he was wearing looked as though it had been used for straining soup at some point;

dark patches of grease were spread across it like cloud shadows on a sunny beach.

He looked me full in the face, cocked his head to one side like a blackbird on a lawn listening for an early worm and said, 'You look like an interesting geezer. What's that you're reading?'

I answered him by reading out the sentence I'd just been trying to decipher: *'The senses are higher than the body, the mind higher than the senses; above the mind is the intellect, and above the intellect is the Atman. Thus, knowing that which is supreme, let the Atman rule the ego. Use your mighty arms to slay the fierce enemy that is selfish desire.'*

'D'you know, you took the words right out of me bleedin' mouth,' he said, pulling up a chair.

And that was it, we spent the rest of the day drinking coffee, eating beans on toast and talking about life, death, literature, philosophy, music – all the things that teenage beatniks talked about in coffee bars in those days.

At first I found his way of speaking almost impossible to follow and it was several days before I began to understand that Bilko spoke a language entirely of his own devising. It was a melange of Yiddish, Mancunian rhyming slang, street trader argot and sheer perverse inventiveness.

A typical Bilko sentence, accompanied by much waving of hands and puffing on his never-ending chain of cigarettes, would go: 'So I'm schleppin' down the frog on the way to the gaff when I sees this reem goy kaif wot I chavvered a few moons back. An' I sez, "Ello," an' she just gives me a load of verbal an' sez, "Wot do I get next time, Bilko? Lobsters?" That's not very kosher, is it?'

This translates as: 'On my way here I met a pretty, young non-Jewish lady I had sex with a few months ago who it seems had contacted pubic lice (crabs) as a result. She asked whether next time she would contact another type of crustacean.'

For hours Bilko would keep up a never-ending monologue. Drunk on life, on words and ideas and often high on Benzedrine, he would talk and talk until everybody around him had either fallen asleep or 'done a swerver'.

So we 'schlepped down the frog' together all around the rainy city that autumn, Bilko and I, gibbering on about being and nothingness and asking such questions as:

BILKO: How do we know that the table still exists in the gaff when we have guided out of the gaff?

ME: We believe it emphatically but according to Plato we can never prove it empirically. Unless somebody stays behind in the room.

BILKO: In which case how do you know that the geezer in the gaff didn't cease to exist once you had left it? He too could have done a swerve and ceased his earthly existence or gone off to somewhere else in the space–time continuum. You see, Sherlock [he too delighted in my nickname], we can never be one hundred per cent sure that all of this ain't an illusion. By the way, do you have enough illusionary gelt for a couple of cups of illusionary Rosie Lea and some Holy Ghost [tea and toast]?

Bilko was very good at picking up girls. He was fearless when it came to 'steaming in' and had an eye for 'reem kaif' that might 'chavver', and might have a 'lettie' (flat) or at least have 'di-los' (parents) who were off the scene for a while.

He was particularly good at picking up sixth-formers from the girls' grammar schools, especially the beatnik types who were transfixed by his direct approach and his mad philosophical ramblings. He was less successful with hairdressers and shop girls in places like the Oasis Beat Club or the Three Coins Coffee Bar where we would often go for a frothy coffee and a banana fritter – man, we were so sophisticated! When he asked them if they had ever wondered whether or not the space–time continuum might be a loop in which we were doomed to repeat the same day for eternity, the hairdressers told him succinctly to 'fuck right off'.

I should never have given him that quote from Eliot's *Four Quartets*, about time present and time past both being contained in time future while all time is eternally present and time itself is unredeemable.

We spent many an hour in the Kardomah café in St Anne's Square, an artists' and con artists' haunt where the bohemian life of

Manchester spent much of its time. The café was below street level and they cleverly roasted their beans close to the gratings so that the smell of fresh coffee ensnared people and drew them down into 'the KD', as it was known. At one time there were Kardomahs all over the country: the one in Swansea was where Dylan Thomas used to hold court. The KD in St Anne's was one of the favourite meeting places of Manchester's Levantine communities and you would hear Arabic and Greek being spoken as well as English, Yiddish and Bilkoese. There was a large fireplace in the KD over which was a motto in Dutch: '*Die werkt met lust verlangt geen rust.*' This translates as: 'He who enjoys his job does not wish for leisure.' Which is probably true but which I am sure some employers would translate as: 'He who likes his job shouldn't expect any wages.'

One day in the KD, Bilko said to me, 'Sherlock, today we are about to beard the bourgeois capitalist lion in its den and show it to be the rubber duck it really is.'

'What are you on about?' I was trying to work out how a lion could be a rubber duck.

'The suits at Burton's have been coming the Tin Man and sending me mail which is of an abusive nature. It is all on account of me extending my credit with them without first going through their ridiculous protocols.'

Half an hour later, we had left our empty coffee cups on the KD table and Bilko's beatnik sandals were planted firmly on Burton's thick carpet, his beret at its usual jaunty angle, his neckerchief askew and his gravy-patterned suede jacket shining under the shop lights. I was wearing a Tyrolean hat, my ex-army combat jacket, mustard jumper and green cords stuffed in cossack boots.

'Can I help you?' an unctuous assistant asked, perhaps wondering if we'd come in to hire morning suits for a society wedding.

'I demand to see the manager,' Bilko said in a firm, magisterial tone. When the manager arrived, Bilko went on at some speed and in a loud voice for several minutes, telling him how disgusted he was at being treated so abominably, how he had held an account here at Burton's for some time and how, if Burton's insisted on sending him letters demanding payment, he was prepared to take his custom (for which read 'debt') elsewhere. The shop was fairly busy, people were listening open-mouthed and the manager looked like a balloon slowly going down.

To this day I still don't know how he did it but, without paying a tin bean, Bilko walked out of the shop having extended his credit to the extent of a new suede jacket and a new pair of strides (pants). He put the jacket on in the KD and spilt half a cup of creamy coffee down it in the first five minutes. I half expected him to take it back to Burton's and complain that it wasn't coffee-proof. Chutzpah is a Yiddish word that translates as 'impudence, gall or audacity' (actually I don't think there can be any single-word English equivalent). However you translate it, chutzpah is what Bilko used for blood.

I was still hitchhiking 'all over the gaff' and, one day in the Sovereign, Bilko, who was very much in favour of vagabondage, said, 'Sherlock, how's about you and me using thumb power and guiding down the Smoke for a couple of days?' The following Friday we set off, together with a girl I was going out with at the time and a sixth-form girl that Bilko had picked up. Getting there was fairly easy even with four of us, though one lift did mean us all sitting in the back of an open wagon as dawn came up over the cold, flat Leicestershire fields. Finding somewhere to doss in London was not easy; the Marquis of Granby in Soho was full of bohemians like us looking for a bed for the night so we failed there. The last I saw of Bilko and his girl they were wandering off through the streets looking for 'a geezer called Scotch John' that Bilko knew who had a doss somewhere. The Crumpsall Kid and his pal ended up dossing in a strange one-roomed building like a Wendy house in the middle of a small park. It was a cold and miserable night and sleep was impossible, made doubly so by the drunks that kept trying to get in, one of whom sounded as though he might be Scotch John. The next couple of nights we spent in a youth hostel. Bilko and his lass had vanished so we made our way back to Manchester alone, arriving just in time for me to meet Pete in the VW van and head out to the Bolton Casino for the Battle of the Bands. This was supposed to be a competition to pick out the best rock bands in the north. There was a revolving stage split into two so that, as one act was playing out front, the next act could be setting up out of sight.

We set up and readied ourselves for the gig, having chosen two numbers: 'I'm a Hog for You Baby' and 'Roll Over Beethoven'. The bloke who worked the revolving stage was either pissed or had it in for us because he sent us round at full belt so that we ended up rolling over as well as Beethoven; only Dave the drummer was semi-upright and that was because he was sitting down holding on to his drums. We didn't win.

I introduced Bilko to some of my grammar school mates but somehow they didn't take to him. They found his patter difficult and they were disconcerted by his habit of going off on surreal monologues then suddenly stopping and asking them something profound and personal such as 'What do you think love is?' I think they were also put off by the way he touched them up for 'gaspers' (cigarettes) and made sure he was in the toilet when it was his turn to buy a round of drinks.

I stayed friends with Bilko for a long time, only losing touch with him when I started going out with the girl I later married. The last I heard of him he was living alone in Salford somewhere.

We Band of Brothers

I was still going to Crumpsall Library a couple of times a week in a pretty hopeless attempt to cram all the stuff I needed to pass the exams into the space between my ears. It was like trying to pack the contents of a large wardrobe into a washbag while the plane is on the runway waiting to take off. But I was still playing in the group and still pretending to be a hipster Beat while wearing a school blazer and it was obvious that something would have to give. One night after a hard gig in Bootle I left the band; we weren't getting any better, weren't getting better gigs and I was a bit tired of the same old stuff. Snogging a girl after the gig who worked at a sardine canning factory and who still had a whiff of the produce about her finally clinched it.

Freed from the band I tried to settle down to some serious revision, but I found it hard. One misty November day I went out of Crumpsall Library where I'd been trying to stuff the dates of the Italian Wars into my brainbox and slid down a side street into the graveyard of St

Mark's church to get some of what passed for fresh air in Cheetham Hill. This churchyard had fascinated me for some time, not least because I had found a large tomb there in which were the remains of Adam Murray from New Galloway who came down from Scotland to Manchester aged fourteen at the end of the eighteenth century to work in the cotton mills and ended up as an inventor, a wealthy man 'who much improved the spinning mule'.

I went back into the library and asked the librarian if there was any information on the church.

'There's a poem by a local poet, Tony Connor, that you should look at.'

That day she put a book into my hand, *With Love Somehow*, that showed me how I could write about the particular, the world I knew, and yet also write about the universal. Just as Hardy, writing his poems about the peasants of Wessex, touched on universal truths, so Tony Connor, writing about the streets I knew in Manchester, was writing more than parochial or provincial verse. I began turning my own poems to things I knew. One of the first of them, 'The Tip', was a short poem about my childhood ICI playground. A few years later I sent it to *The Tribune*, they printed it and paid me a quid; the first money I ever earned from my poetry.

I was still rambling the streets at night when I couldn't sleep and often found myself nattering away to tramps and drunks and other 'characters' in the early hours of the morning. I imagined that I was picking up material for a future novel. One night I ended up sitting by the side of a nightwatchman, warming myself at his brazier. A huge hole had appeared in the road near the Devil's Knock where a burst water main had washed away the sandy subsoil under the road. The first anybody knew of it was when an early morning number 7 bus full of workers had gone half way down it; luckily nobody was hurt, though the driver lost his false teeth scrambling out. The nightwatchman, who was guarding the hole, motioned for me to join him, passed me a mug of hot tea, spat into the glowing coals and said, 'That bastard Churchill!'

I looked around but there was no sign of a fat man with a cigar wearing a onesie siren suit.

'What about him?'

'I would have been a millionaire but for him.'

'How?'

'It was in the war. I invented the sticky bomb. They knew field guns was no use against tanks – the shells just bounced off. What you needed was a bomb that stuck to the tank. One of my kids was playin' in the fields and come home covered in sticky burrs. That give me an idea. If you could cover a big grenade with enough sticky stuff it would stick to the tank and blow a hole in it. I sent the idea to Churchill but he never wrote back. Next thing you knew they was usin' sticky bombs to stop tanks all over the place. It helped win the war did my invention and I never got a penny. That bastard Churchill.'

I thought the best thing to do was humour him so I commiserated, drank my tea then said goodnight and headed home. I was convinced that the nightwatchman was a sandwich short of a picnic and, when I checked, all the books said that the sticky bomb was invented by Colonel Robert Stuart Macrae in what was known as 'Churchill's Toyshop'. Yet, while writing this book, I discovered that all the sticky bombs requisitioned by the army during the war were produced by Kay Brothers of Stockport, a hop and a jump from where we were that night, so perhaps my nightwatchman did have something to do with winning the war – we'll never know. Kay Brothers also made sticky flypaper, by the way, but I don't think the guardian of the hole invented that.

It was about this time that I discovered that pubs weren't just places you went to play rock and roll while an Irish landlady hit punters with a tin tray – they were watering holes, confessionals, marriage bureaux and debating chambers all in one.

There were some great town boozers in Manchester and though we were just underage we could pass for eighteen in a poor light. The Town Hall Tavern, the Seven Stars, the Shakespeare, the Sugar Loaf, the Turk's Head, the Swan With Two Necks, Tommy Ducks – these mahogany, brass and etched-glass palaces were where we spent our Friday nights. We didn't get hammered, we couldn't afford to, but we would sup our half-pints and argue politics and religion for hours. My mate Hughie Jones knew the landlady of the Union in what is now Manchester's Gay Village. In those days, together with the Rembrandt just along the way, the Union was what would now be called a 'gay-friendly' pub and was the favourite hang-out of lesbians, gays, trannies, bisexuals and daft Catholic sixth-formers.

Hughie played a fair jazz trombone and used to bring it down the Union while somebody else brought in a zither banjo. I tuned it like a guitar and knocked out a few blues chords while Hughie blew his horn. We managed 'The Saints' and 'St James Infirmary' without too much trouble and I knew a couple of twelve-bar blues we could hammer through; we would work our way through them and then tag on a handful of the less rude rugby songs. Some of the other lads knew a few monologues, I did a version of 'Abou Ben Adhem' which included signing of an extremely dubious nature ('May his tribe increase' accompanied by slapping of left palm on bicep of right arm while fist clenched etc – perhaps you had to be there) and one of the lads, Tony Morgan, could do the whole St Crispin's Day speech from *Henry V*, Act IV Scene iii. He would be heckled through most of this and would finish by standing on the table and proclaiming the last lines as the heckling grew more inventive:

We few, we happy few, we band of brothers;
[Cheers from our gang.]
For he to-day that sheds his blood with me
Shall be my brother; be he ne'er so vile,
[More cheers from the lads.]
This day shall gentle his condition;
And gentlemen in England now-a-bed …

['I should be so lucky!' and 'Any gentlemen going spare?' from a couple of the trannies.]

Shall think themselves accurs'd they were not here,
And hold their manhoods cheap …

['You can hold my manhood any time you want chuck – and it'll be cheap!' from somewhere close by.]

… whiles any speaks
That fought with us upon Saint Crispin's day!

The last lines were always delivered as though Tony was

addressing the Nuremberg Rally and he would be lifted down to what Hughie Jones called 'rupturous applause'.

The Union had to be one of the most bohemian of Manchester pubs and, since it also sold the cheapest beer, it was one of the most popular. Because it was a safe haven for people who weren't like my Uncle Len it always seemed to be completely relaxed and yet incredibly exciting at the same time. Yet there was something slightly disconcerting about being stood in the gents having a pee and suddenly finding a leggy blonde at the side of you hitching up her mini-skirt, taking out her cock and peeing alongside you while saying, 'It's gone that cold outside I nearly froze me tits off walkin' 'ere from Piccadilly.'

Goodbye School, Hello World

The girls we palled out with were mostly sixth-formers from Notre Dame, Loreto, the Hollies or Chorlton Convent and could give more than as good as they got when it came to arguing politics and philosophy. At the time I was seeing a girl I had met at one of the clubs we played in who was not a Catholic and didn't have too many hang-ups about sex apart from not wanting to get pregnant so I made sure that I always had a 'packet of three' from the barbers with me. My pal Barry was also seeing a girl and, if either of us were short of a condom or three we would share what we had. This was to be my undoing.

The sixth-form common room at school was a smoky den where some of the lads played cards while others read or nattered. It was also the place where somebody obviously just sat and listened and then reported what was going on. One day Barry, who was due out on a date that night, asked me if I had 'any johnnies'. I had two packets in my blazer pocket and gave him one, he gave me three shillings and ninepence, and that was that. No profit was made, I was helping the world population problem and therefore being a good citizen; but the length of Rome's tentacles knows no bounds and the web stretched all the way from St Peter's to the informer in that sixth-form common room in St Bede's College.

It was becoming increasingly obvious that St Bede's and I were going through what marriage guidance counsellors would call 'a rough patch'. Allowing us a modicum of intellectual freedom while expecting us not to question authority seems to me, even now, to illustrate the school's lack of understanding of how the world was changing. In their academic tower with the park on one side and the convent on the other Duggan and the other priests were largely cut off from a world that was changing for ever.

The end came when I was taking my A levels and had grown a pale, gingerish beard in the three weeks allotted for revision and panic before the start of the exams. It wasn't long or thick, but it was most definitely a beard.

As I was sitting in the Great Hall, working my way through an essay on the Dissolution of the Monasteries, Father Burke came from behind, leaned over me and said quietly but with some force, 'Shave it off.' I did – but that wasn't enough to save me.

A day after I finished my A levels my mum got a letter from Duggan which, without offering any explanation (for which I was most glad), read, 'On no account must Michael return to school after the holidays.' I already knew why; a few days before I had met a couple of the lads in town who told me that somebody – they didn't know who – had told Father Burke I was running a vice den in the common room and was selling rubber goods to pure and innocent Catholic schoolboys.

I've wondered, a few times over the last fifty years, whether the boy who grassed me up ever had a twinge of conscience; whether it might have occurred to him that he'd possibly destroyed somebody's career? I was set to do another year at school, may well have got good A levels and gone on to university. I didn't. I've gone on to have a fairly full and interesting life anyway and haven't let what happened hang over me; but as an idle thought from time to time I reflect on that shifty, two-faced, craw-thumping, slimeball, gutless, sneaky Catholic bastard and hope fervently that he is writhing in agony somewhere with his genitals in a jar of piranhas.

Apart from that I have no hard feelings.

One thought has occurred to me over recent years, however: the man who sacked me, the Very Reverend Monsignor Thomas Duggan, stands accused now, long after his death, of having sexually abused a number of boys (in excess of fifty have come forward) during his tenure at St Bede's. So I, who was trying to prevent harm, was sacked by a man who damaged the lives of many of the children in his care. Well, there's a surprise.

And here's a further thought: I have scoured the Gospels and the Apocrypha and the Gnostic texts and nowhere have I found it stated that 'thou must not use condoms'. There is no Aramaic word for 'condom' and nowhere in all his teachings does Jesus mention either 'condoms', 'contraceptives', 'johnnies' or 'French letters'. Like Limbo, all that stuff was made up by men in frocks who weren't having any sex themselves and didn't see why anybody else should have fun without their say so.

However, now I was faced with a couple of problems – if I wanted to carry on and get to uni I would have to get a place to study somewhere else, and if I wanted to have any money over the holidays I would have to get a job. I put the thoughts of another year of A levels to the back of my mind for the moment, got on the 59 bus and went to Middleton Corporation Works Department Depot, where I got a summer job navvying with the council. If nothing else I could at least learn how to use a shovel properly.

That summer was a good one, weather-wise, and working outside doing hard manual labour did me some good mentally and physically. My first job was with the road gang at the upper end of Wood Street, the main road from Middleton to the relatively new overspill estate at Langley. We were working melting the top layer of tarmac off the road and laying a fresh one down. Now they have giant machines that 'plane' off the top layer while another big machine comes and lays a new surface down. We had no great machines, we used what Paddy the ganger called 'handraulics' to do the job. Something slightly bigger than a lawnmower belched out fire and melted the tarmac, which we then stirred about before scattering more gravel on the road then coating it with melted tar from big watering cans. All of this was then rolled flat by a bloke pushing a diesel roller. I was breathing in tar fumes constantly and thought how right my nanna was: I didn't get bronchitis or pneumonia all week. We were a small team of six or so navvies, most of us from the area though the ganger, Paddy, was an elderly Irishman from Mayo who always forgot to bring milk for his morning brew and usually ended up 'mending' his tea by pouring my milky tea into his can to mix with his. He might have been elderly but Paddy was as tough as old clogs and strong with it; he was also the first man I ever saw cooking a fry up on a shovel. We had a brazier to melt the tar buckets and at dinnertime we would gather round it, sitting on upturned wheelbarrows or sacks of cement eating our butties. One dinnertime I watched Paddy cross the road to a shop and come back with a bag containing two eggs, some rashers, a sliced loaf, some butter and a half pound of sausages. He wiped his shovel clean, rubbed butter on it and threw on the rashers, sausages and eggs, holding his 'navvy's banjo' over the fire. While they were frying he buttered himself a heap of sliced bread and ate the lot straight off the shovel using his clasp knife and a fork he'd got from somewhere. Nobody passed comment – probably a good job since Paddy had a very short temper and would use a shovel if need be as well as his boots and his fist.

We worked all that week resurfacing Wood Street and the next Monday I was detailed off with a flagger to work re-laying flags in the old Junction area of Middleton.

I ought to explain here that Middleton was at one time a small town well outside Manchester with its own distinct history and traditions. Archers left there in 1513 to fight with Black Ralph of Ashton at the Battle of Flodden and the beautiful old parish church of St Leonard just across from the Ring of Bells (a folkie haunt of mine in later years) has the earliest memorial stained-glass window in Britain. A small panel shows local men ranked up, their names painted along the sides of their longbows. There is a medieval grammar school, a great old pub, the Boar's Head, and the sixteenth-century Tonge Hall. Middleton became a cotton town during the Industrial Revolution and mushroomed in size. Then it mushroomed again during the 1960s when Manchester Corporation built the vast overspill estate of Langley on farmland at the top of Wood Street and rehoused people from the 'slums' of Harpurhey, Collyhurst and other parts.

The people of Middleton are still known to some as 'Moonrakers', the story being that a couple of local drunks coming back from the pub one night saw the moon shining on the water of a pond, and in a fit of greed/stupidity got a couple of rakes and spent the rest of the night trying to rake the moon off the water.

One of the men in our road gang was a short chap nearing retirement with silver hair, a waistcoat and flat cap, a chippy little character with a constant grin who took no notice at all of Paddy's shouting and bawling and whose nickname was Mau Mau. I asked him why.

'We moved up Langley from Collyhurst. We were t' first to come and when we went into t' pubs in Miggie (Middleton) t' Moonrakers called us Mau Mau – they were trebels who were fightin' t' British in Kenya at the time. That's what t' Moonrakers thought of us lot: we were as foreign to them as t' bloody Mau Mau.' Funny old world: up there in the wilds of Middleton, two tribes shouting at each other over a fence of prejudice.

I was sent to work 'up Junction' with Thompson, one of the council flaggers, just the two of us, pushing a barrow with shovels, brushes and crowbars all the way across town on a roasting hot summer's morning. He was a big, bespectacled, tubby lad; no great fan of work but a Moonraker through and through who knew every ginnel and back court in the area. He showed me how to jockey heavy York flagstones that were almost as tall as me into position and how to lay them onto their beds of compo by sliding them down a long, straight crowbar. Like Big Lou, Thompson was a keen man for the horses and made sure that he got all his bets on in time, leaving me to lay flags while he went to the bookies. The clerk of works used to check on the outlying gangs in a council Land Rover, and if he ever turned up and asked where Thompson was I had to say that he'd been taken short and had gone to find a toilet. After finding me solo flag-laying for the sixth time one day, the clerk of works remarked, 'If there was a Shitting Olympics, Thompson would get gold, silver and bronze.'

Once it rained for the whole day and I spent it sitting in a chicken coop with Thompson who said the owner was a relative of his who wouldn't mind us sitting with his chickens. What a bloody glum day that was: Lancashire rain falling outside, cooped up (literally) in a stinking hut, chickens muttering all round us, pissed off that we'd moved in and taken over their space, and Thompson chain-smoking Park Drive while reading the racing pages of his *Daily Mirror*. There wasn't much conversation between us since the only things he talked about were horses, 'nignogs' and a fat lass he was shagging from the CWS Jam Works down the road.

One of my last jobs on the council had me working with Harold, the sewer man, a little Moonraker who loved his job. He was never happier than when he was scarpering down an iron ladder into the underworld of Middleton to clear some blockage. It was not the best job I've ever had and I remember one Monday morning as we were deep in the bowels (ha!) of the system how Harold pointed at a huge stream of used condoms that were bobbing up and down in the gloop and said, 'They've 'ad a good weekend up at Langley.' Then added with a puzzled expression, 'And most of 'em is supposed to be Catholic!'

He was a pleasant man and happy at his work, though I never got used to his habit of eating his sandwiches down the sewer because, he said, fresh air made them 'taste funny'. I left him down there in the sewer munching his corned beef and brown sauce butties and had mine in the sunshine.

When I wasn't eating my sarnies above a manhole I would go to Lil's Chippy for chicken-liver curry and chips. Lil's was one of the landmarks of Middleton and Lily Kwok who opened the café after the war was a Chinese woman whose amazing life story – which includes murder, gambling addiction, poverty, Triad association, alcoholism and bankruptcy – is told in the book *Sweet Mandarin*, written by her granddaughter, Helen Tse. At the time I knew nothing of Lil's story, but I liked her smiling face and her cheerful banter, and I loved the thick yellow curry sauce, the consistency of custard and with a flavour like no Indian curry you have ever tasted.

Not long before my job with the council came to an end a gang of us were sent to dig up the bottom end of Wood Street; we arrived with Paddy and a lorry full of tools, cordoned off the place we were digging up and set to with pneumatic drills and shovels. Traffic was snarled up, everybody grumbled and those that didn't stood there watching us working. I particularly resented it when blokes who were on 'the pancrack' (signing on the dole) came out of the pub on their way to the bookies and made unhelpful comments as we sweated our gonads off trying to fix a burst water main. These were the 'lozzers' who were working the system, drawing the dole while fencing stolen gear or making a few bob on the horses; there were only a handful in every area and they were disliked by everybody except their cronies.

On this day I was down the big hole, digging deep and throwing the soil up onto the back of a lorry, when a voice shouted, 'What the bloody hell are you doing digging up the roads?'

It was my Uncle Bernard. He was working locally on a plastering contract and was on his way home to Langley for his dinner. He took me home with him and Aunty Barbara filled us both up with a large mixed grill, tea, bread and butter. Bernard was quite upset at having found me down a hole. I told him it was only a summer job but he wasn't convinced.

'You shouldn't be diggin' roads. That's why you went to grammar school – to get away from all that. You should have got a holiday job in an office.'

He was even more shocked a year or so after when he found me handing him a ticket in my bus conductor's uniform. But that's a story for another time.

A few days later, still digging and still in the same hole, I saw a pram approaching on the pavement above. Pushing the pram was a dark-haired girl my age or younger, wearing a summery blouse and quite a short skirt. I had dug myself down well below street level and could see that she had an extremely fine pair of legs.

'Does your mother know you're out?' I asked – not one of my best chat-up lines ever, but it would do.

'Yes, and she's right behind her!' said the Scouser who would become my mother-in-law.

INDEX